Effective Appellate Advocacy
REVISED EDITION

Frederick Bernays Wiener

The *Litigation Bookshelf* Series

FREDERICK BERNAYS WIENER

Effective Appellate Advocacy
REVISED EDITION

Christopher T. Lutz and William Pannill, Editors

**Defending Liberty
Pursuing Justice**

SECTION OF LITIGATION
American Bar Association

Cover design by ABA Publishing

Printed in the United States of America.

08 07 06 05 04 5 4 3 2 1

Library of Congress Cataloging-in-Publication Data

Wiener, Frederick Bernays
    Effective appellate advocacy / by Frederick Bernays Wiener ; edited by
Christopher T. Lutz and William Pannill.
        p. cm.
    Originally published: New York : Prentice-Hall, 1950.
        ISBN 1-59031-234-1
        1. Appellate procedure—United States. 2. Trial practice—United
States. I. Lutz, Christopher T. II. Pannill, William. III. Title.

    KF9050.W5 2004
    347.73'8—dc22

                                                        2003021497

Discounts are available for books ordered in bulk. Special consideration is given to state bars, CLE programs, and other bar-related organizations. Inquire at Book Publishing, ABA Publishing, American Bar Association, 750 North Lake Shore Drive, Chicago, Illinois 60611.

www.ababooks.org

Contents

PART I. GENERAL PRINCIPLES

PART II. EFFECTIVE BRIEF-WRITING

PART III.   ARGUING THE APPEAL

PART IV. OTHER ISSUES

Foreword to the Revised Edition

This volume brings a great book to the contemporary audience it deserves. Frederick Bernays Wiener first published *Effective Appellate Advocacy* in 1950. Eleven years later, in 1961, Colonel Wiener—he had served as an Army lawyer—made many changes for a second edition that was focused on federal appellate practice and procedure as it existed in the 1950s and 1960s. A third, and slightly revised, version of the federal appeals book appeared in 1967. Then, the book went out of print. Aside from a recent verbatim reproduction of the 1967 edition, Colonel Wiener's book was never again printed before his death in 1996.

In the 35 years since the last edition, Colonel Wiener's book has developed a devoted following. Many regard it as the best guide to appellate advocacy ever written. Its advice is as practical and useful, its style as clear and distinctive, and its opinions as forceful and pungent as the day the book first appeared. Those who could locate it—on the back shelves of law libraries or tables at used book stores—had a treasure, and many kept it to themselves.

In 1999, one of us wrote an article about Colonel Wiener's lost classic. Pannill, "Appeals: The Classic Guide" 25 *Litigation* No.2 (Winter 1999) at 6. The enthusiastic response from readers led the Book Publishing Board of the Section of Litigation to embark on a new, revised edition. With the cooperation and patience of Doris Merchant Wiener, Colonel Wiener's widow, and that of his son, Captain Thomas Wiener, U.S.N. (ret.), a new edition of *Effective Appellate Advocacy* is now a reality.

Some may wonder what it means to "revise" a classic, and so an explanation is in order. But first, what has *not* changed: We have retained virtually every word of the advice in the book. Where Colonel Wiener changed his 1950 phrasing or added advice in the two 1960s editions, we have included those changes. We have also kept most of the examples from actual cases that he used to illustrate matters like the choice and ordering of arguments or the phrasing of argumentative headings in briefs.

We have dropped some material. That includes discussions of specific federal appellate procedures or rules from the 1960s, as well as long footnotes citing cases on matters such as regulation of interstate commerce 40 or 50 years ago. We have condensed accounts of how each state supreme court dealt with argument and briefs in the 1940s. In the 1950 edition, Colonel Wiener included appendices with more than 100 pages of briefs and transcripts of arguments. He dropped that material from later editions, and we have not revived it.

Apart from deletions, there are few changes in the words that Colonel Wiener wrote. Most involve time references. Thus, if the 1950 edition speaks of something happening "a few years ago," this edition says "many years ago." When Colonel Wiener produced the 1960s editions, he made similar alterations, so those here seem appropriate to us.

Our method has been to take the 1950 edition as the starting point, and to add later revisions of its text, but we have incorporated only some of the material from the 1961 and 1967 versions. We think this retains everything useful from prior editions, along with many examples of Colonel Wiener's legal erudition, and eliminates material now obsolete. In addition to keeping the book's unequalled advice, we have retained Colonel Wiener's distinctive voice—a combination of wit, strong opinions, and a superb writing style.

Despite these changes, it is important to remember that most of the text was written more than a half century ago, and its author was a product of his time, an era when most lawyers were men and the profession was more formal. Phrases and terms that reflect the times and the author ("pulmotor job" and "soft-toned shortstop") appear occasionally. We have not updated case citations, but they are secondary to the advice contained in the book. Colonel Wiener did not write a legal treatise. In addition, Colonel Wiener was not—to put it mildly—a fan of Blue Book citation formats, and so we have maintained his citation form.

This book is a tribute to Colonel Wiener himself. Besides being one of the great appellate lawyers, he was a forceful and distinctive personality, a formidable scholar, and a man who knew how to win a case on appeal. We have included a brief remembrance by Jacob Stein, a lawyer who knew Colonel Wiener. We have also included from prior editions the forewords (written by Justice Sherman

Minton and John W. Davis) and acknowledgments (written by the Colonel himself). They too give a picture of the man behind the book.

The Section of Litigation is pleased to present this book to the bar.

CHRISTOPHER T. LUTZ
WILLIAM PANNILL
October 2003

There Was a Giant in the Land

I first recall seeing Fritz Wiener at Connecticut Avenue and L Street in Washington, D.C., in front of the Stoneleigh Court Building (no longer there), an attractive, old-fashioned apartment house converted, with few changes, into an old-fashioned office building. I place the time around 1960. Although I did not know who Fritz was, I knew he must be somebody. His posture was militarily correct. He wore a cowboy hat that conflicted with his otherwise conservative 1930s double-breasted suit. He sported mustachios in an Oliver Wendell Holmes, Jr., style.

Some time later, I was introduced to him by a friend with whom I was taking a walk along Connecticut Avenue. "There is Fritz," said my companion; "I want to say hello to the Colonel." We approached and my friend introduced me. Pleasant words were exchanged. We resumed our walk. I asked who Fritz Wiener was. "Fritz is the leader of the appellate bar. He was in the Solicitor General's Office. When he was with the Judge Advocate General he became the authority on military law."

Months later I called Fritz to ask him to take the appeal of a criminal case. Fritz suggested I come by his office at Stoneleigh Court to discuss it. Fritz had a working fireplace, a large library of law books, bound copies of his appellate briefs, and an assortment of general literature heavy on the military and the Revolutionary War. There were comfortable leather chairs. He lit up a big cigar and analyzed the facts I gave him five different ways, reciting as he went along the relevant precedents. He enjoyed astonishing me and others with his remarkable memory of the Supreme Court reports, citing cases by name, date, and the U.S. volume and page number.

Although Fritz was a great-nephew of Sigmund Freud, I have my doubts concerning his belief in the curative power of psychoanalysis. He graduated cum laude from Brown University and magna cum laude from Harvard Law School. He was assistant to the Solicitor General from 1945 to 1948 when he entered private practice.

Fritz found time in his busy private practice to write law review articles including often-quoted comments on military law. He wrote for the Selden Society, the organization devoted to the discovering and the publishing of the reports from the earliest days of the English Law. I have re-read Fritz's reviews of two books, which reflect his reactions to a book he liked and one he disliked. The reactions show much about the man.

First the book he liked: the Oliver Wendell Holmes, Jr./Harold Laski correspondence. Here is Fritz's opener:

For sheer entertainment, for unsurpassed intellectual delight, these two volumes of letters will assuredly have few equals—and no superiors. The correspondence which they preserve ranges widely over the whole gamut of human activity: philosophy, law, government, the history of ideas, literature, art, events of the day, and, above all, people. It would be invidious to attempt a more detailed catalogue; suffice to say that almost every page suggests an essay.[1]

Holmes (like Fritz) did not believe that mankind was improvable or that government could solve life's major problems. Laski believed that mankind was improvable and the right kind of government (radical socialism) could solve life's major problems. This conflict in points of view did not inhibit the writers. In the few pages of his review, Fritz tells some interesting things about Justice Holmes and much about Harold Laski's complicated and ultimately tragic life that was missing from Kingsley Martin's full-length biography.

Now the book Fritz did not like: the 1961 McNaughton revision of Wigmore on *Evidence*. In criticizing McNaughton's effort, Fritz gives his views on the care that must be taken in legal writing.[2] Please excuse the length of the quotation that follows: It has many things close to Fritz's heart.

The mass of current legal materials is, all too obviously, tremendous, although to measure it, as Mr. McNaughton does, simply by piling up volumes in vertical stacks, is plainly inaccurate; one contributing reason for the multiplication of reports is that the West Publishing Company now prints fewer words on a single page and fewer pages in a single volume than it did fifty or even twenty-five years ago.

Nonetheless, while it may well be impossible for a single individual today even to revise an extensive work already written, certainly not without years of labor, so that collaborators must be employed, I suggest that McNaughton's system of scholarship by committee, whose unhappy results have marred

---

[1] 2 JOURNAL OF PUBLIC LAW 136 (1953).
[2] 75 HARVARD LAW REVIEW 136.

the pages under review, is not the answer. Collaboration, yes; divided responsibility, no.

This is a problem not unique to the academic world; every private law firm, every public law office, faces it daily; the dilemma is the imperative truism that a chain's strength is the strength of its weakest link. Four months out of law school I was plunged into the vortex of a stockholders' suit, occasioned because the partner in a large and respected firm, who had in writing advised the corporation that it had power to buy its own stock, neglected to add three all-important words: "out of surplus." A year out of Government, once more in private practice, I won a significant courtroom victory because government counsel had collectively contended, contrary to the demonstrable fact, that a particular objection was not made on the record.

Complete freedom from mistakes is, it goes without saying, unattainable. Nonetheless, large organizations that are well run follow two built-in admonitions in order to catch (or at least substantially minimize) avoidable errors.

First, they hire competent help. This is too often a counsel of perfection, not only in public offices where statesmen have obligations to constituents, but also in private offices where senior partners all too frequently have less gifted junior relatives.

Second, they check. The articles of partnership can easily provide that every opinion going out over the firm name must first be initialed by two or more partners. (If as many as two or three of them do not know that a corporation cannot properly buy its own stock except out of surplus, perhaps that particular firm had better close up shop.) And, in any kind of a law office, public or private, whenever a brief that bears the names of, and is frequently reviewed by, several lawyers, contains a statement that "this contention was not made at the trial, as the present record shows," that circumstance should, automatically, require at least one reviewing lawyer to read the record himself for verification. Otherwise everybody's business becomes nobody's business, and vital interests are risked on the accuracy or otherwise of the rough-drafter at the foot of the totem pole.

This passage brings to mind Fritz's own definition of a perfectionist: A person (Fritz) who takes infinite pains himself and gives infinite pain to others.

Fritz's book *Civilians Under Military Justice* (University of Chicago Press) was published in 1967. He did much of the research in London where he and his wife, Doris, were in residence at Brown's Hotel, where they cut quite a figure. If Fritz had had two lives to live, one of them would have been as a bewigged barrister with a thriving appellate practice, a writer of books on the history of English law, and a permanent resident of Brown's Hotel.

As you will read in the text that follows, Fritz is the only lawyer in the history of the Supreme Court of the United States to lose a case, with a published adverse opinion against him, only to win the very same case (*Reid v. Covert*) on rehearing without a controlling change in membership of the Court. *Reid v. Covert* held that Congress has no constitutional power to subject to trial by court-martial Army wives who accompany their soldier-husbands overseas in time of peace, only to murder them on military bases.[3]

In 1972, Fritz had a victory before the Supreme Court in a case involving the rights of a private club. He was then retained to file the petition for certiorari in another case with similar issues. He had every reason to believe the petition would be granted. It was denied. The only Justice who voted to grant certiorari was a Justice for whom Fritz had a minimum of high regard.

Fritz took this very hard. He said that things had reached the point where it was time to call it quits. Doris and he had decided to say goodbye to the law practice and settle in Phoenix, Arizona. Perhaps the cowboy hat he wore was a clue to his desire to wind up way out west. He made it. Colonel Wiener is buried at the foot of Thunder Mountain, at Fort Huachuca, a U.S. Army Post in Sierra Vista, Arizona.

While he was packing up to leave, Fritz's friends convened a going-away party at the Army–Navy Club in suburban Virginia. In attendance to wish Fritz and Doris goodbye were a group of well-wishers that included solicitor's office veterans, judges, and lawyers. The evening came off very well with Fritz's friends telling stories of Fritz's star performances before the Supreme Court. There were descriptions of Fritz in his swallowtail coat, the only remaining private practice practitioner who dressed with such formality.

A friend recalled that in one of his appearances, Justice Frankfurter commented to Fritz "You are speaking of the conduct of the prosecutor. Let me say that when I was a prosecutor in the Southern District of New York we would not think of doing such a thing that you describe." Fritz's reply: "Justice Frankfurter, there were giants in the land in those days."

After Fritz left town we exchanged letters. He decorated his remarks with citations to authority. As an illustration, I recall his letter in which he chastised me for writing that someone had come up with a unique idea. He said the idea was neither original nor unique, citing a patent case. In another letter he commented that a

---

[3] 351 U.S. 487, 76 S. Ct. 880 (1956) [*Covert* I—Defeat] and 354 U.S. 1, 77 S. Ct. 1222 (1957) (on rehearing) [*Covert* II—Victory].

politician caught in a scandal was not a reasonably prudent man, followed by a cite defining a reasonably prudent man.

The ABA, in republishing Fritz's book, does a service to the Bar. It also puts a stop to an epidemic of biblioklepty. The original edition has a way of disappearing from one library and reappearing in another.

There is much more to be said about Fritz. The person to do it is Professor Paul R. Baier of the Louisiana State University Law Center. He is at work on the full biography of the Colonel. It will, of course, replace, correct, and put in proper perspective this impressionistic sketch of one of the most interesting and accomplished leaders of the bar.

JACOB A. STEIN

Foreword to the 1950 Edition

Of all the demands his calling makes upon an advocate, none is more weighty than the preparation and argument of an appeal. For one thing, it represents the last chance for a client who has lost below. Or, if he has been fortunate enough to win, it is the last effort necessary to save the advantage he has gained. The argument of the appeal is, therefore, a breathless moment for the lawyer and the client alike.

Yet the task of the advocate assumes a much broader scope when one reflects that the decisions of appellate courts are rarely confined in their influence to the fortunes of the instant case. They are the precedents in which are to be found not only the law of the past and the present but also the foreshadowing of the law of the future.

A cynic has borrowed the words of Byron to describe the volumes of appellate decisions as:

> Smooth solid monuments of mental pain,
> The petrifactions of the plodding brain.

The advocate has his share in building these monuments, and his brain must plod alongside that of the judge in this construction. It is important, therefore, that his work be well and skillfully done and especially that he lend to the court all the assistance in his power.

Mr. Wiener has written a book that outlines in great detail and with copious illustrations how this part of an advocate's duty can best be performed. The raw recruit at the bar as well as the veteran will be helped by its perusal.

JOHN W. DAVIS

Foreword to the 1967 Edition

To get into court and to maintain your right to be there is the object of all pleading and is as important in an appellate court as in a trial court.

In the courts of the United States with which this book deals, one is seldom thrown out of court because of poor pleading. If the jurisdictional facts are there, the court will consider your case. Nevertheless the lawyer will be well advised to pay careful attention to his pleading, since that is his first introduction to the court. A case well pleaded is a case half argued.

In cases on appellate review there are, in addition to pleading, the problems of briefing and oral argument. A brief should be *brief* and concise, while at the same time it is elaborating in written form the propositions laid out in your pleading. Skill in presentation and in arguing those propositions, first in writing and then on your feet, will challenge and command the attention of the court.

This book is a guide to handling of cases on appeal in the Federal courts by one who is eminently qualified to instruct and direct in this field. The author is a distinguished and able advocate at the bar of the Supreme Court of the United States with wide experience in appellate work, stemming from his position as a former Assistant to the Solicitor General of the United States and then from an extensive private practice.

SHERMAN MINTON

Acknowledgments [1950]

Traditionally, a preface consists of a list of the reasons an author assembles to indicate why the book to which it is affixed should not have been written, after which it is expanded by him to set forth the even more numerous reasons that in his opinion justify the fact that his work was written.

In this instance the reasons why the present work was produced will be self-evident to anyone who reads it. Thereafter, the readers rather than the author can more appropriately formulate and expand upon the grounds why it should have remained unwritten. Accordingly, this book will not be introduced by any preface.

The listing of those who contributed to the finished work, however, stands on a different footing, and at this juncture it is a genuine pleasure to acknowledge an indebtedness to the many persons who assisted in the enterprise.

Two such groups, however, must necessarily be nameless. The first consists of numerous judicial friends whose counsel and insight are responsible for much of what appears in the following pages. Failure to acknowledge their help individually is a consequence of the feeling that many of their remarks, having been privately made, must remain anonymous; and that, in any event, to mention these distinguished gentlemen by name might be thought to import an approval on their part of the author or of his views. I hope that they will not disapprove too strongly of either; but my thanks to them will, for the reasons just suggested, be expressed otherwise than in print.

The second group consists of all those who, since the time when I first emerged from law school, have shaped my thinking and my practice in the present field. All men are the product, in greater or lesser degree, of their environment and associations, and certainly a practicing lawyer's credo is necessarily shaped by many influences. I acknowledge a deep indebtedness to the influence of erstwhile seniors and colleagues—an indebtedness, however, that I deeply regret not being able to allocate accurately.

February 1950

Acknowledgments [1961]

"No man is an island," and therefore even one's most personal, individualistic, and single-handed productions necessarily reflect the impact of others.

This book, now in a revised version, is no exception. In the remarks affixed to the earlier edition—written just eleven years ago this month—I listed the many kind friends to whom I was then indebted, some named, others necessarily nameless. Those acknowledgments assuredly carry over into the present volume.

On this occasion, also, my thanks for help and, above all, for additional insights into the subject matter are due many persons. Again there are many members of the bench who should not be more particularly identified, but who have continued to shape my thinking and approaches in the field of appellate practice.

And this time, far more than before, I owe a genuine debt to the many doughty opponents whom I have faced in appellate courts over the last ten years. Not infrequently, as indeed the pages that follow bear witness, I did not fully approve of all of their techniques in particular instances. But their talents and resourcefulness have called forth on my part the best that I could muster, and for that I am truly grateful.

And now it is a particular pleasure to express my deep appreciation to named individuals:

To the judges, listed in Chapter 2, who were good enough to answer my questions regarding the operating methods of their several courts.

To Saul Gordon, Esq., of the New York Bar, my colleague in some uphill battles, for suggesting many helpful revisions of the earlier text.

To my wife, Doris Merchant Wiener, not for reading the manuscript—that, after all, was a chore she could hardly avoid—but for the unerring critical sense that she brought to bear upon it.

To Charles J. Alexander, Esq., of the District of Columbia Bar, for checking every citation. (He volunteered for that detail; I didn't dare request him to assume such drudgery, however necessary.)

To my secretary, Mrs. Hazel Shadix Whitehead, for typing the manuscript.

To the editors of the *American Bar Association Journal,* for permission to reprint a chapter that first appeared in their pages.

And, not least, to the editorial staff of BNA, Incorporated, for assistance in seeing the book through the press, and for the numerous succulent lunches that they contributed in the process.

F. B. W.

Washington, D.C.,
February 1961

PART I

GENERAL PRINCIPLES

CHAPTER 1

Why Advocacy?

Section 1. Scope of the book.—This book tells how to brief and how to argue a case on appeal. It deals exclusively with Appellate Advocacy: how best to persuade an appellate court to decide a case in your favor. It is neither a practice manual nor a text on appellate procedure. It is written on the assumption that all the necessary procedural steps to perfect the appeal have already been or will be timely taken, and it is addressed to the problems common to cases wheresoever they may be argued on appeal—in the state courts, in the federal courts, or in the Supreme Court of the United States.

A good many of the principles discussed herein are equally applicable to the arguments of questions of law and fact, written and oral, in courts of first instance. The task of presenting the facts effectively, the psychology of persuasion, the requirements of candor and accuracy—these are matters common to forensic efforts in any courtroom, at any stage of a litigated proceeding. But it seemed more conducive to clarity to avoid the lengthy list of qualifications and exceptions that a broader scope for this book would necessarily have involved. Consequently, for that as well as other reasons, the present work is limited to Appellate Advocacy.

Section 2. Importance of Appellate Advocacy.—Counsel defeated in the trial court—the licked lawyer—is recognized as having twin rights: (1) he may go down to the inn at the county seat, or to his club in town, and cuss the court and/or jury; and (2) he can take an appeal. The shelves of American law libraries, which groan under the constantly accumulating load of reports of decisions in appealed cases, are living proof that the second right has been exercised times without number.

Appeals are therefore important, whether one lawyer seeks on behalf of the appellant to undo the great injustice done his client at the trial, or whether another lawyer, on behalf of the appellee, strives to support the judgment or decree so justly entered in the court of first instance. And, for the same reason, effective appellate advocacy, which is the technique (or, if one prefers, the art) of persuading appellate courts to decide in one's favor, is likewise important.

Once in the appellate court, the lawyer is addressing a tribunal that, individually and collectively, is seeking to do substantial justice. He will be writing and speaking to judges fired by a desire to reach a just result, who in consequence are sensitive to the equities of the particular case. But they must necessarily rely on the opposing advocates to make them aware of those equities, and to point out the facts of record and the applicable rules of law that compel a just decision.

This book endeavors, among other things, to tell lawyers how to stress the equities of their cases persuasively, to the end that they may win their cases on appeal.

Section 3. Can Appellate Advocacy be learned?—It may be urged—and some friends have suggested—that it would be just as impossible—and quite as unhelpful— to attempt to teach advocacy as to write a learned tome on how to paint a picture or how to write a novel. That stricture may well be true as to some of the finer points of the process; certainly neither the writing of a brief nor the oral presentation of an appeal can qualify as an exact science. Nor is there, as to either activity, any single "approved solution." Mr. Wellman entitled his classic guide for the trial lawyer *The Art of Cross-Examination,* and it may well be that appellate advocacy, at least when it is skillfully and effectively practiced, is also something of an art. Nonetheless, the process in its essentials can be stated in terms of rules, or at least of standards of fairly general application. It can therefore be taught—and learned; learned, too, more quickly and somewhat less painfully than simply through one's own mistakes. For in law, as in other fields of human endeavor, it is only the fool who needs to learn by experience: the wise man learns, and profits, from the experience of others.

Section 4. Should advocacy be taught?—Anyone who has ever spent any length of time in an appellate court, whether for instructional purposes or by way of busman's holiday, or even simply waiting for his own case to be reached, will answer that question with a resounding "Yes." Advocacy needs to be taught, and it needs to be learned. Too many, far too many, lawyers burden courts of appeal with poorly prepared, poorly presented, and thoroughly unhelpful arguments—for which they receive, and clients pay, substantial and not infrequently handsome fees. Lawyers, like other professionals, can be divided into the classic three-fold scale of evaluation as able, unable, and lamentable. Nonetheless, and after making due allowance for the frailties of mankind, it is really amazing how few good arguments are presented and heard, quite irrespective of the tribunal concerned. I was once told by a justice of the Supreme Court of the United States that four out of every five arguments to which he was required to listen from that bench are "not good." And comments from judges of other appellate courts give me no reason to suppose that the percentage of good arguments is perceptibly higher elsewhere.

It would seem to be, therefore, high time for the subject of appellate advocacy to be given some attention. The present book is a response to the conviction that there is nothing mysterious or esoteric about the business of making an effective written or oral presentation to an appellate court, that the governing principles of that process can be extracted and articulated and therefore taught, and that any competent lawyer has the ability, with study and proper application, to write a brief and make an argument that will likewise be competent—and that will further his client's cause.

Section 5. Why bother with advocacy at all?—A representative cross-section of the graduates of one distinguished law school were once polled by the faculty, and asked to rank "the skills of a lawyer" in the order of their importance in their particular branches of practice. "The lowest rating, by a fairly wide margin, was given to skill in advocacy."[1]

Even if this simply means that most alumni of the particular institution never get to court, but instead devote most of their energies to the office or to conferences or consultations with clients, the rating is amazing—and, it is submitted, amazingly wrong. For whenever a lawyer negotiates, or puts a proposition to a client, or even when he discusses a difference of opinion with a partner, he is engaged in advocacy, viz., the process of trying to convince people of something, the technique of persuasion. It is significant that Sir Winston Churchill, speaking of the thirty most active and fruitful years of his life, refers to them as "years of action and advocacy."[2] And it is likewise significant that the very same group of lawyers, especially the older graduates, gave to "the ability to understand and marshal facts" "the highest rating by a considerable margin."[3] Now the marshalling of facts is not a talent *in vacuo*; it is one of the vital elements of advocacy. And, as will be demonstrated below at length and in some detail, frequently it is the most vital element.

---

[1] Fuller, *Work on the Curriculum*, Harvard Law School Bulletin, No. 2, July 1948, p. 3.

[2] Churchill, *The Gathering Storm* (1948), p. iv. (Copyright by Messrs. Houghton, Mifflin & Co.)

[3] Note 1, *supra*.

The low rating given to advocacy therefore does more than illumine and underscore the estimate of my distinguished judicial friend that four out of every five lawyers appearing before him have forensic halitosis (or such other oral ailment as may be suggested); it indicates that too many members of the bar fail to understand what advocacy really is. It is not simply haranguing a jury about "this poor boy" or the unwritten law, so called. It is not simply screaming at an appellate court or being "positive" in the Ambrose Bierce sense, which is to say, wrong in a loud tone of voice. It is, whether in court or out, an exercise in persuasion. And that, after all, is why a lawyer appears before an appellate court: to persuade the tribunal to decide the case in his favor. And since when has skill in persuading a particular group of hearers to decide in his favor become a minor factor in the skill of a lawyer?

But it may be urged, and frequently is, that it should be possible to submit the entire case or controversy to the court without any argument, either written or oral. Why not, so the question goes, why not simply hand up the record and the relevant authorities? After all, the judges are disinterested, they are learned in the law, and many of them have bright young law clerks to assist them in their researches. The judges either make or find and declare the law—depending on one's particular jurisprudential views. Therefore, why not leave the whole matter to them, and avoid the contentiousness and the expense and the artificiality of litigation?

The best answer to these suggestions is to apply a technique borrowed from one of the so-called exact sciences. When doctors wish to learn the function of a particular human gland whose workings are not too clear to them, they remove the corresponding gland from a dog or other animal in their laboratory, and then study the effects of the excision. Thereafter, when they have observed the behavior of the poor pooch minus that particular organ, they generally acquire some considerable insight into what the X gland really does.

I propose to apply the same technique to a still somewhat cloudy realm of law, and to answer the question, "Why bother with advocacy at all?," by taking an actual case that was not presented in true advocate's fashion in the brief and by then examining the result.

Section 6. What happens when a case is not presented in advocate's fashion?—The guinea pig experiment for present purposes will be *Cramer v. United States*,[4] the first case in which the

---

[4] 325 U.S. 1.

Supreme Court of the United States ever considered a conviction for treason on the merits. It is now over fifty years old, but its date is immaterial to the principle about to be considered.

Here are representative excerpts from the Supreme Court's opinion:

[The Treason Act, 25 Edw. III] cut a bench-mark by which the English-speaking world tested the level of its thought on the subject until our own abrupt departure from it in 1789.[5]

* * * necessity as well as desire taught a concept that differed from all historical models in the drafting of our treason clause.[6]

The framers combined all of these known protections and added two of their own which had no precedent. * * * And a venerable safeguard against false testimony was given a novel application by requiring two witnesses to the same overt act.[7]

So [the framers] added what in effect is a command that the overt acts must be established by direct evidence, and the direct testimony must be that of two witnesses instead of one. In this sense the overt act procedural provision adds something, and something important, to the definition.[8]

In the *Cramer* case, the petitioner's conviction was reversed, five to four, and the majority opinion, just quoted, asserts that both the constitutional concept of treason and the two-witness requirement were new. Both points are developed at some length in the Court's opinion, which extends to nearly 46 pages in the official reports.

Section 7. More data on the laboratory example.—Actually, the definition of the crime of treason was taken from the English Statute of 25 Edward III, and the two-witness requirement, which had been in and out of English law since 1547,[9] derived from the English Statute of 7 William III. This appears clearly from an examination of the text of the three provisions.

(i) Constitution of the United States, Article III, Section 3:

Treason against the United States, shall consist only in levying War against them, or in adhering to their Enemies, giving them Aid and Comfort. No Person shall be convicted of Treason unless on the Testimony of two Witnesses to the same overt Act, or on Confession in open Court.

---

[5] 325 U.S. at 17–18.

[6] 325 U.S. at 20.

[7] 325 U.S. at 24.

[8] 325 U.S. at 30.

[9] See 7 Wigmore, *Evidence* (3d ed. 1940), sec. 2036.

(ii) St. 25 Edward III, stat. 5, ch. 2:

* * * if a man do levy war against our Lord the King in his realm, or be adherent to the King's enemies in his realm, giving to them aid and comfort in the realm, or elsewhere, and thereof be provably attainted of open deed by the people of their condition: * * * that ought to be adjudged treason.[10]

(iii) St. 7 & 8 William III, ch. 3, sec. 2:

* * * noe person or persons whatsoever shall bee indicted tryed or attainted of high treason whereby any corruption of blood may or shall bee made to any such offender or offenders or to any the heir or heirs of any such offender or offenders or of misprision of such treason but by and upon the oaths and testimony of two lawfull witnesses either both of them to the same overtact or one of them to one and another of them to another overtact of the same treason unlesse the party indicted and arraigned or tryed shall willingly without violence in open court confesse the same or shall stand mute or refuse to plead or in cases of high treason shall peremptorily challenge above the number of thirty five of the jury any law statute or usage to the contrary notwithstanding.

So far as an indictment for treason alleging only a single overt act is concerned, the quantitative requirement of the St. 7 & 8 Will. III is, of course, identical with that of the Constitution of the United States.

And Mr. Justice James Wilson of the Supreme Court of the United States, who had been a member of the Constitutional Convention and in that capacity had drafted the treason clause,[11] had this comment to make about the constitutional definition of the offense in a series of law lectures delivered in 1790 and 1791:

* * * This single sentence comprehends our whole of national treason; and, as I mentioned before, is transcribed from a part of the statute of Edward the Third. By those who proposed the national constitution, this was done, that, in a subject so essentially interesting to each and to all, not a single expression should be introduced, but such as could show in its favour, that it was recommended by the mature experience, and ascertained by the legal interpretation, of numerous revolving centuries.[12]

The paradox or, if one will, the mystery of the *Cramer* case is twofold. First, the St. 7 & 8 Will. III, which settled the two-witness rule in the law of treason,[13] was not cited in either opinion; second,

---

[10] Original text in Norman-French; translation from *Rex v. Casement,* [1917] 1 K.B. 98, 99.

[11] See Hurst, *Treason in the United States,* 58 Harv. L. Rev. 395, 404-406.

[12] 3 Works of James Wilson (1804), 99-100.

[13] See 7 Wigmore, *Evidence* (3d ed. 1940), sec. 2036. England repealed the requirement in 1945. St. 8 & 9 Geo. VI, c. 44 (The Treason Act, 1945).

the opinion of the Court refers to the treason clause of the Constitution as representing a novel application, a new concept, and an abrupt departure, in the face of Mr. Justice Wilson's statement in 1790—and he had drafted the clause in 1787—that the old language was employed because of a desire to carry over the old interpretations.

How to account for this extremely curious result?

Section 8. Explanation of the mystery.—Both the St. 7 & 8 Will. III and Mr. Justice Wilson's statement were before the Court in the *Cramer* case.[14] But the Government did not file an advocate's brief after the Court set the case down for reargument. The Government filed, in an Appendix, a very scholarly historical study of the law of treason, running to 404 pages. It was not, nor did it purport to be, an argument; it was an impartial discussion.[15] In addition, the Government also filed an 88-page brief that was in the nature of a commentary on the Appendix.

The realm of "might have been" is traditionally an unprofitable source of speculation. Whether the *Cramer* case could have been won, whether a fifth Justice might have been persuaded to vote the other way if the Government had filed a real brief, i.e., an argumentative document, a written argument instead of a colorless, "dispassionate," impartial, and necessarily discursive treatise, is not a question that can be helpfully discussed. But whatever a fighting, argumentative brief might or might not have done, it would certainly have saved the Court the embarrassment of the whopping historical boner as to the concept of treason.

The dissenting judges expressed the views of Mr. Justice Wilson. They said:

There is * * * no evidence whatever that the offense of adhering to the enemy giving him aid and comfort was designed to encompass a narrower field

---

[14] See, for the latter, *Appendices to Brief for the United States on Reargument,* No. 13, Oct. T. 1944, p. 2.

[15] "The following appendices [App. A, Civil and Canon Law Materials; App. B, Anglo-American Materials] have been prepared at the request of the Solicitor General. The authors of the appendices were requested to avoid argumentative support of any particular position, and to select material for inclusion or exclusion solely on the basis of its reliability and its relevance to the questions under review by the Court. The appendices are submitted to the Court in the belief that they constitute a fair, dispassionate, and informative analysis of the law of treason; but the Government does not in any way assume responsibility for, or necessarily agree with, the inferences drawn or the conclusions expressed by the authors." *Appendices to Brief for the United States on Reargument,* No. 13, Oct. T. 1944, p. iii.

than that indicated by its accepted and settled meaning. Nor is there the slightest indication that the kind or character of overt acts required were any different than those which had long been recognized or accepted as adequate.[16]

But they had no documentation to support these assertions, because the crucial contemporaneous comments of Wilson, J., had been lost, literally lost, somewhere in the 404 pages of "fair, dispassionate, and informative analysis."

Section 9. The advocate's duty.—The basic premise of common law jurisprudence is the view that the best and surest way of ascertaining the truth and arriving at a just result is to have an impartial tribunal make its decision after first hearing the opposing parties present their conflicting contentions in the strongest and most forceful way.

The corollary of that premise is that when the opposing positions are not strongly or argumentatively presented, the tribunal does not necessarily reach a sound result, does not necessarily ascertain the truth, and may be led into egregious error. It is my own considered view, reached after a good deal of searching cogitation, that the *Cramer* case stands as a living monument to that corollary.

Therefore, it may be safely laid down that any lawyer who fails to brief and argue his case so as to present his position in the most effective manner fails in his duty, not only to his client but also to the court whose officer he is.

A court must be impartial. An advocate must be fair and accurate, but he has no business being impartial. An impartial advocate not only fails in his duty, he fails in his function as well. He is, actually and inescapably, a contradiction in terms.

---

[16] 325 U.S. at 76.

CHAPTER 2

Methods of Appellate Courts in Considering Appeals

Section 10. In general.—The mechanics of the appellate process as applied by appellate judges is a topic related to the one just discussed, because once the actual functioning of appellate courts is studied and appreciated, the need for effective advocacy becomes even more apparent. Sometimes, as in the *Cramer* case, the impression left by the briefs is the controlling factor. In other instances, the oral argument is more apt to be determinative.

Some lawyers feel that oral argument is unimportant, because "the judges will study the briefs"—and the briefs are written by the bright young lads in the office, who are sometimes very bright indeed. But this assumes that an appellate court functions like a radar-operated fire-control director, which causes the projectile always to hit the target provided only that all the relevant data have been correctly supplied. That assumption, in many instances, is neither a safe nor even a correct one. Because the fact of the matter—the brutal, hard fact of the matter—is that cases frequently are won and lost on oral argument.

This is particularly true of the indifferent cases, in which a court is not much interested as an original proposition. There are some cases, of course, that no one can lose—cases that could safely be entrusted to the office boy. There are other cases that no one can win, regardless of the skill or learning or persuasive powers of the advocate concerned. But there is a large intermediate zone of cases, running in my judgment to perhaps a quarter of the total, that do not present pressing problems or burning issues, and as to which it is perfectly obvious that no one would suppose "that civilization will come to an end whichever way this case is decided,"[1] where oral argument plays a very substantial if not a decisive part in determining the issue. This conclusion may shock some persons,

---

[1] Holmes, J., dissenting, in *Haddock v. Haddock*, 201 U.S. 562, 628.

11

and lead others to suggest that its statement is not sufficiently deferential or respectful to the courts. I can only say, in the words of the countryman who was queried as to his belief in baptism, "Good Lord, yes! I've seen it done." I have seen cases won and lost on oral argument. And the reason for this phenomenon will appear more clearly when the mechanics of the appellate process are examined.

There are two phases to be examined under this heading, the process before argument and the process after argument.

Section 11. Before argument; Practice in the Supreme Court of the United States.—To what extent do appellate judges study the record and briefs before counsel get up?

In the Supreme Court of the United States, the justices know in a general way what a case is about before it is argued on the merits, because they have already examined the jurisdictional statement when the case comes up on appeal as of right, or the petition for certiorari when it comes up for discretionary review. Whether thereafter, before the argument on the merits but after the noting of probable jurisdiction or the granting of the writ of certiorari, they read the briefs on the merits, is something that varies with the individual Justice and with the burden of work at any particular moment. It varies also with the same Justice. My impression is that most of the Justices do not regularly read the briefs on the merits before argument, except in selected cases in which they are particularly interested; and I have heard it said, by one who had reason to know, that only the late Mr. Justice Cardozo made an invariable practice of reading the briefs in advance.[2]

Editor's Note: Previous editions set out the results of Colonel Wiener's exhaustive investigation of whether the judges of the federal courts of appeal and justices of state supreme courts read briefs before or after oral argument. The specifics, which have little current application, add up to this: On some courts, judges invariably read briefs before argument. On others, they never did. And, on still others, practice varied from judge to judge. Finally, on a few courts, a single judge was assigned to read the briefs before argument. Judges who did not read briefs before argument gave workload and a desire to be open-minded at oral argument as the main reasons for their practice.

Nowadays, there is probably similar variation, though experience suggests that at least some members of most appellate panels are familiar with the issues. This may mean that pre-argument brief reading is more prevalent or it may reflect the increased presence of law clerks, who do read briefs. Read-

---

[2] This has been checked and is believed to be entirely authoritative.

ers are advised to consult court rules or other published information, or to speak with experienced appellate practitioners. Given the time that has passed since Colonel Wiener's research on brief-reading, only a few examples of his findings appear in this edition.

Section 12. Before argument; Practice in the United States Courts of Appeals.—

First Circuit. Chief Judge Magruder writes: "I cannot say that we 'invariably' read the briefs before argument, but I think it is the general practice of all of us to do so."[3]

Second Circuit. Judge Frank writes: "I think that (with me as an occasional exception) the judges of our court (almost) never read the briefs before the argument. With our heavy docket, we don't set a case for a day certain. Wherefore, many a case goes over to another week, when a different bench is sitting. If a judge reads the briefs before argument, he may thus be acting futilely."[4]

Third Circuit. Chief Judge Biggs writes: "The judges make a point of reading the briefs before argument. They do so in every instance except where some unforeseen event occurs, such as a judge being ill or some other emergency arising which requires another member of the court to take his place on short notice."[5]

Fifth Circuit. Judge Sibley, formerly Senior Circuit Judge, indicates that the practice in this court has changed in recent years. He says

When I came on the appellate bench in 1930 neither briefs nor records were examined in advance of argument, the judges preferring to have perfectly open minds until oral argument was heard, and no expression of opinion was made till briefs and record had been read and we went into conference about the case several weeks later. There was quite a lag in making decisions, and some forgetfulness of details. For the past few years we have usually looked over briefs and record in advance of argument, so as to have a general idea of the points in the case, and at the time of argument frequently so tell counsel, and that they need not expend much time in stating the case, but go at once to the discussion. We are rather given also to asking questions about what seem to us the most pressing points. This has all tended to save time and concentrate the argument, and I believe has not produced much prejudgment of the cases.[6]

---

[3] Letter from the Hon. Calvert Magruder, Chief Judge, July 27, 1948

[4] Letter from the Hon. Jerome N. Frank, Circuit Judge, July 27, 1948. *Accord:* Circuit Judge Charles E. Clark, quoted in Hicks, *Materials and Methods of Legal Research* (3d ed. 1942), p. 380.

[5] Letter from the Hon. John Biggs, Jr., Chief Judge, September 11, 1948.

[6] Letter from the Hon. Samuel H. Sibley, Circuit Judge, August 17, 1948.

Eighth Circuit. Chief Judge Gardner writes: "I read all briefs before the argument, not with a view to determining how the case should be decided, but with a view of determining in advance what the issues are. This practice is, I think, generally followed by all our Judges," although "the practice varies to some extent with the individual Judge."[7]

District of Columbia Circuit. Until late in 1949, there were six members of this court; Chief Judge Stephens then wrote that "five of us read before the argument, one does not."[8]

Section 13. Before argument; Practice in state and territorial courts of last resort.—Below is listed, in alphabetical order by states, the practice before argument in nonfederal courts of last resort.

Supreme Court of California. "Each Justice of the Supreme Court receives and examines a copy of the petition for hearing in this court after decision by the District Court of Appeal. A conference memorandum on the case is prepared by one of the justices who, in addition to the petition, reads the briefs in the case. In his memorandum he summarizes the contentions of the parties, discusses the authorities and expresses his own views upon the issue or issues involved. This memorandum is circulated to all of the other justices and a conference is thereafter held on the case at which time it is determined whether or not the cause should be taken over by the Supreme Court. Therefore, if a hearing is ordered in this court all of the justices have read the petition for hearing before argument of the cause."[9]

Supreme Court of Florida. "Inasmuch as this court hears about 750 cases a year," writes Chief Justice Thomas, "it has never been practicable for the judges to read the briefs before the arguments. Personally I think this is a splendid system, but we are always so pressed that we have never been able to inaugurate it here."[10]

Supreme Court of Iowa. "Some of the Judges of this court read the records and briefs and arguments before oral submission of the case. Many of the Judges go over the briefs and arguments a day or so before the submission. The practice varies with the individual Judge."[11]

---

[7] Letter from the Hon. Archibald K. Gardner, Chief Judge, July 29, 1948.

[8] Letter from the Hon. Harold M. Stephens, Chief Judge, August 5, 1948.

[9] Letter from William I. Sullivan, Esq., Clerk of the Supreme Court of California, August 6, 1948.

[10] Letter from the Hon. Elwyn Thomas, then Chief Justice, July 28, 1948.

[11] Letter from the Hon. John E. Mulroney, Associate Justice, September 22, 1948.

Supreme Judicial Court of Massachusetts. Chief Justice Qua writes: "No point is made of not reading the briefs before the argument. It is not, however, our practice to read them before the argument and none of our justices regularly does so. It is my personal opinion that in most instances counsel would rather come to a court which they can be sure has not prejudged the case."[12]

Supreme Court of Minnesota. Chief Justice Loring writes

Whether or not the briefs shall be read before the oral argument is a matter of choice with the individual judge. Some judges feel that they bring a more open mind to the oral argument if they do not read the briefs prior thereto. In this court, cases are assigned some days ahead and undoubtedly the judge to whom a case is assigned examines the briefs and record very carefully so that he is able to check the verity of the facts stated in the arguments, and due to our custom of immediately after the oral arguments are finished on any given day to have a conference so that each judge may state his impressions of the case, the one to whom it is assigned usually has to state his impressions of the case quite formally and thoroughly. In order to do that, of course, he must have examined the briefs and records carefully.[13]

New York Court of Appeals. Judge Bromley writes: "* * * it is not my practice—and I believe it is generally true of the other judges of the Court of Appeals—to read briefs before argument. This is certainly the general rule, although in important cases there are exceptions. I think the majority of sitting judges would prefer to read briefs in advance of argument, but in a court as busy as ours, where we generally listen to seven appeals a day, the pressure of work is so great that it has seemed to me—up to date, at least—to be impossible to read briefs in advance."[14]

Supreme Court of Oklahoma. Chief Justice Hurst writes that "all nine of the justices do not read the briefs before argument, but, ordinarily, the Justice to whom the case is assigned does."[15]

Supreme Court of Pennsylvania. Chief Justice Maxey writes: "Occasionally, in very important cases, we read the briefs before argument. I assume that the practice varies with individual judges. I am quite certain that most of the judges do not read the briefs before argument."[16]

---

[12] Letter from the Hon. Stanley E. Qua, Chief Justice, August 3, 1948.

[13] Letter from the Hon. Charles Loring, Chief Justice, July 29, 1948.

[14] Letter from the Hon. Bruce Bromley, Associate Judge, June 22, 1949. The Chief Judge is specifically on record as not reading briefs in advance of argument. Loughran, *The Argument of an Appeal in the Court of Appeals,* 12 Ford. L. Rev. 1,4.

[15] Letter from the Hon. Thurman S. Hurst, Chief Justice, September 24, 1948.

[16] Letter from the Hon. George W. Maxey, Chief Justice, July 28, 1948.

Section 14. Practice after argument; In general.—Here two basic questions arise, the answers to which condition the task of the advocate. First, when is the vote taken? Do the judges study the case first and then vote, or do they vote first and then write an opinion after study of the records and briefs? If the vote is taken first, the opinion is very apt to become, certainly in effect, a brief in support of the majority vote[17]—another factor that emphasizes the importance of the impression left at the close of the oral argument.

Second, is the writing of the opinion assigned before or after the argument? If it is assigned before, according to a prearranged system of assigning opinions seriatim, obviously the judge to whom it is assigned will necessarily exert a greater influence on the final result, and there develops a tendency toward one-man opinions. If, however, the opinion is assigned afterwards, the argument may have succeeded in interesting other judges in the case and thus have influenced the final result. Under either method, the more fully draft opinions are discussed, the less likelihood there is of one-man opinions and the greater is the probability that the opinion finally handed down will represent the composite views of the entire court.

Editor's Note: Again, Colonel Wiener conducted a detailed survey of the practice in many appellate courts. His correspondence with judges and justices across the nation revealed great variation in the procedures for reaching decisions and writing opinions. Because these results defy easy summary, a few are set out below—with the caution that they likely do not reflect current practice in specific courts. As always, it is essential to read what courts print and appellate practitioners say.

Section 15. After argument; Practice in the Supreme Court of the United States.—In this Court, two weeks of argument are followed by two weeks of recess; in each of the first two weeks, Monday through Friday are devoted to arguments, and Saturday to conference; there is a further conference on the second Saturday of the second two weeks; and opinions are announced on every Monday, except only the second Monday of the recess fortnight.

---

[17] "At Conference he was open-minded. But once he had come to a conclusion neutrality ceased. He then became an indefatigable proponent for the position he had reached, an ardent advocate and a forceful writer for the ground that he deemed solid. The Chief Justice delighted to take on all comers around the conference table and armed with precedent and reason to battle, more often successfully than not, for his views." Address of Mr. Justice Reed on the Occasion of the Dedication of the Birthplace of Chief Justice Stone, Chesterfield, N.H., August 25, 1948.

At the conference, the case is stated by the Chief Justice, and then discussed by each Associate Justice in order of seniority. It is then voted on, in inverse order of seniority, the junior Associate Justice voting first. The writing of the opinion is then assigned by the Chief Justice, or, if he is in dissent, then by the senior Associate Justice of the majority. The draft opinions are then circulated. Thereafter, depending on the difficulty of the case, the opinions are considered at one or more further conferences. Written comments of considerable length are often made by Justices to the writer of the opinion and personal discussions take place in chambers between those on the same side of a legal question. I have been told that frequently the form of the opinion is changed and that in unusual cases there are as many as ten or fifteen draft circulations before final acceptance.

Frequently, the critical factor is thus the length of time between argument and conference. If a case argued on a Wednesday is voted on by Saturday, necessarily the impression left by the oral argument is tremendously significant. To the extent that the vote is postponed to the following Saturday or to the conference a fortnight hence, the briefs or the Justices' independent research looms larger in the final determination; the greater the time lag, the more independent study possible. No definite information on this variable is available; all that can be said is that it depends on the apparent complexity of the case, on the state of the calendar, and, of course, on the writer of the opinion.

Section 16. After argument; Practice in the United States Courts of Appeals.—

First Circuit. Chief Judge Magruder writes:

At the conclusion of a given sitting, the members of the court invariably have a conference in which the cases are discussed one by one, a tentative vote is taken, and the assignment for opinion writing is made. It is not our practice for each judge to prepare a memorandum on the case. After a draft opinion is ready, it is circulated by mail. Sometimes this gives rise to extensive correspondence back and forth, when disagreements develop or when suggestions for change are made. Occasionally, a further conference is held, either by special arrangement, or more often when the court is assembled in Boston for a later sitting.[18]

Second Circuit. Judge Frank writes:

Each of the three sitting judges, before the conference, reads the briefs and as much of the record as is pertinent. Each then prepares a memo. (I've sometimes

---

[18] Letter from the Hon. Calvert Magruder, Chief Judge, July 27, 1948.

written memos as long as 15 pages.) These memos are then distributed *inter sese*. Thereafter, and for the first time (usually about a week after that in which we sat), the three judges confer. It's amazing how often one of us sees an aspect of the case (re facts or legal rules) which the others overlooked. Sometimes a conference on a single case will last for an hour. Not infrequently, one or two of the three abandons the position he took in his memo. (The chance composition of the court thus some times affects the decision.) No vote whatever occurs until after conference—except in the very, very few cases decided from the bench.

After conference, that one of the three sitting judges who is senior in service assigns the writing of the opinions. The assignment is very informal: If one of us asks to be assigned, his request will ordinarily be granted.

The opinion, when circulated, is of course subject to criticisms and suggestions, freely given and usually accepted.

Obviously, the result of our method is that we do not have "one-man" opinions. The style of writing, however, is left to the opinion writer.[19]

Third Circuit. The judges invariably confer with each other immediately after the argument, according to Chief Judge Biggs,

usually on the afternoon of the same day on which argument is had unless (a rare occasion) the court sits so late that it is impossible to confer conveniently. In this event a conference is held as soon as possible, either the following afternoon or within two or three days. There is no time lag unless a judge has been called in emergency and has had no opportunity to examine the record and briefs in which event the interim will be sufficient to let him make the examination. (Note that we use the appendix system rather than the full record.)

The practice of having each judge prepare a memorandum was abandoned about seven years ago. In exceptional cases where there is a difference of opinion one or more judges may prepare memoranda for a second or even a third conference.

There is usually no conference to discuss the draft opinion. These are simply circulated to all members of the court, including those who did not sit in the panel as well as those who did sit. This gives an opportunity for rehearing before the court en banc, a privilege rarely availed of. If more than one conference is had and there are memoranda, the latter are usually discussed. The members of the court vote at the conference usually immediately after argument. In some difficult cases some member of the court will be assigned the duty of preparing a draft in the form of an opinion and the vote will be taken by letter after the draft is circulated or at a later conference. The opinions are

---

[19] Letter from the Hon. Jerome N. Frank, Circuit Judge, July 27, 1948.

assigned usually at the end of a week of sittings so that opinion writing can be fairly distributed.[20]

Fifth Circuit. Judge Sibley, formerly Senior Circuit Judge, writes:

We ordinarily hear argument Monday, Tuesday and Wednesday. On Friday we have a conference touching the cases heard that week, and any others held over from previous weeks. No written memorandum is usually presented then. The discussion is informal, and we will likely agree on the proper decision of over half the cases heard that week, and assign them for the preparation of an opinion. Those in which there is doubt or disagreement are held over for further investigation and discussion. Opinions when written are marked with a concurrence separately by each judge if entirely satisfactory. If not, objections are brought under discussion. A separate concurring opinion sometimes results, or a dissent. Our present practice is a great time saver, for we now have opinions filed in a majority of our cases within thirty days after argument, and we have little need to reread anything, since it is promptly acted on. I believe the quality of our work has not suffered.

We vote on a case ordinarily after conference and before opinion is written, but each judge is at liberty to change his vote at any time before the opinion is filed, or to call for further conference.[21]

Eighth Circuit. Chief Judge Gardner writes:

The Judges invariably confer with each other at the close of the arguments submitted each day and before the preparation of a memorandum or opinion. The Judges also confer on all the cases at the close of the term. At these conferences we determine on what cases, if any, we are clear what the decision should be. On these we have no further conference. In all other cases each of the participating Judges prepares memoranda. A later conference is held to discuss the memoranda or conference opinions.

On the cases in which we are very clear, we vote at the conference held at the close of the term; on others we vote after the memoranda have been submitted and discussed at a conference. The cases are not assigned for final opinion until after all conferences have been held.[22]

Section 17. After argument; Practice in state and territorial courts of last resort.—

Supreme Court of Arkansas. The judges invariably confer with each other after the argument; the time varies, but it is sufficiently long to permit examination of the records and briefs. The only written memorandum is prepared by the judge who writes the opinion,

---

[20] Letter from the Hon. John Biggs, Jr., Chief Judge, September 11, 1948.

[21] Letter from the Hon. Samuel H. Sibley, Circuit Judge, August 17, 1948.

[22] Letter from the Hon. Archibald K. Gardner, Chief Judge, July 29, 1948.

unless another judge desires to write; it is then discussed in conference. The judges vote after the preliminary conference and again upon acceptance or rejection of opinion. The writing of the court's opinion is assigned when the cases are submitted.[23]

Supreme Court of California.

After the granting of a hearing a calendar memorandum is prepared by one of the Justices and circulated to all of the Justices prior to oral argument. Following argument on the cause, time permitting, a conference is immediately held on the cause; otherwise, the conference is held within a few days thereafter. At this conference a vote of the Justices is taken with respect to the possible disposition of the cause. All members may not at that time be ready to express a definite conclusion with respect to the issues involved but they at least express tentative conclusions. The Chief Justice thereupon assigns the cause for the preparation of a written opinion to a Justice who expressed the majority view of the court. After the opinion is prepared by that Justice and circulated among the other Justices, any one of the other Justices may write a memorandum thereon or concur in the opinion as written, or prepare a dissent.

Following the circulation of the opinion, conferences are frequently held but not, of course, in every case. Should the Chief Justice or any other Justice, however, desire that a conference be called on a case following the circulation of the opinion, it is called and the case is again discussed. When all, or at least a majority of the court, have signed an opinion it is filed, together with any concurring or dissenting opinions that have been prepared in the matter.[24]

Supreme Court of Delaware. Chief Justice Richards writes:

After the case has been argued all of the Judges who hear it confer before a memorandum or opinion is prepared. Notice of this conference is given to all the Judges by the Presiding Judge and sufficient time is allowed to permit an examination of the record and briefs. At times more than one memorandum is prepared but often there will be only one written memorandum which is by the Judge who writes the opinion. Drafts of opinions are sent to all the Judges who sit in the case and usually a conference is held to discuss them. The Judges usually vote after the first conference has been held, but at times more than one conference is held before a final vote is taken.[25]

Supreme Court of Indiana. Here the assignment is done by the secretary of the court in rotation, any judge having the privilege to refuse a case and have it reassigned. The judges confer immediately

---

[23] Letter from the Hon. Griffin Smith, Chief Justice, September 25, 1948.

[24] Letter from William I. Sullivan, Esq., Clerk of the Supreme Court of California, August 6, 1948.

[25] Letter from the Hon. Charles S. Richards, Chief Justice, November 1, 1948.

after argument. The practice is for the judge to whom the case is assigned to write an opinion in rough, which is then submitted at a full conference of the five judges. The final vote is taken after submission of the rough draft of the opinion (or opinions, if there be dissents or concurring opinions).[26]

Supreme Court of Iowa. Mr. Justice Mulroney writes

At the close of each day during which cases have been submitted the entire court meets in consultation and discusses the cases that have been submitted that day. No memo is prepared but the case is assigned (by rotation) to one Judge to prepare an opinion. Thereafter at the next meeting of the court, three weeks later, the opinions that have been prepared are discussed. I might add that as soon as an opinion is prepared a copy is immediately given to each Judge and if any Judge desires to make written comment, a copy of such comment is also sent to each Judge. In other words, the opinion and all of the written comments are discussed and if any Judge is in disagreement with the opinion, time is given to that Judge to prepare a dissent, or if a majority of the court is in disagreement with the opinion written, the case is reassigned to someone of the majority view for another opinion.[27]

Supreme Judicial Court of Massachusetts. There is a preliminary conference immediately after the argument, on the same day, and tentative opinions are expressed at that time. The cases are then assigned for the writing of the draft opinions, which need not necessarily follow the views expressed at the preliminary conference. Generally the judge who is assigned the opinion brings in a draft, which is thoroughly discussed orally; after this each judge may prepare a memorandum and usually does if there is any disagreement. A vote is taken after the draft opinion is brought in. If this vote shows disagreement or if any judge desires further discussion, the case goes over until the next conference. The final vote takes place when agreement has been secured or when it becomes plain that agreement cannot be secured.[28]

New York Court of Appeals. Each judge in rotation takes a case in his turn. The judges confer with each other after argument, and in fact consultation is held on every case and every motion after ample time has been afforded for examination of records and briefs. Chief Judge Loughran writes that "there is consultation on every case and every motion whether memoranda are circulated or not and irrespective of the writing of any opinion. This consultation

[26] Information furnished by the Court.

[27] Letter from the Hon. John E. Mulroney, Associate Justice, September 22, 1948.

[28] Letter from the Hon. Stanley E. Qua, Chief Justice, August 3, 1948.

is the most important phase of the work of the court." Any judge may write a memorandum of opinion in any case, and the members of the court vote "when an agreement is reached at consultation and not before."[29]

Supreme Court of Ohio. There is a conference after the arguments, either on the same or the following day. The members of the court vote after the discussion in the Court Consultation, and the writing of the opinion is then assigned, when a majority concur. Except in the case of dissents, only the judge to whom the opinion is assigned prepares an opinion. Each opinion is read in the Court Consultation, and each judge has a copy and makes suggestions as the opinion is being read.[30]

Supreme Court of Pennsylvania. There is a conference on the morning after argument. Chief Justice Maxey writes

After the tentative vote is taken on the next morning [after argument] the Chief Justice assigns the case to one of the majority. The latter writes the opinion. Occasionally some other judge writes a concurring opinion and quite frequently some judge writes a dissenting opinion. After the opinions are received there is a further discussion. It quite often happens that the vote changes.[31]

Supreme Court of Vermont. The late Chief Justice Moulton wrote:

We always confer informally directly after the argument and before the preparation of the memorandum or opinion. At this conference each judge expresses himself as to the merits of the case, and the judge to whom the writing of the opinion has been assigned takes notes on what is said by each one of his associates. The opinion is then prepared and submitted to the others, each one of whom prepares a memorandum concerning any criticism, comment or proposal of change. All these papers are returned to the writer, after which a conference is held at which all matters of disagreement are discussed and resolved if possible. It is at this time that the opinion is put in its final shape. The members of the Court are assigned to the writing of opinions in rotation.[32]

Supreme Court of Appeals of Virginia. In this court, there is invariably a conference after argument, usually on the afternoon of the day the case is argued. Chief Justice Hudgins describes the practice as follows:

A majority of the justices prepare a memorandum of the case sometime before the argument—that is, they make a note of what they regard as the

---

[29] Letter from the Hon. John T. Loughran, Chief Judge, July 31, 1948.

[30] Information supplied by the Hon. Carl V. Weygandt, Chief Justice, July 29, 1948.

[31] Letter from the Hon. George W. Maxey, Chief Justice, July 28, 1948.

[32] Letter from the late Hon. Sherman R. Moulton, formerly Chief Justice, October 7, 1948.

decisive points in the case. Frequently, during the argument these notes are extended. At the conference after argument the different points are discussed rather fully. Sometimes the views of the justices are taken down in shorthand and a typewritten copy furnished each justice. The final vote on the case is not taken until each member of the Court has studied the opinion and furnished the other justices with his criticism of it. Before oral argument the case is assigned to a justice to prepare the opinion. If, at the first conference, he does not agree with the majority, the case is reassigned. Sometimes the justice who is preparing the opinion changes his views. If so, he writes the opinion in accord with his own concept of the principles involved. If the majority of the Court do not agree with the opinion as he writes it, it is reassigned and his opinion becomes the dissenting opinion.[33]

Section 18. Importance of the first impression.—The foregoing detailed review of the mechanics of the appellate process documents, underscores, and above all explains the assertion made earlier in this chapter (*supra*, Sec. 10) that many, many cases are won or lost on oral argument. Necessarily and inescapably, the impression derived from the oral presentation is vital wherever and whenever the briefs are not read before argument, or when the first vote is taken immediately thereafter. And, whether the decision in a particular case reflects what is basically a joint endeavor, or whether, realistically viewed, it is (at least initially) the determination of the single judge to whom the case was assigned in advance of hearing, the impression derived from the argument is bound to carry over into the later, detailed study of the record and briefs. This is particularly true when one considers the pressure of court calendars. Mr. Justice Holmes noted, many years ago, that "one has to consider this element of time. One has to try to strike the jugular and let the rest go."[34] And, fifty years later, the bar had occasion to get, from a Supreme Court Justice since deceased, a revealing glimpse of "the few hours that can be given to consideration of this case."[35] Thus the time element interacts with the factor of appellate mechanics to add still further significance to the oral presentation.

Only occasionally do judges steel themselves against the impression obtained from the argument. A distinguished state judge, of over twenty years' appellate experience, once wrote: "I am reluctant to reach conclusions at the close of the oral argument lest my later consideration of the case be influenced thereby." And another

---

[33] Letter from the Hon. Edward W. Hudgins, Chief Justice, July 28, 1948.

[34] Holmes, *Walbridge Abner Field* [1899] in *Speeches* (1913) 75, 77.

[35] Jackson, J., dissenting in *Jungersen v. Ostby & Barton*, 335 U.S. 560, 572.

wrote that "because of the thoroughness with which cases are reviewed in conference, * * * we do not attempt to obtain impressions on the argument." Then, too, as another judge indicated, "Personally I take in more through the eyes than through the ears."

More frequently, however, appellate judges endeavor to obtain a full understanding of the case from the argument, and, when the presentation has been clear, they succeed in doing so. It goes without saying that they are very substantially assisted in their work when the argument enables them to obtain such an understanding.

Section 19. Coincidence between first impression and final vote.—I made inquiry of the judges who were good enough to contribute the data collected in this chapter as to the extent to which their impressions at the close of the oral arguments coincided with their final votes, and have set forth below the percentage of such coincidence.

By way of preliminary comment on the figures that follow, it should be noted that, as one judge pointed out, "the case may be such that the same result would follow a mere reading of the briefs."

By way of further preliminary, it should also be noted that an argument that is unclear or ineffective will leave no impression save one of confusion. Thus, one able and distinguished federal judge (whose name had better be withheld out of consideration for the sensibilities of the bar of his jurisdiction) wrote in these terms:

It may be heresy to say so, but in my experience, oral argument is not as helpful as it should and could be if the advocates would reach the simple point in the lawsuit and discuss it intelligently. The difficulty with the average advocate is that he succeeds primarily in confusing the court rather than clarifying the issues. Many times the logical answer falls into place with a proper understanding of the facts and the issues. In sum, my answer * * * is that most of the arguments leave me in doubt of the conclusion. I do usually manage to gain a clear-cut understanding of the case, even if it be necessary to pull it out of the lawyers.

Another distinguished and learned jurist, a personal friend of long standing who, for a number of reasons, cannot be identified, went even further:

Once in a while, I may confess, at the close of the oral argument none of us seems to know what the hell the case is about; but I assume you won't quote that literally in your forthcoming book on *Appellate Advocacy*.

Well, I do quote it literally—with his later permission—because every appellate judge will admit privately that, after the worst of arguments, the same thing happens in the best of courts.

Finally, a third preliminary warning: there are many close and difficult cases that no judge will feel ready to decide without further and very close study of the record and of the authorities even after model arguments on both sides.

In the ordinary case, however, good oral argument is very important, far more than even many able lawyers realize. I quote at random from a few letters received from appellate judges:

I think all our judges desire to hear oral argument, and that the argument is helpful. When the lawyers appear to know their case, and to have examined the law well, it helps the judge to feel that he has heard pretty much all that he should hear, and saves him much labor in independent checking up.

I am one of the judges whose mind is stimulated by argument. With a prior study of the record and briefs and after the interrogation at argument, which proceeds about as it does in the House of Lords, I have usually reached the conclusion which I bring to the specific conference of the judges, though sometimes intervening further study changes the conclusion reached at the termination of argument.

Personally, I consider argument of prime importance, particularly where cases are assigned in mechanical rotation as in our Court.

For those of us who have not read the briefs in advance of oral argument, that is the first information we receive about the case. Quite naturally the argument is material.

For a while I read the briefs prior to argument, but I soon abandoned the practice because I found it more interesting and helpful to read the briefs after the lawyers on oral argument had breathed the breath of life into them. I can read a brief much more profitably after my interest has been aroused. * * * Oral argument is of great importance. As I said in the beginning, it breathes the breath of life into the briefs. Without argument, a brief is a cold and uninviting thing. The argument serves at least the purpose of arousing the interest of the judge. If well done, they frequently create in the judge's mind an impression that is not easy to remove.

My own philosophy is that, if a case is worth appealing, it is worth arguing. I think its principal value is in the interest and stimulation which it creates as to the issues and questions, not in the answers which it provides. It adds the only human touch there is to the dull impersonal processes of appellate review. It enables me to see through a lot of strengths and weaknesses which the stultified expression of a brief sometimes disguises or leaves colorless. I enjoy the task of opinion writing much more in an argued case than one submitted on briefs. And frankly, I think most judges will write a better opinion under the direct challenge of an oral argument from its psychological impact than otherwise.

It is almost a commonplace that every trial lawyer senses how there generally comes a particular point in the proceeding where the scales have been irrevocably tipped in favor of the side that ultimately prevails. Indeed, when reviewing the transcript of testimony, it is very frequently possible to pick the very turning point of the trial, the moment after which the result was never in doubt.

In many appellate arguments, it is similarly possible to pinpoint this same instant. An appellate judge once said to me, "Majorities in our court pile up very rapidly." Consequently the task of the appellate advocate in every instance is to endeavor, while he is on his feet and while he can impress the judges with the impact of his presentation, to persuade the judges that his cause is the better one. To the extent that the legal authorities are balanced, so that the decision could go either way, the impression made at the argument may well be the determinative factor in inducing the court to reach its ultimate decision in accordance with that impression. Accordingly, to document this view, inquiry was made of appellate judges.

Apparently there is a closer coincidence in courts that deal largely with private rather than public law controversies. In the first edition of this work, in which were included data from thirty-eight State and Territorial courts of last resort, in addition to data from Federal appellate courts, the percentage of coincidence was very high; the largest group of judges wrote that their final vote coincided with the impression at the close of the argument in 90 percent or more of all the cases heard. This figure is in accord with what an outstanding state judge revealed several generations ago to Mr. Charles Evans Hughes, then teaching law at the Cornell Law School.[36]

In the 1967 edition, which was limited to federal appeals, the reported percentage of concordance was substantially lower, varying from "a large majority" and "usually" to several estimates of

---

[36] Hughes, *The Supreme Court of the United States* (1928) 61–62:

"I suppose that, aside from cases of exceptional difficulty, the impression that a judge has at the close of a full oral argument accords with the conviction which controls his final vote. A Judge of the Court of Appeals of New York told me some years ago that he had kept track for a time of his impressions after the oral arguments and found that in ninety per centum of the cases, although, of course, he reserved his vote until after a thorough study, his final judgment agreed with his view at the end of the oral argument. This is so because the judges are conversant with their special material, that is, the prior decisions of the court, and when they apprehend the precise question to be decided they are generally not slow in reaching a conclusion."

about 80 percent, with only one judge placing the percentage of concordance at 90 percent or higher.

Probably—for this cannot rise higher than informed conjecture—the difference reflects a difference in subject matter. Constitutional cases, particularly, require reflection, and cannot always be safely decided on the impression, however persuasive, that is made orally. The same is true of cases turning on the interrelationship of complex statutory provisions. This is not to say either that oral argument can be omitted in constitutional or statutory cases, or that a substantial question can safely be left to an insubstantial argument. In this field, also, "Few cases are won but many are lost."

But, whether the issue is one that lends itself to virtual resolution at the argument, so that further study will vary the judicial impression then formed in only a tenth of the cases, or whether it is one of such complexity that oral argument merely provides suggestive topics for judicial reflection, the brief is vitally important also. There must be a brief, to summarize the evidence, to set out record references, to collect citations, to discuss the authorities—to do all that oral argument cannot do and at the same time to buttress and support and substantiate the impression made by oral argument. The inescapable fact of appellate work is that both brief and argument are necessary, that neither can safely be omitted, and that, for effective appellate work, both must reflect the best work of which the advocate is capable.

Please note that I say "effective" rather than "successful" appellate work. There is no way to guarantee success on appeal. Indeed, if there were, if such a secret were known to me, I should hardly undertake to share it with others.

All I can fairly or properly assert is that success on appeal is far more likely to follow from effective than from ineffective briefs and arguments, and that the remainder of this book will endeavor to show how to write effective briefs and how to make effective oral arguments.

PART II

EFFECTIVE BRIEF-WRITING

CHAPTER 3

Essentials of an Effective Appellate Brief

Section 20. Introductory.—An appellate brief is a written argument in support of or in opposition to the order, decree, or judgment below. This part of the book attempts to tell how to write a good appellate brief. The subject may seem at first blush to be dull as last night's dishwater, but it is a very important one indeed. When a court, as frequently happens, reads briefs in advance of argument, then your brief is the first step in persuasion. When a court reads briefs only after argument, then, if it is persuaded to decide the case your way after hearing the oral presentations, your brief becomes the peg on which to hang its collective judicial hat. And in a close case, where the issue is uncertain and where the legal materials must be studied at considerable length, the brief becomes the factor on which the entire case will be won or lost.

The present chapter covers the essentials of effective brief-writing, the next one considers helpful techniques in writing and research, and Chapter 5 discusses the finer points and the details of the process. It is a process that entails, in my judgment at least, a quest for perfection—a quest pursued under the pressure of dead-lines and the demands of other cases, a quest perhaps foredoomed to failure by the eternal fallibility of man.

The name of the practitioner, so say the scholars, is writ in water. Certain it is that he has but few tangible mementos of his labors— his name in the reports (misspelled, likely as not) and a few bound volumes of briefs on his shelves, gathering dust. (After all, briefs and the opinions they assisted in shaping and influencing represent the preservation of his professional skill.) For my part, I should like some day to write the dream brief, one wholly free from misprints and from awkward expressions, which, on rereading five years later, I would not want to change by so much as a comma (except possibly to add citations to cases subsequently decided that confirm the contentions made). To the extent that time and other cases permit, I still strive for that goal—but without success up to now.

Such a standard of perfectionism in a brief is doubtless just that—a dream. But there is nothing dreamy about an effective appellate brief—and it is the effective rather than the impossibly perfect brief that is the subject of this chapter.

For the rest, it is really not profitable to discuss an effective brief in terms of abstractions. Too many otherwise excellent discussions of brief-writing are of very little use except to the expert, simply because they are abstract; and, *ex hypothesi*, the expert does not need them. What follows, therefore, will be concrete and detailed.

Most of the examples discussed in the pages that follow will be taken from my own practice. That choice is dictated by convenience, not by egocentricity. Of course there are plenty of other and, I have no doubt at all, better examples. But the briefs discussed here are the ones that arose out of the cases with which I have wrestled; they are the ones I have personally sweated out, where I had intimate acquaintance with the details of the problems presented and with the processes by which ultimate solutions for those problems were reached. Nevertheless, although the examples chosen are thus limited, I have sought to select, not esoteric specialties, but topics of general interest and techniques of general application.

For extended research, the best sources are the libraries of courts, bar associations, and law schools, many of which preserve the records and briefs in appellate cases. There is no better guide to good brief-writing anywhere than the examination and study of briefs written by leaders of the bar and (by and large) by such Government agencies as handle extensive litigation. Briefs in those categories are highly instructive as to form, substance, and technique.

Section 21. List of the essentials.—The really essential features are:

(a) Compliance with rules of court.

(b) Effective statement of facts.

(c) Good, clear, forceful English.

(d) Argumentative headings.

(e) Appealing formulation of the questions presented.

(f) Sound analysis of the legal problems in argument on the law.

(g) Convincing presentation of the evidence in argument on the facts.

(h) Careful attention to all portions of the brief.

(i) Impression of conviction that allays the reader's doubts and satisfies his curiosity.

These essentials are discussed in order below. The details and the finer points, i.e., those that help to make the difference between a really good brief and one that is merely adequate, are considered in Chapter 5.

Section 22. Compliance with rules of court.—Compliance with rules of court is stated as the first requirement, because even if you should succeed in writing that dream brief, the clerk would not permit it to be filed if it exceeded the permitted length or if it violated in other obvious respects the rules of the court to which it is tendered. So—first essential—familiarize yourself with the *current* rules of the court where your brief is to be filed, and comply with them. The word "current" is advisedly emphasized; failure to heed the obsolescence factors in rules of court can be extremely dangerous.

Since this book is not a practice manual, it will not attempt to collect the provisions concerning briefs as they are written in the rules of American appellate courts. The only safe procedure, if you are new at the game or are writing a brief for a strange court, is to read the rules, check with the clerk or an older practitioner, and examine and follow some briefs that have already passed muster.

Three points that are dealt with in the rules of most appellate courts must be carefully checked:

First. Many courts require a particular and frequently somewhat arbitrary arrangement of briefs, with respect to color of cover, rigidly detailed arrangement of matter, summary of argument and of the principal authorities, and prescribed position for the statement of questions presented.

Second. Most clerks, reflecting the views of their courts, are quite fussy about untimely filings.[1]

---

[1] Many circuits have rules to the effect that late filing constitutes a ground for dismissing the appeal, and on occasion such dismissals are noted in the Federal Reporter. In one instance, an appellant filed no brief for three years!

Similarly, these instances have been noted in the course of currently scanning the Federal Reporter: (a) Appeal dismissed because record not in shape for review. (b) Failure to print any evidence in the appendix. (c) "It may be wondered how appellate could have expected the district court to rule other than it did on the very meager record in this case."

It is believed that no useful purpose would be served by supplying citations in these instances.

Third. Most appellate courts limit the length of the briefs that may be filed without prior express permission.

One additional but extremely important caution must be noted here: Be sure to ascertain the limitations on the reviewing powers of the appellate court. Some courts lack the power to review questions of fact in particular circumstances. On occasion, the time and form of the exception to the adverse ruling conditions the reviewing court's appellate jurisdiction. Since this is not a practice manual, the details in the several jurisdictions will not even be suggested. But the basic admonition is the same: The brief-writer must be aware of the limitations under which his appeal will be considered.

Section 23. Effective statement of the facts; In general.—In many respects, the Statement of Facts is the most important part of the brief.

The greatest mistake any lawyer can make, after he has written a fine brief on the law, is to toss in a dry statement of facts and send the thing off to the printer. My chief, when I first came to the bar (now more years ago than I like to recall), used to insist that that was the common error made by the young men in the office—and everything I have seen since then has served only to confirm the truth of his admonition. I owe it to him to acknowledge that I have profited by his wisdom, and learned the great lesson that, in writing a brief, the facts should first be studied, mastered, sweated over— and written out into an acceptable draft before the rest of the brief is even touched.

For facts are basic raw materials of the legal process, as all great lawyers, from ancient worthies down to the great judges of modern times, have recognized. *Ex facto jus oritur*—the law arises out of the fact—is a well-worn maxim of old, to the point of being hackneyed. But it expresses a fundamental truth that, within the memory of most of us, Mr. Justice Brandeis regularly put into practice. As Professor Freund, one of his former law clerks, has written:

His belief in the primacy of facts was apparent even in the process of preparing an opinion. However much he encouraged his law clerks to present the results of their legal research in a form which might be directly useful in drafting an opinion, he took on himself the burden of drafting the statement of facts. This was his private assurance that he would not be seduced by the fascination of legal analysis until he had grounded himself in the realities of the case as they were captured in the record.[2]

---

[2] Freund, *On Understanding the Supreme Court* (1949), 50.

While the advocate's task and function differ from those of the judge, in that the advocate must persuade while the judge has only to decide, the foregoing excerpt emphasizes the vital significance of bringing the facts of the case to the judges' attention with a view to shaping their decision.

Remember, courts are not automatons, and judges do not cease to be human beings, however much they may—as they very properly should—steel themselves against emotional bias. The constantly repeated demonstration that "hard cases make bad law" is living proof of that proposition. The real importance of facts is that courts want to do substantial justice and that they are sensitive to the "equities." Consequently the first objective of the advocate must be so to write his Statement of Facts that the court will want to decide the case his way after reading just that portion of the brief.

Section 24. Effective statement of the facts; Formulating the statement.—First of all, when you write a Statement of Facts, you must remember that you are trying to reach another person's mind, and you must also remember that any person's acquisition of knowledge is a cumulative process. Therefore, you must state facts of the case in your brief as you yourself would wish to read them— the introductory summary first, the details later—in order to get a clear, consecutive, understandable picture of what the case is really about.

A lawyer engaged in stating facts is telling a story, a story the court should accept and understand as it reads along, without having to supplement your narrative by its own independent efforts. Or, to use a different metaphor, the lawyer stating the facts is painting a picture—and those who look at that picture should not be troubled by the details of how the artist mixed his colors. To the extent that the reader may want to check the facts of the story, or the art-lover those of the picture, the record references supply the necessary assurance that what has been depicted is real and not imaginary. See Sections 44 and 76, below.

Therefore, avoid the lazy kind of summary that says, "The witness Quackenbush testified that _____; that _____; that _____; that _____," and so on *ad infinitum* and *ad nauseam.* Any literate stenographer can do that; most lazy lawyers do it; but it isn't very helpful to the court and it doesn't forward the case, so a good lawyer will not do it.

Similarly, it is a mistake to assume, as many lawyers apparently do, that it is necessary to set out the testimony in the same order in which it was presented at the trial. The trial lawyer must take one witness at a time, and develop what witnesses X, Y, and Z know about incidents A, B, and C. There is generally no other way in which he can get that evidence into the record. But the appellate lawyer writing the Statement of Facts should marshal his evidence, not according to witnesses, but according to topics. True, it takes more work, which is why so often it is not done. But the topical arrangement is really the only effective one.

No matter how long or short a Statement of Facts may be, it should always be written in such a way as to advance the cause of the party on whose behalf it is prepared. It must not argue or editorialize; its strength lies in selection and juxtaposition, without of course ever appearing to involve the irrelevant.

In many instances, you can add immeasurably to the effectiveness of your Statement of Facts by simply quoting the opinion below, varying it only by adding appropriate record references enclosed in square brackets. If you represent the appellee, this treatment gives the Statement of Facts the additional and very substantial weight that attaches to findings made by the tribunal that saw and heard the witnesses. If you represent the appellant, the same technique gives you the freedom from distracting minor issues that comes from saying that, accepting fully the facts found below, you pitch your entire case on questions of law. Or, otherwise stated, use the opinion below supplemented by references to the record when you are appellant as to the law or when you are appellee as to the facts.

Frequently a Statement of Facts will be long, particularly when the record is long. In that event it should not be written as one continuous screed, but should be divided up, through the use of subheadings, so that the reader can more easily grasp the relevance of what he reads.[3]

---

[3] Here are examples of subdivisions of statements in two cases, one civil, the other criminal.

    (a) *Federal Trade Commission v. Cement Institute,* 333 U.S. 683:

        "The Federal Trade Commission's complaint.

        "The findings of the Commission.

        "The cement industry and respondents' position therein.

        "Absence of competition in the industry.

        "Respondents' multiple basing-point delivered-price system.

        "Collective action to prevent competition and to maintain respondents' pricing system.

        "Effects of respondents' combination.

        "Violation of Section 2 of the Clayton Act.   (continued)

When the Statement of Facts is long, it is even more necessary to write it so that the judicial reader's interest will never flag, but will always be held, and will always be carried in the direction that the advocate wishes it to go. That endeavor must never be permitted to sag, even at the end, when the proceedings in the court below are being discussed.

It is a mistake to write simply, "The court below affirmed (R. 74)," when you could have written, "The court below affirmed on the ground that the evidence amply justified the jury in finding petitioner guilty as charged (R. 74)."

Frequently the Statement of Facts can be, as it were, neatly buttoned up by a juicy quotation from the findings or opinion below. If you are appealing, summarize or quote the opinion below when it seems pretty obviously wrong, or summarize or quote from the dissenting judge, or both. If, on the other hand, you are for the appellee, set out the conclusions or the apt quotation from the majority opinion, or do the same for the dissent when it seems unsound on its face.

In short, write your Statement of Facts from beginning to end, from the first paragraph to the last, with this one aim always before you: to write your Statement of Facts so that the court will want to decide the case in your favor after reading just that portion of your brief.

It is doubtless tiresome to reiterate all this. But the fact is that the fault most universally found in Statements of Facts is that they are too dry, that they do not make the most of what the record affords, and that in consequence they do not advance the case.

"The Commission's conclusion and order.

"The decision of the Circuit Court of Appeals.

    (b) *Chandler v. United States,* 171 F.2d 921 (C.A. 1), certiorari denied, 336 U.S. 918:

        "A. Appellant's activities prior to Germany's declaration of war against the United States on December 11, 1941.

        "B. Appellant's broadcasting activities in Germany, 1942-1945.

        "C. The substance of appellant's broadcasts and his intent to betray the United States.

        "D. The overt acts submitted to the jury.

           "(i) Arranging for and making recordings.

          "(ii) Participating in conferences for the improvement or formulation of broadcasts.

         "(iii) Participating in conferences for the resumption or continuation of broadcasting activities.

        "E. Appellant's apprehension and his return to the United States in custody.

        "F. Appellant's alleged insanity."

Section 25. Effective statement of the facts; The atmospheric trimmings.—Once the basic arrangement has been blocked out, with proper topical introductions and with the facts arranged in logical order—and generally the chronological order is the most logical one—it is time to consider the next step, which is, succinctly, to incorporate the atmospheric trimmings.

Here the task is to present the facts, without any sacrifice of accuracy, but yet in such a way as to squeeze the last drop of advantage to your case—and that is a task which in a very literal sense begins with the first sentence of your Statement of Facts and continues through the last one (in which you set forth the opinion or judgment below).

Examples of how to do it and of how not to do it will be considered later; here will be noted some general admonitions.

(a) First and foremost, you must be accurate. You owe that duty to the court, and, equally, you owe that duty to your client. And, for the same reasons, you must be candid. If the court finds that you are inaccurate, either by way of omission or of affirmative misstatement, it will lose faith in you, and your remaining assertions may well fail to persuade. See Section 44, below, for a discussion of the application, in this connection, of the maxim *Falsus in uno, falsus in omnibus.*

A Federal appellate judge once remarked that "Skilled advocacy is not a substitute for operative facts though that art may supply emphasis and delicate nuances of evidence clearly established by the record."[4]

That statement marks, about as well as it can be drawn in the abstract, the line between the proper use of atmospheric trimmings and the improper use of imperceptible slanting that results in intentional misstatement. It is just as much the duty of the advocate to present his facts favorably as it is his duty to present the law forcefully. It is not in any sense "cute" to wring every advantageous fact out of your record—just so long as the full Statement of Facts is fair, honest, and accurate. I emphasize both aspects because—as a matter of actual fact—quite a number of appellate judges seem to feel that any advice to stress the favorable facts is tantamount to urging deception as an aid to winning on appeal. Any such reaction is the result either of a failure to understand the office of advocacy, or of a failure to analyze one's own thinking—or of both.

---

[4] Finnegan, J., concurring in *Lusk v. Commissioner of Internal Revenue,* 250 F.2d 591, 595 (C.A. 7).

The mark of really able advocacy is the ability to set forth the facts most favorably within the limits of utter and unswerving accuracy.

(b) Second, grasp your nettles firmly. No matter how unfavorable the facts are, they will hurt you more if the court first learns them from your opponent. Draw the sting of the unpleasant facts by presenting them yourself. To gloss over a nasty portion of the record is not only somewhat less than fair to the court, it is definitely harmful to the case.

If you fail to heed this injunction, if you omit salient and significant but unpleasant facts, the opposition will rub your nose in them. Consider, for example, the execution done by the following excerpts from an answering brief on a brief in chief that omitted pertinent facts. (Proper names have been changed.)

We have documented the United States Attorney's argument on the defense of extortion with record references, not only in order that it might be considered against the context of the evidence in the case, but also because the Smiths' brief falls considerably short of reflecting all of the pertinent facts.

(1) The Smiths start by saying that Milton Smith and Morris Brown voluntarily enlisted in the Air Corps (Br. 7). They fail to state that Sam Smith had them volunteer for the Air Corps in order to avoid having them drafted and assigned to the infantry (R. 184, 276-277).

(2) The Smiths admit that their concern, the Paris Thread Corporation, paid the Berg Company for the uniforms furnished to Jones and other officers of the First Bomber Command (Br. 9). They fail to state that, at Sam Smith's request, the Berg Company's books were later altered to show that the officers themselves paid for the uniforms (R. 190-195; Govt. Ex. 5, 6, 7, R. 192, 193, 195, 1219, 1221, 1223).

*   *   *   *   *

(5) The Smiths quote Sam Smith as urging Jones to leave the boys at Westover and Bradley Fields with the Airborne Engineers because they were happy there (Br. 13, 15). "I said" 'Warren please let's forget all about the kids, they are very happy, they met a nice captain, a nice sergeant.' ... I said Warren I told you once before please let's forget all about the kids, they are happy and I am happy." (R. 1228, 1229.) The Smiths do not say in their brief, nor did Sam Smith tell the United States Attorney, that in fact he approached Colonel_____, Colonel_____, Major_____, and Captain_____ in his attempts to have the boys transferred out of the Airborne Engineers, and that he fainted when Colonel_____ told him that nothing could or should be done (supra, pp. 16-18).

(6) The Smiths place Jones in New York on the morning of November 25, urging Sam Smith to come to a decision on whether he will pay $5,000 to keep

the boys from being sent to the Pacific (Br. 16, 35). But their own motion for new trial, on which they rely to establish error here (Br. 33-36), shows that Jones was in Washington on the night of November 24/25, that he left Washington at 9:30 A.M. November 25 and flew to Connecticut, and that he did not arrive at La Guardia Field, New York, until 4 P.M. on that day (Motion, p. 48; U.S. Br. 82-83).

(7) The Smiths twice state that the order transferring the boys from the Air Commando Group at Goldsboro into the Air Transport Command in Wilmington was dated November 29 (Br. 17, 35). This is literally true (R. 1218). But they fail to state that this transfer was directed by a letter from Headquarters Army Air Forces dated November 25 (R. 123, 1218), and that this letter was written in consequence of Jones's telephone call to Miss Graham on November 24 (R. 256-257). Consequently, even if, as the Smiths now assert (Br. 16), the $5,000 was paid not later than November 27, it is still clear that, when the payment was made, Jones had put it out of his power to take Milton and Morris to the Pacific.

(c) Never argue or editorialize in your Statement of Facts. Always be straightforward; indicate the conflict in the evidence, gain whatever advantage you can out of the order of its presentation, but save your argument for the body of the brief. The temptation to slip in a sly remark is sometimes pretty strong; let it go into an early draft, if you must, and get what fun you can out of it; but be sure it is out of the final product.

In short, present your facts accurately, candidly—but always favorably, and always strive to make the most favorable impression, short of actually arguing, with the facts that you have.[5]

---

[5] I may perhaps be pardoned for quoting from a reply brief which passed over my desk:

"An appellant does not often use much space in a reply brief to praise a brief for the appellee. Here, then, though we think commendation due, a few words may seem enough.

"In general, the appellee's brief recites the evidence fairly. Of course, quite properly, the statement is of that most favorable to the Government, but there is little at which to quibble. * * *

"The argument seems to us to say all that can be said for the Government on the points raised, and to say it with great skill; e.g., how much more effective the connotations of the words in the brief * * * than those in the indictment * * *.

"We do not suggest that the choice of words employed in the brief for the appellee goes beyond the license of an advocate. * * *

"Our praise of the appellee's brief is, therefore, tempered with a note of caution. Its art is in its color, not applied in crude daubs, but with restraint that sometimes requires scrutiny to perceive its fundamental flaws. * * *"

Section 26. Examples of effective and ineffective Statements of Facts.—It remains to illustrate the foregoing generalizations with specific and concrete examples.

(a) Courts dislike to referee ideological contests, or to be asked to umpire disputes that exude even the faintest suggestion of mutual zeal to get a question decided,[6] or to assist the litigant who goes to law to vindicate a principle rather than a substantial legal right, or to take advantage of a situation at the expense of the public. The problem in such cases is to make the court aware of what is going on—which obviously cannot be done by calling one's opponent a strike-suitor or his cause a cooked-up case. Usually, in such a situation, the facts of record speak for themselves, and all the advocate need normally do is to set them out, without comment.

An example that comes to mind is that of a bitterly contested proceeding involving a tract of public land that was of no possible value except as a source of rock for a nearby breakwater. If the claimant had succeeded in obtaining it, the neighboring municipality would of necessity have had to pay handsomely for the stone it wanted. In order to convey the desired impression, the brief for the public official commenced its statement as follows

> Whaler Island is a small rocky island in the harbor of Crescent City, California, some 3.65 acres in extent (R. 17-18). It is without value for agricultural purposes, is not adapted to ordinary and private occupation, and is of utility only in connection with the improvement and development of the harbor (R. 31).

> This island is the land for which the appellant Lyders seeks a patent (Bill, pars. V, XVIII; R. 4, 15-16).[7]

In that case, the matter was dropped with its mere statement, and was not further pursued. There was nothing to argue about, because the circumstances in question were atmospheric only, and legally irrelevant.

In other cases, however, facts going to the infirmity of a party may become relevant, in which event they are properly taken up for subsequent argument. Then the problem is to distinguish between the Statement of Facts and the Argument, to keep the first absolutely straightforward, and to put the editorializing and characterization where they belong, viz., in the portion of the brief designated as "Argument."

---

[6] Cf. *United States v. C.I.O.*, 335 U.S. 106.

[7] *Lyders v. Ickes*, 65 App. D.C. 379, 84 F.2d 232.

Examples of the second category arise in situations where review by a higher court is discretionary and not as of right, and where accordingly the appellate court must be convinced, not so much that the decision below is correct or incorrect, but rather that the question is important and is one that deserves or requires review. In such a situation any fact tending to show that a litigant is more interested in obtaining an advisory opinion than in vindicating his legal rights becomes not only relevant but important and, it may be, controlling.

A case arising out of a World War II removal order, but coming up sufficiently long after V-J Day to be of essentially academic interest, illustrates the point. The plaintiff had been individually ordered excluded from the sensitive West Coast area after having been convicted of conspiracy to commit sedition.[8] He sued the Commanding General for damages, a judgment in his favor was reversed on appeal, and he petitioned for a writ of certiorari to review the result. The statement in the Commanding General's brief opposing the petition therefore pointed out:

The complaint asked damages in the sum of $3500, but subsequently petitioner filed a waiver of all damages in excess of $100 (R. 83, 291, 296, 303).

In the portion of the General's brief headed Argument, he adverted to this fact and argued that

* * * the circumstance that, after bringing suit for $3500 (R. 11), petitioner subsequently stipulated that he would waive all damages over $100 (R. 83, 291, 296), strongly suggests that the object of this proceeding for damages was not so much redress for injuries sustained as the obtaining of abstract pronouncements from the courts as to respondent's authority. This he cannot have * * *.

Certiorari was denied,[9] and the factor just mentioned may well have contributed to that result.

(b) It is a commonplace that a very bad man may have a very good case. But judges are human, they want to do substantial justice, and therefore in close cases they are, more or less unconsciously (depending on the individual judge), bound to be influenced by the character of the litigant, particularly when he appears before them as a crusader for the right.

Without doubt, the Jehovah's Witnesses spearheaded much civil rights litigation in the 1940s, and much of our constitutional law

---

[8] Distinguish the mass exclusion orders considered in *Hirabayashi v. United States*, 320 U.S. 81, and *Korematsu v. United States*, 323 U.S. 214.

[9] *Wilcox v. Emmons*, 67 F. Supp. 339 (S.D. Cal.), reversed *sub nom. DeWitt v. Wilcox*, 161 F.2d 785 (C.C.A. 9), certiorari denied, 332 U.S. 763.

was written—and rewritten—around their activities. It is not necessary to collect at this point either the cases or the commentaries thereon or even to set out at length the situation out of which the next example arises. Suffice it to say that two members of the sect, Kulick and Sunal, were separately classified as I-A for the draft. When they failed to report for induction, they were indicted, and at their separate trials neither was permitted to attack his draft classification; each was convicted, neither appealed.

Shortly thereafter, the United States Supreme Court held, disagreeing with some 40 circuit judges in the process, that, in criminal prosecutions under the Selective Training and Service Act of 1940, defendants did have the right to attack the correctiveness of their draft classifications. *Estep v. United States* and *Smith v. United States*.[10] Accordingly, Kulick and Sunal separately petitioned for habeas corpus, alleging that they were detained without authority of law—on the ground of denial of the right to defend at their original trials. One circuit held that habeas corpus lay in these circumstances, another that it did not, and both cases came before the Supreme Court.

The facts were that Kulick had originally been classified as I-A, i.e., available for immediate military service, and then been reclassified as IV-D, viz., minister of religion. Thereafter, to quote from the Statement of Facts in the Government's brief,

Nothing further occurred until August 23, 1944, when the local board was indirectly informed by one of respondent's neighbors, who was identified, that respondent spent most of his time at home, except when working as a professional model, in which capacity he sometimes posed in military uniform. Apparently as a result of this information the local board reclassified respondent I-A. He then requested a hearing * * *. Respondent appeared before the local board on August 30, 1943, and at the conclusion of the hearing the following notation was made as a minute entry in respondent's file:

"When registrant appeared it was learned after interrogation that he was an artist model—and has been photographed in military uniform; when further questioned regarding C.O. in military uniform his reply was evasive." The board continued respondent in I-A * * *.

The other individual, Sunal, had originally claimed exemption as a conscientious objector; in his questionnaire, he had stated that his occupation was "automotive carburetor and electrical mechanic," and that "I am not a minister of religion." He was classified I-A. Five days after that classification was made, Sunal for the first time

---

[10] 327 U.S. 114.

claimed classification as a minister of religion. Hearings and appeals ensued, and he was finally classified in IV-E as a conscientious objector; thereafter, failing to report, he was tried and convicted, and served a term of imprisonment. All these facts were set forth in the Government's brief. Then, as has already been noted, Sunal petitioned for habeas corpus, challenging the validity of his conviction for failing to report for induction in respect of a new classification made after his release from confinement, on the ground that he had not been permitted to attack his new draft classification at that second trial.

The Supreme Court held that the rulings by the convicting courts in the two cases, though erroneous in the light of the subsequent *Estep-Smith* decision, did not deprive either Kulick or Sunal of their constitutional rights, and that accordingly, since they had failed to appeal, they could not thereafter review their convictions on habeas corpus. *Sunal v. Large* and *Alexander v. United States ex rel. Kulick*.[11] The Court's opinion did not discuss the particular facts of the two cases; it said:

> The local boards, after proceedings unnecessary to relate here, denied the claimed exemptions and classified these registrants as I-A * * *.

> The same chief counsel represented the defendants in the present cases and those in the *Estep* and *Smith* cases. At the time these defendants were convicted the *Estep* and *Smith* cases were pending before the appellate courts. The petition in the *Smith* case was, indeed, filed here about two weeks before Kulick's conviction and about a month after Sunal's conviction. The same road was open to Sunal and Kulick as the one Smith and Estep took. Why the legal strategy counseled taking appeals in the *Smith* and *Estep* cases and not in these we do not know. Perhaps it was based on the facts of these two cases. For the question of law had not been decided by the Court; and counsel was pressing for a decision here * * *.[12]

Can it therefore fairly be said that, in deciding the dry and technical question of the scope of habeas corpus, the Supreme Court was entirely uninfluenced by the circumstance that, at the very least, the *bona fides* of the individuals seeking release from confinement was open to question?[13]

---

[11] 332 U.S. 174, affirming *Sunal v. Large*, 157 F.2d 165 (C.C.A. 4), and reversing *United States ex rel. Kulick v. Kennedy*, 157 F.2d 811 (C.C.A. 2).

[12] 332 U.S. at 175, 181.

[13] Rehearing denied, 332 U.S. 785; motion for leave to file second petition for rehearing denied, 333 U.S. 877.

(c) Similarly, the most important function of the Statement of Facts in a brief in a criminal case is to indicate something of the party's guilt or innocence. If you represent the prosecution, your aim must be to convey the impression that the convicted man is just as clearly guilty as he can possibly be; if you represent the defendant, you must strive to show that he has been greatly wronged. This is true in both instances not only when the question concerns the sufficiency of the evidence to support the verdict, but whatever the question is, quite regardless of the formal issues raised on the appeal. "Courts delight to do substantial justice."

A striking instance for the employment of this technique was presented by the sordid *Restaurant Longchamps* tax fraud case, which arose near the end of World War II. Three of the convicted persons appealed without success and then petitioned for a writ of certiorari. At the trial and again in their petition these defendants indicated that there was no denial of the tax frauds charged, and raised only issues arising out of their alleged disclosure prior to the Treasury investigations, and out of the use of their admissions and of the books of their corporations.

Notwithstanding the admission of the tax frauds thus made in the petition, the Government's Brief in Opposition to the granting of certiorari discussed the facts relating to the fraud in as great detail as if the issue had been the sufficiency of the evidence in the Circuit Court of Appeals rather than the importance of petitioners' questions for purposes of review of their case by the Supreme Court.[14] All the shabby details were set out, the evidence relating to the alleged disclosure was discussed at length, and the facts on the credibility of one of the defendants and on his contradiction were stated *in extenso*. (This lad had made the grave mistake, *inter alia*, of testifying to a meeting with the Collector of Internal Revenue, alleged to have taken place at the precise time when that worthy was in fact meeting with eight very substantial and prominent fellow-citizens in connection with the affairs of the Governor Smith Memorial Fund.) Moreover, the findings of the district court, to the effect that the alleged disclosures were neither full nor frank nor voluntarily made, were not simply summarized, but were quoted in full.

The consequence was, not so much that the Brief in Opposition was able to brush off the questions sought to be raised as never

---

[14] Indeed, the Statement was simply lifted verbatim from the Government's brief in the court of appeals.

having been reached,[15] but that there was necessarily generated a feeling in the mind of any reader that, whether the questions were reached or not, these petitioners were so clearly guilty of such a particularly outrageous crime that jail was doubtless much too good for them.[16]

(d) Emotions that sway a jury will frequently backfire in an appellate court, or at least prove notably ineffective. But while most appellate judges cannot be charged with being, in the current idiom, bleeding hearts, they are still human beings, and thus are necessarily shocked by anything in the nature of unjustified cruelty.[17] If, therefore, the facts of your case are such as will cause a revulsion of feeling on the part of a juryman, they are bound to have at least a modicum of similar effect on the members of an appellate court.

The case of *Hatahley v. United States*[18] involved, on its face, cold jurisdictional and legal problems: Were rights under the Taylor Grazing Act, a federal law, affected by a state statute regulating abandoned horses? Had there in any event been compliance with the state statute's terms? Did the Federal Tort Claims Act[19] cover intentional trespasses with the scope of federal agents' authority? The injuries for which redress was sought were the carrying off of horses and mules belonging to the plaintiffs, who were Navajo Indians.

Actually, the depredations were committed with extreme brutality, so much so that an observer commented, "I didn't know they were still doing that to Indians." Here is how the facts were set forth in petitioners' brief:

---

[15] "The petition in this case presents arguments resting and depending on an assumption which is entirely hypothetical, viz., that petitioners made a voluntary disclosure amounting to a confession which was induced by a promise of immunity. That assumption is quite without support on the present record, in consequence of which the questions sought to be presented are never reached."

[16] *United States v. Lustig*, 163 F.2d 85 (C.C.A. 2), certiorari denied, 332 U.S. 775, rehearing denied, 332 U.S. 812.

[17] See *Francis v. Resweber*, 329 U.S. 459, holding that neither double jeopardy nor cruel and unusual punishment is involved in executing a death sentence after an accidental failure in equipment had rendered a previous attempt at execution by electrocution ineffective. The dissent was written by a justice who more normally voted the other way in similar constitutional and criminal cases, but who appears to have been sufficiently impressed by the rather grisly facts of the first attempt at execution to set them forth in full. 329 U.S. at 480–481, note 2.

[18] 351 U.S. 173.

[19] 28 U.S.C. §§ 1346(b), 2671–2680.

The animals were rounded up on the range and were either driven or hauled in trucks to a Government owned or controlled corral 45 miles away. Horses which could not be so handled were shot and killed by the Government's agents on the spot. The remainder were accorded brutal treatment: the horses were so jammed together in the trucks that some died as a result, and in one instance, the leg of a horse that inconveniently protruded through the truck body was sawed off by a federal employee, one Dee P. Black. (Fdg. 23, 25; R. 33-35.) Later, the animals were taken in trucks to Provo, Utah, a distance of 350 miles, where they were sold to a glue factory and as horse meat for about $1,700—at around 3 cents a pound (R. 93, 293)—no part of which was received by petitioners (Fdg. 24; R. 34).

It may well be that the circumstances above detailed made no impression whatever on the members of the Court. But if those facts led any of the judges to the conclusion that, for such a wrong, there must be a remedy, then setting out the facts as quoted necessarily contributed to the holding that "These acts were wrongful trespasses not involving discretion on the part of the agents and they do give rise to a claim compensable under the Federal Tort Claims Act."[20]

Section 27. Use of the Statement of Facts to advance one's case; Illustrative examples.—The application of the foregoing techniques will perhaps be more clearly perceived by examining, not examples from different cases, but comparative instances from successive stages of the same case.

In *Von Moltke v. Gillies*,[21] the question raised in a habeas corpus proceeding was whether petitioner had freely, intelligently, and knowingly waived her right to assistance of counsel, and whether she had freely, intelligently, and knowingly pleaded guilty. Her contention was that she had been induced to plead guilty by an F.B.I. agent who, so she alleged, had, by misinforming her as to the law, convinced her that she would be found guilty if she went to trial. The habeas corpus judge had found against her, the circuit court of appeals had affirmed, and she sought certiorari.

The difficult feature of the case, from the Government's point of view, was the dissenting opinion in the court of appeals, which had espoused and believed petitioner's story.[22] Moreover, the F.B.I. agent had not been a good witness; his denials left something to be

---

[20] 351 U.S. at 181. For sequels, see *United States v. Hatahley*, 257 F.2d 920 (C.A.10), certiorari denied, 358 U.S. 899; *United States v. Ritter*, 273 F.2d 30 (C.A.10), certiorari denied, 362 U.S. 950.

[21] 332 U.S. 708.

[22] See 161 F.2d at 116–121.

desired.[23] The strong points of the case, for the Government, were the favorable findings of the habeas corpus judge; the strong indications in the record that petitioner's story had originally germinated in the otherwise unfertile atmosphere of the House of Correction; and the fact that petitioner was, throughout, consistently contradicted by other witnesses as well as by herself.

The Brief in Opposition to the petition for certiorari was written under the pressure of meeting a deadline,[24] and in the rush incident to the end of the particular term of court. The Statement of Facts which that document contained did not, therefore, succeed in dispelling the unfavorable impression produced by the dissenting opinion below, and accordingly certiorari was granted.

Preparation of the Government's brief on the merits, however, could proceed in the comparative leisure of the summer "vacation." In the new Statement of Facts, the relevant facts in the record were first divided into undisputed and conflicting evidence, and the latter heading was broken down into some seven separate incidents.

Those incidents were taken up, witness by witness, and were set out in such a way as to emphasize the innumerable instances wherein petitioner contradicted herself or was contradicted by others. The Statement of Facts, which had covered some 15 pages in the Brief in Opposition, was expanded to 29 pages in the brief on the merits, and almost all the material that had originally been left to footnotes was carried into the text. The result was a far more convincing presentation, and although the Government did not win the case in the Supreme Court, it did not lose it either. Three justices voted to affirm, four to reverse and to set petitioner free, and the other two were of the opinion that they could not recreate the crucial incident from the dead record, and so voted to remand to the district court "for further proceedings with a view to a specific finding of fact regarding the conversation between peti-

---

[23] Here was the critical portion of his testimony:

"Q. And did you during that discussion use an illustration about a rum runner?

"A. Well, I heard Mrs. Von Moltke say that, and since she did I have been trying to recall, and I cannot remember such an illustration.

"Q. I see.

"A. But it is quite possible that Mrs. Von Moltke's memory is better than mine, and I may have used such an illustration."

[24] Under the rule of court then in effect, only twenty days were allowed, after the service of the Petition, for filing the Brief in Opposition; and at that time it took not less than seven days to get a brief through the Government Printing Office.

tioner and the F.B.I. agent, with as close a recreation of the incident as is now possible."

Section 28. Matters that must be avoided in a Statement of Facts.—Below, in Section 79, under the heading of "Things You Cannot Afford to Do," are collected four outstanding horribles in brief-writing: inexcusable inaccuracy, unsupported hyperbole, unwarranted screaming, and personalities and scandalous matter.

Most of these unpardonables crop up in portions of the brief other than the Statement of Facts; and, at least in my experience, even the most unprofessionally unprofessional inaccuracy is generally met with in the argument portion of the brief (after the writer's ardor has really been inflamed).

Subject to what is said—and collected—in Section 79, a common fault in many Statements of Facts is the tendency to editorialize and to argue. These are faults, because a court reading a Statement of Facts wants to feel that it is getting the facts, and not the advocate's opinions, comments, or contentions. Here are some examples of argumentation in Statements of Facts, taken quite at random, followed by comments:

(a) It is perfectly apparent from a cursory reading of the decision of the Commission (see particularly pp. 489a-499a) and of the Court (R. 597-601) as against the relevant portions of the testimony (61a–182a) that the decision of both Commission and Court is based upon the social philosophy inherent in the "no profit to affiliates" theory, and not on the record facts which the Commission should have found or at least considered and passed upon in this particular case. In other words, we do not have an administrative finding of relevant facts, but refusal to consider such facts because of the adoption of standards created ad hoc by the Commission itself.

(b) Only three of these customers were called by the Commission to testify and give evidence at the hearings. The other customers did not appear at the hearing and no evidence as to them was adduced except the figures set forth in the appendix, which were taken by the Commission's agent from the petitioner's books and records. Therefore there is no complete picture of the transactions between them and the petitioner and no sufficient basis for determining main issues with respect to their transactions. Apparently the Court below has assumed that the practices employed by registrant in dealing with these other customers were the same as those followed in dealing with the customers who testified.

(c) There was substantial, affirmative and uncontradicted evidence that the actual purpose of the accumulation of profits was wholly other than that of avoidance of surtaxes. There was no affirmative evidence that surtax avoidance was a motivating purpose.

The foregoing examples are perfectly proper argumentation, and, had they been included as part of the Argument in each instance, would have been thoroughly effective. All were, however, found in Statements of Facts—where they have no place.

(d) It is to be observed that petitioners did not move for a directed verdict in the trial court, but they sought a review by the United States Circuit Court of Appeals for the ___ Circuit of the entire record upon the proposition that there was such a lack of evidence in this cause as to make the convictions of the petitioners a miscarriage of justice. It is also to be observed that the petitioner, Richard Brown, was represented in the trial court by counsel other than those now appearing for said petitioner.

Example (d) is editorialized rather than strictly argumentative, but illustrates a tendency on the part of some appellate practitioners to hold trial counsel responsible for the state of the record. It is a natural enough tendency, for all too often new counsel on appeal is called in to do a pulmotor job on the stretcher case left at his door. But, on appeal, you are bound by the record that has been made, be it good or bad. If it is good, fine; if it isn't, you are stuck with it, warts and all, and you help neither yourself nor your case by intimations, however veiled, to the effect that you would have tried it differently had you been counsel at the trial.

(e) Petitioner's effort to show the reason for the juggling of his classification, and unwarranted denial of his rights by the local and appeal boards, was thwarted by the rulings of the trial court (App. 16) in denying G_____'s counsel the right to pursue the inquiry on cross examination of the Secretary of the local board, the Government's witness, upon whom it relied to prove its case against defendant G_____.

* * * His testimony proved not only such fact [that the Order was void] but his good-faith action, honest conviction of his stand in the premises, which motivated him in his actions in answering the charge of the indictment; questioning the validity of the Order to Report, want of jurisdiction of the board, and no need to report for induction as a condition precedent to challenge such order.

(f) Frank O. and Andrew E. Wilson, doing business under the trade name of Lone Star Oil Company, a partnership, own and operate a chain of seven retail gasoline filling stations in the City of _____, Texas. And they also own the real estate on prominent business corners of the City of _____, upon which they have erected magnificent structures and equipment to house their business.

Examples (e) and (f) illustrate the fault of editorializing and of using characterizations in the Statement of Facts. In (e) the characterizations would probably have been relevant if included in the Argument, but what difference did it make in (f) whether the structures were magnificent or just hovels? The case involved either taxation or an alleged OPA violation—my own notes on it are unclear—but the nature of the structures was irrelevant in either situation.

Finally, by way of extreme instance, there is an example taken from the Statement of Facts in a brief arguing a draft evasion case; further explanatory comment, other than to point out that the capitalization appeared in the original, is surely unnecessary:

> (g) Petitioner has advanced the principle of law of self defense as applicable to the facts of this case. A defendant who fails to co-operate with government BECAUSE HE BELIEVES THAT IT MEANS THE LOSS OF IMMORTALITY, even to the extent of refusing to take human life, should be allowed the legal defense which in all the courts of the land permits the TAKING OF HUMAN LIFE when the defendant is in fear of losing his mortal life. Constitution of the United States, Article I Amendments fully justifies this extension of the law of self defense to such a situation as this, since it guarantees the free exercise of religion. The inherent powers of the courts to re-define all defenses to apply to new situations should also be sufficient authority of the Court herein to so extend the law of self defense.

Section 29. Good, clear, forceful English.—Good English is the next essential, though I shall do little more than state it. I don't pretend to be an expert on syntax or rhetoric, and so far as I am personally concerned, I write, for better or worse, entirely by ear. But the observations that follow may be suggestive, and possibly helpful. A brief should be well written, but to be effective it must be clearly written. You are endeavoring to reach the minds of others, and therefore what you say must, above all, be clear. Clarity is more important in a brief than literary excellence.

Next, what you write should be grammatical. A lawyer is a professional man, in whom poor English should not be tolerated. I know that a good many brief-writers do not (perhaps because they cannot) use good English, but there is really no excuse for any such performance. Offhand I should say that the only justified departure from the rules of grammar for a lawyer is the split infinitive, "to specifically perform." In that instance alone, the English Department is of no help to the equity practitioner.

I think, also, that a lawyer should be at pains in his briefs, whatever may be the case in pleadings and contracts, to minimize legal formalisms such as "the said," "hereinbefore," "thereinafter," and the like.

Nor is it any longer a sign of learning to encumber a brief with excerpts from the Latin—unless they are very pat indeed. But, with the decline of the classics in the secondary schools and colleges, and a waning of the notion that the citizens won't think a man a lawyer unless he constantly spouts legal jargon in his everyday speech, there is much less of that nowadays than there once was.

The Statement of Facts, as has already been indicated at length, should be straightforward, without embellishments and with a minimum of adjectives. It is not until the Argument portion of the brief is reached that you change the pace, so to speak, of your prose, and (if I may mix a metaphor by mechanizing it) really turn on the steam. From then on out, you argue!

Of course, it is well not to press too hard at your own weak points, for frequently the skill of the advocate consists in skating deftly where the ice is thin (or even where there isn't any ice at all). A good many situations will call for what has been aptly called "walking violently on eggs."

But you can't write an Argument without arguing, and therefore statements that might well be preceded in law review articles with the professional "it would seem" must be introduced in briefs by "it is therefore abundantly clear," or, at the very least, by "it necessarily follows."[25]

Moreover, when you really get to the heart of the case, don't be afraid to hit hard, and don't hesitate to write a fighting brief. There is nothing in brief-writing quite so fallacious as what, for want of a better term, I like to call the striped-pants complex, namely, the notion that it is somehow undignified to make a strong, hard-hitting argument. That idea is really on a par with the view that an advocate should be impartial, or has any business being so—as to which see Sections 6 to 8, above, and the example there dissected and displayed. You simply can't write an argument on a la-di-da basis or after the manner of that well-known Milquetoast, the soft-toned shortstop.

Style is of course an individual matter. It may be that the Frenchman was right who said that the style is the man. Certainly there is full opportunity in this field for the exercise of individual and personal judgments, since many different styles of writing may be equally effective. There is a wide range of styles in which good

---

[25] It is said in Kalven, *Law School Training in Research and Exposition* (1948) 1 J. of Leg. Education 107, 117, "We believe the law-review note is a more fundamental form of legal exposition than the brief." The answer to this proposition in the present connection is that, whether or not the law review note may constitute more fundamental exposition, it is not argumentation; and a brief must, above all, be argumentative.

argumentation can be written, a range as broad as the personality spectrum of effective advocacy, and within that range it would be silly dogmatism to insist on any particular manner of expression. Literary style after all is a form of art, and in the latter field we may all disclaim technical competence and yet know what we like. That circumstance alone makes style such a difficult matter to discuss.

Ideally, the raw material for such a discussion in the present field would be a library full of briefs, with representative examples of good, bad, and indifferent extracted and compiled within the covers of a single casebook. But there are no such casebooks, and the available libraries are few and necessarily inaccessible to many practitioners. Therefore, I have selected my examples of good, clear, forceful English from opinions of former members of the Supreme Court, which are of course readily available in the reports. The portions of such opinions that follow the statement of the facts and issues are generally written in a more or less argumentative style, and thus are helpful here; and it may be noted that, since dissenting opinions are normally written with more zeal (if not indeed with somewhat less restraint), dissents are an even more valuable source of forceful legal writing.

In terms of familiar opinions, my own view—and I put the matter in terms of personal preference because it very largely comes down to that—my own view is that the most effective argumentative style is one like that of the late Chief Justice Hughes, with possibly a touch of Holmes for the snappers at the ends of significant passages. There is something powerful and inexorable about a Hughes opinion—I cite a few at random in the footnote.[26] Read those opinions, note how their reasoning develops logically step by step, get the feel of the pulsating, rhythmical, irresistible argument rolling on towards its predetermined end, and you will appreciate the force of really argumentative writing. Chief Justice Stone also wrote some good, strong opinions, notably in dissent. Those collected in the footnote seem to me outstanding, and to merit reading and rereading.[27]

---

[26] E.g., *Sterling v. Constantin*, 287 U.S. 378; *Retirement Board v. Alton R. Co.*, 295 U.S. 330, 374 (dissent); *Morehead v. N.Y. ex rel. Tipaldo*, 298 U.S. 587, 618 (dissent); *United States v. Wood*, 299 U.S. 123; *Labor Board v. Jones & Laughlin*, 301 U.S. 1; *Apex Hosiery Co. v. Leader*, 310 U.S. 469, 514 (dissent).

[27] E.g., *United States v. Butler*, 297 U.S. 1. 8 (dissent); *Morehead v. N.Y. ex rel. Tipaldo*, 298 U.S. 587, 631 (dissent); *Helvering v. Gerhardt*, 304 U.S. 405; *United States v. Darby*, 312 U.S. 100; *United States v. Local 807*, 315 U.S. 521, 539 (dissent); *Schneiderman v. United States*, 320 U.S. 118, 170 (dissent); *Girouard v. United States*, 328 U.S. 61, 70 (dissent).

Other judges have their admirers also—but, I repeat, these are personal preferences. Cardozo, J., wrote beautiful English, but his opinions are too limpid and too lyrical to constitute the most effective argumentation. Holmes's opinions are generally too epigrammatic for brief-writing, except as to the snapper sentences; a judge can rest on neatly phrased assertion, but an advocate needs something more. The judge needs only to decide; the advocate must persuade.

Some lawyers and judges urge that a brief should always contain short sentences. It is true that excessively long sentences result in turgidity. The force of Chief Justice White's later opinions was very perceptibly marred by this quality, though assuredly they rolled onward to a powerful conclusion.[28] But the constant use of short sentences to the exclusion of longer ones imparts a staccato quality to prose writing that also detracts from the final results. Mr. Justice Brandeis's opinions always seemed to me to fall into that category; they were, however, crystal-clear and wholly devoid of verbal embroidery.[29]

As I say, I'm no English professor, and I don't expect my literary preferences in argumentative writing to coincide with those of others. I can only repeat that good, clear, forceful English is an essential; that in this particular activity one learns by doing (particularly with a more experienced person at hand to edit one's early doings); and that there is a lot of pay dirt in the dusty volumes of other folks' briefs on the library shelves.

Section 30. Argumentative headings.—Headings should always be argumentative rather than topical or even assertive. For instance, say "This suit is barred by laches because brought twenty-five years after the issuance of the original certificate" rather than "This suit is barred by laches." The first gives the argument in a nutshell, the second does not—though certainly the second assertive heading is infinitely more effective than the merely topical "The question of laches." Similarly, say "Appellant had notice of the defect and therefore is not a holder in due course" in preference to "Appellant is not a holder in due course" or to "Appellant's contention." Otherwise stated, employ the technique of the American newspaper headline rather than that of the English: our

---

[28] E.g.., *Minneapolis & St. Louis R. R. v. Bombolis,* 241 U.S. 211; *Selective Draft Law Cases,* 245 U.S. 366.

[29] E.g., *Wan v. United States,* 266 U.S. 1; *New State Ice Co. v. Liebmann,* 285 U.S. 262, 280 (dissent); *Louisville Bank v. Radford,* 295 U.S. 555; *Ashwander v. Tennessee Valley Authority,* 297 U.S. 288, 341 (concurring opinion).

journalists say "Bums Down Braves, 9–2," whereas theirs write "Test Match at Lords."

Perhaps the greatest disservice an appellee's lawyer can do his case is to write, "Replying to Appellant's Point I." This is not even topical, and in consequence is completely blind, giving the judicial reader no clue whatever to the substance of the argument. It follows that the "Replying to" type of heading is completely unhelpful—and it is just as bad when used in an appellant's reply brief.

Always set out your contentions affirmatively—and for maximum effectiveness formulate your headings so that they will be argumentative.

Subheadings should likewise be argumentative rather than topical or merely assertive, primarily because all are collected in the index at the beginning of the brief, and are thus frequently read first by any judge who wants to get the argument in abbreviated compass.

You lose a lot, therefore, if your subheadings are not precise and specific. If your headings and subheadings are properly argumentative, your argument starts with the index at page (i) of the brief, and the court will not need to go beyond that point to catch the essence of your position.

Collecting all the headings and subheadings in the index has also this important incidental advantage: it discloses whatever lack of uniformity may have crept into them in the course of your writing, and so provides a convenient opportunity for strengthening revisions (and, it may well be, for catching misprints and other infelicities).

Perhaps this is as good a place as any for the admonition that a main heading should never be followed by just a single subheading. If a proposition cannot be divided into more than one part, it is merely being restated. Therefore, if you find yourself unable to work out more than one subheading, the difficulty is that your main heading is improperly formulated; you had better rewrite it. (I know that the old books on argumentation used to prescribe something that went like this: "Oscar is entitled to rights and privileges, for: (a) Oscar is a citizen." My point is that effective argumentation for briefs requires that this proposition be rewritten, either as "Oscar is a citizen and is therefore entitled to rights and privileges," or as "Oscar is entitled to rights and privileges because he is a citizen." The first is probably preferable, and it certainly is so if Oscar's citizenship is the real issue.)

Here is an example of some argumentative headings and sub-headings, taken from the index page of the prevailing brief in a fairly celebrated case,[30] that are sufficiently detailed and precise to give the reader the very heart of the party's contentions immediately:

I. It has always been held that one of the incidents of a lawful arrest is the right to search the premises under the control of the person arrested for the instrumentalities of the crime of which he is accused, and that such a search is a reasonable one within the Fourth Amendment.

A. The cases in this Court prior to 1927 establish that the right to search premises for instrumentalities of crime is an incident of a lawful arrest therein.

B. There may be an exception permitting search of the premises for evidentiary papers incident to a lawful arrest in cases where a crime is actually being committed in the presence of the arresting officers.

C. The *Go-Bart* and *Lefkowitz* cases have been uniformly understood to hold that a search of premises incident to a lawful arrest has as wide a scope as a search authorized by a search warrant, and is limited to the objects for which such a warrant could issue.

D. The right to search premises under the accused's control for instrumentalities of crime as an incident to his lawful arrest is of ancient origin, and its recognition by the courts represents not an encroachment on constitutional protections but rather a reaffirmation of their original boundaries.

You may read all this and disagree, and certainly later decisions may have whittled down the propositions established in the particular case. No matter; the point made here is not whether the quoted assertions are still good law; it is that, after reading these detailed, specific, and argumentative headings, you know precisely the substance and scope of the argument.

Here is another example, likewise taken from a prevailing brief in a case decided some years back,[31] that also sets forth a party's arguments, in this instance in step-by-step progression:

I. The railroads' refusal to make direct delivery of livestock to sidings located on their line is a breach of their legal duty to the public as common carriers, which the Commission had power to remedy by its order.

A. If Track 1619 were owned by the New York Central, then clearly the Interstate Commerce Act has been violated, and the Commission's order would be unassailable.

B. In view of Section 1(3) (a) of the Interstate Commerce Act, the situation is not altered in any respect by the circumstance that Track 1619 is owned by a non-carrier.

---

[30] *Harris v. United States,* 331 U.S. 145.
[31] *United States v. Baltimore & Ohio R. Co.,* 333 U.S. 169.

C. Nor is the situation altered by reason of the New York Central's contract with the Stock Yards which provides expressly for discrimination against livestock, since common carriers cannot by contract relieve themselves from their duties to the public.

D. The Stock Yards' right, if any, to compensation from the New York Central for the use of its land has no bearing upon the validity of the Commission's order requiring the railroads to perform their duties to the public.

There were additional points, but the foregoing was the nub of the argument. Here again, the reader is left in no possible doubt as to the substance or the progression of the propositions presented.

Here is another example, this time of reasonably argumentative headings, but of only ineffective topical subheadings:

I. Section 266 of the Judicial Code, requiring the hearing and determination by three judges of applications for certain interlocutory injunctions, is not applicable to this case. Therefore the three-judge trial court convened pursuant to section 266 was without jurisdiction to issue the interlocutory injunction and abused its discretion in doing so.

No state statute involved.

As to order of administrative board or commission.

_____ v. _____ discussed and distinguished.

Section 266 inapplicable where order affects only particular district and is of limited scope.

Conclusion.

*   *   *   *   *   *   *

III. This action is a suit against the State of _____, of which the Supreme Court has exclusive jurisdiction awarded in section 233 of the Judicial Code. Being without jurisdiction for this reason, the trial court abused its discretion in granting the interlocutory injunction.

Statutes.

Officers' authority as to state court suit.

Grounds for state court suit.

As to agreement discharging liability.

This is a suit against the State.

Quite apart from any substantive aspects, the main headings are weakened by being divided into two sentences, and of course the force of the subheadings is almost completely lost by being rendered topical; the reader does not and cannot obtain any clue to the party's position from reading them.

Specifically, "_____ v. _____ discussed and distinguished" would have been much stronger had it been rendered as, "_____ v. _____

is not controlling because * * *," going on to indicate briefly why it is not controlling.

"This is a suit against the State" is assertive rather than topical, but, since it does not go on to say why the suit is one against the state, it is not argumentative.

"Section 266 is inapplicable where order affects only particular district and is of limited scope" is the best of the lot—but it would have been even better if instead of "where order" there had been written "because the order here." Then the subheading would have read, "Section 266 is inapplicable because the order here affects only a particular district and is of limited scope"—and then it would have been a good, thumping, argumentative sentence.

Perhaps it should be added, with reference to the main heading under III, that if the trial court was really without jurisdiction, its issuance of an interlocutory injunction would have been somewhat worse than an abuse of discretion—the latter expression being one that implies the existence of jurisdiction. It is therefore not a good heading. A heading should, at the very least, be consistent with itself, and should not generate disbelief or opposition on a first reading.

Let me take another example of how not to do it:

II. The Rule of Jurisdiction Invoked by the Court Below Is Not Unconstitutional.

A. The Intent of Congress.

B. The Constitutional Considerations.

C. The Application of the Constitutional Considerations to This Case.

D. The Effect of Petitioners' Contentions.

Every one of the subheadings is blind, giving the reader no clue whatever to the substance of the argument; and the principal heading is only assertive. It falls short of being argumentative because it does not explain why the rule being appealed from is not unconstitutional—a matter of more than passing importance, since that was the vital issue in the case.

Possibly there is one situation where merely topical headings are justified, namely, when you are simply analyzing the authorities, and are presenting them in a spirit of sweet reasonableness, i.e., where it doesn't make much difference which of several lines the court will take since they all lead to the same result. But with that single exception, failure to set off the various stages in the Argument portion of the brief with full and detailed argumentative headings detracts materially from the brief's effectiveness.

One additional comment, suggested by a learned friend, may well be added: The reader should never need to refer back to the heading in order to grasp the full sense and meaning of the opening sentence. As phrased by him:

> The text of an argument ought not to depend upon a heading or subheading for an understanding of its meaning. My theory of a heading or sub-heading is that it ought to be something that the reader can take or leave alone. (I apply the same rule to footnotes.) In reading a brief, a book, or an article, I am annoyed, after I have got into a sentence, to find that I must refer back to a heading to understand the sentence. I test my own work by asking myself whether the text is complete and is understandable without reading either the headings or the footnotes. If so, then I consider the headings and the foot-notes as aids which will assist in the reading of the text, but which will not impede that reading.[32]

Section 31. Appealing formulation of the questions presented.— Another essential of an effective appellate brief is the appealing formulation of the questions presented on the appeal—and "appealing" in this connection means the phraseology that will most effectively impel the reader to answer the question posed in the way the writer wants him to answer it. Consequently this is an extremely important item, particularly since by stating well the question presented you are really choosing the battleground on which your litigation will be contested.

The formulation of the question is particularly important whenever review is discretionary, the most usual example certio-rari in the United States Supreme Court. In that situation, permission or refusal to go higher frequently depends in very large measure on the framing of the question. On behalf of the petitioner you help induce review by making the question appear important and the result below wrong. Contrariwise, when the object to be obtained is the denial of review, the question should be framed in such a way as to minimize the importance of what is involved.

Two forms will fit almost every case. The first and more usual form is to use a sentence beginning with "whether"; e.g., "Whether post-mortem declarations are admissible." The second, usually appropriate only for the more complicated cases, is to state the salient facts and then to add, "The question presented is whether in these circumstances the later proceeding is barred by the earlier judgment." This second method may also be appropriate whenever

---

the simple statement of the question does not make the case appear to be sufficiently interesting or appealing.

Some judges seem to feel that advice to phrase a question appealingly is tantamount to a suggestion for deceiving the court, so that by slanting the question, or even by twisting it out of shape, a busy tribunal may be led to reach an answer favorable to the party. Here again, this is a view that reflects misapprehension of the purpose and content of advocacy.

The essential technique, generally, is so to load the question with the facts of the particular case or with the relevant quotations from the statute involved, *fairly stated,* that you can almost win the case on the mere statement of the question it presents. Please observe the caveat: *fairly* stated. If an excess of zeal leads you to state the question unfairly, the thing will boomerang and explode in your face—or, perhaps more to the point, in your client's case.

Here are some examples:

The first one illustrates the problem of how to phrase an issue appealingly, with minimum mention of facts.

The case turned on the income tax liability of a very wealthy father in the surtax brackets. Papa owned lots of gilt-edged bonds and stuff; before the coupons matured, he clipped them and gave them to his son as a gift. When the coupons matured, sonny boy cashed them, and returned the proceeds as income on his return. This young lad, as it happened, was a substantial distance from the breadline, but he still wasn't up in Papa's tax range. So the revenuers undertook to tax the old man for the income from the coupons.

How to phrase the question? The Commissioner of Internal Revenue could have stated it as "Whether a man is taxable on income that his son receives"—but that would hardly have induced any court to say "Yes." So he stated the question as follows (first example is from the petition, second from the brief on the merits):

1

Whether the owner of coupon bonds should include in his gross income the amount of coupons which he detached and gave to his son several months prior to maturity.

2

The taxpayer owned coupon bonds. Several months prior to maturity of the interest coupons he detached them and gave them to his son, retaining the bonds themselves. Is he relieved of income tax with respect to such interest coupons?

Both are well-formulated questions. The second is probably a shade the better because it stresses that the taxpayer retained the bonds and then asks on top of that whether he is relieved from tax. (The Supreme Court, by six to three, held that he was not.[33]) Note also the change in the form of the question presented, from the one-sentence "whether" form to the fact-statement-plus-question form, all in the direction of adding appeal. The significant point is less the result in the case than the way that case illustrates to what extent phrasing the question may be a problem in applied semantics.

The next two examples illustrate the permissible use of the loading-with-facts technique:

The first concerned a man drafted in 1918 and ordered to report on November 11, 1918. On that day, of course, all draft calls were cancelled. So, after lunching with his draft board, this lad went home, and, in due course, received a "Discharge from Draft." For some years thereafter he enjoyed the tax exemption accorded by the state legislature to all honorably discharged soldiers of the war with Germany. Subsequently the local tax officials tightened up, decided he was not an honorably discharged soldier, and refused to recognize his exemption. After suit, the Supreme Court of the state decided that he was not within the statute.[34] Nothing daunted, he communicated with the Secretary of War; declared that in 1918 he had been ready, willing, able, and fully qualified, and that his service (such as it was) was honorable; and demanded an Honorable Discharge from the Army. Being refused, he brought suit—and the appellate court held that he was entitled to such a Discharge. On its face the thing had all the earmarks of a comic opera, if not an exaggerated farce. Actually, however, the decision was a very serious matter for the Army: there were over 45,000 others in like circumstances and issuing Honorable Discharges to all of these would have involved a very considerable administrative chore, and would in addition have placed a substantial financial burden on the United States (and on the states) in view of the mass of veterans' benefit legislation on the books.

The Secretary of War, therefore, petitioned for review. Here is how he framed the question presented:

Whether a court may, by mandamus, order the Secretary of War to issue an "Honorable Discharge from the Army" to an individual who received a "Discharge from Draft" in 1918, over 25 years prior to the institution of suit,

---

[33] *Helvering v. Horst*, 311 U.S. 112.
[34] *Lamb v. Kroeger*, 233 Iowa 730, 8 N. W. 2d 405.

where such individual simply reported for induction on November 11, 1918, returned to his home on that day because of the cancellation of all draft calls by order of the President, never entrained for travel to a military camp, never wore the uniform, and never was accepted for military service by the Army.

The entire case was thus set forth in the question, whose very phrasing underscores the untenability of the "veteran's" position. In the actual case, certiorari was granted, and the decision below unanimously reversed—a mere thirteen days after oral argument.[35]

The next example—a similar unfounded claim similarly dealt with—was the case of the Week-End Sailor—the member of the Temporary Reserve of the Coast Guard who patrolled the waterfront in his spare time and then insisted that he was entitled to veterans' preference in subsequent federal employment. Here again, the question states the case, and here again, certiorari was granted and the decision below, which held such an individual to be a veteran, was promptly reversed.[36] The question was stated as follows:

Whether members of the Volunteer Port Security Force, a branch of the Temporary Coast Guard Reserve, who were assigned duty periods (here, of less than six hours a week) in order to interfere as little as possible with their hours of regular civilian employment during their enrollment, who could be disenrolled at their own request upon representation that their duty assignments conflicted with such civilian employment, who were not subject while on duty to transfer away from their homes without their consent, and who remained at all times subject to the draft provisions of the Selective Training and Service Act, 1940, are entitled to preference in federal employment as "ex-servicemen . . . who have served on active duty in any branch of the armed forces of the United States, during any war," within the meaning of the Veterans' Preference Act of 1944.

It should be remembered that these techniques are equally applicable to every kind of case, and are not in any sense limited to the somewhat esoteric public law cases that fall to the lot of Government counsel to handle.

Here is an example involving a real estate title that could well arise in any country lawyer's office at the courthouse square. The question as phrased was:

Whether a lost grant of a fee simple title may be presumed when there has been only spasmodic possession at long intervals, where the original grant and the first mesne conveyance in a complete chain of title disclose the defect in the claimed title and show that only a five-year lease was granted by the

---

[35] *Patterson v. Lamb*, 329 U.S. 539.
[36] *Mitchell v. Cohen*, 333 U.S. 411.

sovereign, and where no record of a grant from the sovereign appears although the law required records of such grants to be kept.

There's your chain of title—and your case—in a nutshell. And that is an example of almost universal utility, since a land-title dispute could and does arise anywhere.[37]

Section 32. Examples of helpful and unhelpful formulation of the question presented.—It goes without saying that not all situations are adapted to the loading-with-facts technique of formulating the question presented. But the question presented in any case can be clearly and appealingly stated—or, contrariwise, unclearly and unappealingly. It will probably be helpful to set out here as examples the questions presented in each of four cases. The first statement in each instance is the petitioner's formulation of the question; the second is the respondent's. As it happens, review was denied in each instance, but nothing turns on that for present purposes. The significant point for the student of the process is to inquire which of the rival statements is more effective, and why; and whether in his judgment the parties could have stated the problem for their purposes more effectively than they did. (For convenience in reference, the citations to the opinions below are included in the footnotes.)

(A)

Petitioner: "Did the Circuit Court of Appeals for the Sixth Judicial Circuit err in overruling petitioner's contention that until there had been an adjudication by the proper military tribunal, that the soldier involved was guilty of violating the Articles of War relating to desertion, the District Court was without jurisdiction to try the issue presented by the indictment?"

Respondent: "Whether petitioner could be prosecuted under Section 42 of the Criminal Code for aiding a deserter from the Army before the soldier had been convicted of desertion by a court-martial."[38]

In the foregoing case, the petitioner's statement is defective principally because it is unclear; it refers to "the issue presented by the indictment" without any clue to what that issue is. Thus it fails to do what the correct formulation of "question presented" must always do, viz., tell the court what the case is about. Respondent's statement does just that, though it presents the matter plainly, without forensic sex appeal.

---

[37] This particular one arose in Hawaii. The Ninth Circuit decided it twice, once for one side and then for the other, and the Supreme Court split *5–4. United States v. Fullard-Leo,* 331 U.S. 256.

[38] *Beauchamp v. United States,* 154 F.2d 413 (C.C.A. 6), certiorari denied, 329 U.S. 723.

(B)

Petitioner: "1. Is the Petitioner a native, citizen, denizen or subject of a 'hostile nation or government' liable as such 'to be apprehended, restrained, secured and removed' as an alien enemy?

"2. Is the Petitioner a citizen of the Third German Reich or the German Nation or Government?"

Respondent: "Whether an alien, born in Bohemia, then a part of the Austro-Hungarian Empire, in 1905, who later became a Czechoslovakian citizen when the place of his birth was included in that country after World War I, and who, after the Munich Pact of 1938, while in the United States, petitioned to be and was recognized as a German citizen, is now a citizen or subject of an enemy country within the meaning of the Alien Enemy Act of 1798, despite the re-occupation of the territory of his birth and former residence by Czechoslovakia."[39]

Petitioner's questions are too generalized to be informative. Respondent, on the other hand, has set forth the facts in his question, through use of the "loading" technique, and has framed it in such a way that there is but little doubt of the answer.

(C)

Petitioner: "Whether petitioner, a former reserve officer of the Army (and thousands of other reserve officers, whose rights are vitally affected by this, the first case involving their right to retirement pay) may sue in the District Court under the principles enunciated by this Court in *Dismuke v. United States,* 297 U.S. 167, and similar cases, to recover the retirement pay provided by Congress in Section 5 of the Act of April 3, 1939, as amended, when he is deprived of such pay by the arbitrary, discriminatory and capricious acts of those charged with administering that statute, such conduct being aimed at preventing petitioner in particular and reserve officers in general from obtaining the benefits promised them by Congress."

Respondent: "Whether a reserve officer can sue in a district court to establish his right to retirement pay on account of alleged disability incident to his military service, where he has not pursued the administrative remedies made available by statute and executive order for the assertion and review of such claims, and in the face of the Tucker Act's specific denial of jurisdiction over 'claims for pensions.' "[40]

Here petitioner has resorted to the "loading" technique, perhaps to an unwarranted degree; respondent has also loaded his question, but without resort to epithetic adjectives. The first makes a good jury speech; the second is a compact plea to the jurisdiction.

---

[39] *United States ex rel. Reichel v. Carusi,* 157 F.2d 732 (C.C.A. 3), certiorari denied, 330 U.S. 842.

[40] *Randolph v. United States,* 158 F.2d 787 (C.C.A. 5), certiorari denied, 330 U.S. 839.

(D)

Petitioner A: "The question presented is whether or not a retired United States District Judge is entitled to increased compensation at the rate of $15,000 per year provided for District Judges by the Act of July 31, 1946 (Public Law 567, 79th Congress), in lieu of the salary of $10,000 per year currently being paid."

Petitioner B: "1. Whether the new salary law applies to retired judges of whom petitioner is one; whether it is open to construction and legislative history to impose upon it an implied exception of 'retired' judges and petitioner from it and the increase of salaries granted by it to all district judges.

"2. Whether the so-called retirement law is 'a special reference' or 'specific aspect' or consideration of salaries of 'retired' judges and 'fixing' the same; whether exercise of the privileges or options of said law is acceptance of an offer on condition that 'he should continue to draw the salary he was receiving when he retired' and restricting him thereto despite the subsequent new salary law and its increase of salary; whether it operates as an implied exception imposed on the new salary law to exclude 'retired' judges and petitioner from the grant thereof; and whether the 'retirement' law is of any *legal* effect save to conditionally authorize appointment of additional judges without permanent increase in the number thereof, and in all else futile, superfluous verbiage affecting the status and salary right of petitioner not at all."

Respondent: "Whether petitioners, who had retired as United States District Judges prior to July 31, 1946, are entitled to be paid at the rate of $15,000 per year, as provided by the Act of July 31, 1946, for 'each of the judges of the several district courts' when the judges' retirement act provides for payment to a retired judge of 'the salary of which he is * * * in receipt' at the time of retirement, and when the salary received at that time was $10,000 a year."[41]

Petitioner A has stated the question clearly and without trimmings. Petitioner B's statement is—well, not very helpful; but respondent, by quoting the two statutes in his question, has made it pretty plain that the judges retired prior to 1946 were just out of luck—which is what was held.

Additional examples are legion. But the principle is always the same: The most appealing statement of the question is always the one that most effectively impels the reader to want to answer it as the writer of the question wanted him to.

Section 33. Unappealing formulation of the questions presented in order to defeat review.—When you are petitioner or appellant, you must dress up your questions appealingly in order to induce the higher court to take your case. But, when you represent

---

[41] *Bourquin v. United States,* 108 Ct. Cls. 700, 72 F. Supp. 76, certiorari denied, 332 U.S. 762.

respondent or appellee, you are perfectly satisfied with the *status quo,* and consequently your duty to your client requires that you minimize the questions presented by your adversary, in order to make them appear unimportant, or uninteresting except to the parties involved, or as turning on a mere question of fact. Here are some examples of effective depressants, taken from successful Briefs in Opposition.

(a) Whether the evidence is sufficient to support the verdict.

(b) Whether there is substantial evidence in the record to support the finding that * * *.

(c) Whether the concurrent findings of the two lower courts that * * * are correct.

(d) Whether petitioner may now rely on Section _____ of the Act of _____, which it failed to call to the attention of either of the courts below.

(e) Whether, in a prosecution for making sales at over-ceiling prices, where the sole question at issue was whether petitioners demanded and received more than the ceiling price, the judge's omission to charge on willfulness constituted prejudicial error requiring reversal of the convictions, where petitioners' counsel specifically acquiesced in the charge.

One caution may be in order when, on behalf of the winning side below, you employ the "always belittlin'" technique. There is always a tendency to add, by way of conclusion, that the question presented for review is not an important one. Very often, however, the question is important, but review is not, since the case was rightly decided. Therefore, unless you are prepared to concede that the question would not have been important even if you had lost below, don't yield to the tendency. For example, if a court decides that a valid contract requires consideration, the decision is right but the question is clearly of importance, as will be clear by considering the situation if the ruling had gone the other way. Therefore, in the usual situation, don't urge that the question is unimportant; say rather that the decision does not require further review.

Be careful, also, how far you go in asserting that a case is "*sui generis*"; you may be seeking review of the same kind of question later on, and, if your opponent is alert, he is in a position in a close case to persuade the court to make you eat your words.[42]

---

[42] In the first Palmyra Island case (*United States v. Fullard-Leo,* 133 F.2d 743 (C.A. 9), certiorari denied, 319 U.S. 748), the Government argued (Br. Op. 8; No. 883, Oct. T. 1942) that "This case is, in petitioners' words (Pet. 5), *sui generis.* Thus it presents no conflict of

(continued)

Section 34. Sound analysis of the legal problem in argument on the law.—We come now to the body of the brief, the Argument proper. If and to the extent that a question of law is to be argued, the essential for an effective brief is that the legal problem involved be carefully and soundly analyzed. Here the basic problem for the brief-writer is to determine which are the principal questions and which the subsidiary ones; what to do when there are alternative propositions, any one of which is sufficient to prevail; and in which order the points on which one relies should be presented. These are, obviously, not matters as to which one can profitably be dogmatic, but a good working principle is to put one's best foot forward.

(a) Where there are no alternatives, i.e., where you must prevail on every point in order to win, the only solution is to set forth your points in logical, step-by-step progression. This is subject to the qualification that, if there is no particular logical sequence, the point that goes to the very heart of the matter, that strikes the jugular, should always be argued first.

Let me take some examples:

(i) In the *Harris* search-and-seizure case,[43] the officers arrested Harris under a warrant, then searched his apartment for the instrumentalities of the crime for which he was arrested, and in the course of that search found the contraband for the possession of which he was tried and convicted. In order to sustain the conviction, it was first necessary to show that the officers had a right to search, next that this right extended to all of Harris's apartment, and finally that they could retain any contraband discovered in the course of that search. The point first mentioned was basic and hence it was argued first; the others followed logically thereafter. Here was the sequence of points:

I. It has always been held that one of the incidents of a lawful arrest is the right to search the premises under the control of the person arrested for the

---

decisions and moreover is correct." But the second decision by the Ninth Circuit sitting *en banc* went the other way (156 F.2d 756), and this time the Government had to seek review. No opposition was filed, and certiorari was granted. (329 U.S. 697.) I have often wondered whether the Supreme Court would have agreed to review the case on the second occasion if the claimants had opposed and quoted the former characterization.

Probably, however, the decisive factor in the grant of certiorari was the public importance of determining the ownership of this strategically located island.

[43] *Harris v. United States,* 331 U.S. 145.

instrumentalities of the crime of which he is accused, and that such a search is a reasonable one within the Fourth Amendment.[44]

II. The search was not a general exploratory search for evidence of crime.

III. The search was not improper because it extended beyond the precise portion of the premises where petitioner was arrested.

IV. The seizure of the Selective Service documents and their introduction in evidence were proper.

(ii) In the *Hackfeld* Alien Property case,[45] the facts, briefly, were that Hackfeld's Hawaiian property had been seized during the first World War; that it was returned to him, pursuant to an Executive Allowance signed by the President, on a determination that he was an American citizen; and that thereafter he sought a further recovery, after which the Government brought a cross-action for the return of alleged overpayments, asserting that Hackfeld had never been an American citizen as a matter of law, and that he had, through his fraud, induced the determination that he was one. The trial judge directed a verdict in favor of the Government on the sole basis that Hackfeld had always been a German and that the additional payments had in consequence been made without authority of law. Hackfeld's estate appealed.

On the appeal, the Government had to show first, that the court had properly gone behind the Presidential Allowance; next, that a certain tax proceeding was not *res judicata* as to Hackfeld's citizenship; third, that the trial judge was right as a matter of law in ruling as he did; and, finally, that the facts of record as to Hackfeld's fraud were sufficient for alternative support of the judgment. So the brief filed in the Second Circuit presented the main points in that order:

I. The Executive Allowance in No Way Constituted a Bar to This Action.

II. The Federal Estate Tax Preceding Is No Bar to This Action.

III. Hackfeld Never Became an American Citizen.

IV. The District Court Should Have Directed a Verdict in Appellees' Favor on the Ground of Fraud.

It is proper to note, however, that these last headings are assertive and not argumentative, and therefore not to be commended as headings.

---

[44] For the subheadings under this point, see p. 56, *supra.*

[45] *United States v. Rodiek,* 117 F.2d 588 (C.C.A. 2), rehearing denied 120 F.2d 760, affirmed by an equally divided court, 315 U.S. 783. See also *Rodiek v. United States,* 100 C. Cls. 267.

(iii) In the *Douglas Chandler* treason appeal,[46] the defendant raised numerous objections to his conviction—that he had been tried in the wrong district, that Congress had not made specific provision for the trial of offenses committed abroad, that he had been improperly returned to the United States, that treason could not be committed by adherence to the enemy by an American residing in enemy territory, that the overt acts were insufficient and were insufficiently proved, and that the court made errors in the admission of testimony and in its instructions to the jury.

In order to sustain the conviction, it was just as important for the Government to establish that Chandler was tried in the proper district as it was to prove that his acts amounted to treason. But the heart of the case was the proposition that broadcasting propaganda on behalf of an enemy was treason, and so that point was argued first. The details as to the arrangement of the Government's points are set forth below in Section 47 under the heading, "Never Let the Other Side Write Your Brief." That is to say, select your own battleground; do not permit opposing counsel to choose it for you. That is an admonition almost universally applicable.

(b) When you have alternative grounds, place the most appealing one first—and by "most appealing" in this connection is meant the proposition that evokes the least judicial sales resistance.

(i) For instance, in cases involving judicial review of administrative action, when you are appearing for the agency, show that the agency was right before you start to argue that, right or wrong, its determination is not subject to judicial review. The other order may be more logical, but it involves substantially more judicial reluctance; courts don't like to be told that their jurisdiction to review is limited.

Thus, in the case that involved the scope of a railroad's release under the Transportation Act of 1940,[47] the two main headings in support of the administrative action giving that release full effect were as follows:

I. Claims to lands granted by the Acts of 1874 and 1904 in lieu of lands granted by the 1866 Act and thereafter relinquished were extinguished by the release here executed pursuant to the Transportation Act of 1940.

II. Apart from the merits, the Secretary's construction of the interrelationship between the Acts of 1866, 1874, 1904, and 1940 involved the exercise of discretion, was reasonable, has not been shown to be clearly wrong, and thus is impregnable to mandamus.

---

[46] *Chandler v. United States,* 171 F.2d 921 (C.A. 1), certiorari denied, 336 U.S. 918.

[47] *Krug v. Santa Fe P. R. Co.,* 329 U.S. 591.

As it happened, the court went directly to the merits and upheld the Secretary,[48] but the same technique employed in similar cases may well lead to decisions resting on nonreviewability. In any event, courts are much more inclined to withhold their hand after first being convinced that the administrative officer was right—which is simply another illustration of the principle that courts delight to do substantial justice or, at the very least, that they are perceptibly influenced by "the equities."

(ii) Similarly, where one alternative involves distinguishing away a recently decided case while the other has a clear path not thus obstructed, argue the latter alternative first to avoid the reluctance courts always feel when asked to reshape their recent precedents. Requesting a court to overrule or modify a case but lately decided, after full consideration and over strong dissent, always involves a heavy uphill pull.

Thus, in the *Knauer* denaturalization case,[49] the argument in support of the judgment below, which had cancelled Knauer's citizenship, rested on two elements: fraud in the oath of allegiance, and fraud in his representation that he was attached to the principles of the Constitution. The latter problem had been before the Supreme Court in *Schneiderman v. United States*,[50] a case that was twice argued, and that had not only narrowed the scope of denaturalization proceedings, but had substantially (and, in the view of the dissenting judges, unduly) narrowed the concept of "attached to the principles of the Constitution." Moreover, in *Baumgartner v. United States*,[51] the Court had held that the facts there presented did not establish "beyond a troubling doubt" that Baumgartner had committed fraud in taking the oath of allegiance.

Each of these decisions placed a heavy burden on the Government, but the *Schneiderman* case was the more impressive and difficult obstacle, partly because it had been a more hotly contested litigation, but essentially because it involved a fuzzier and more debatable concept, viz., the principles of the Constitution. In

---

[48] "We agree with the District Court. We think, as it held, that the Secretary of the Interior's construction of the 1940 Act was clearly right. Therefore, we do not discuss the Government's contention that, since the Secretary's construction was a reasonable one, it was an allowable exercise of his discretion which should not be set aside by injunction or relief in the nature of mandamus. See *Santa Fe P. R. R. v. Work*, 267 U.S. 511, 517; cf. *Santa Fe P.R.R. v. Lane*, 244 U.S. 492." *Krug v. Santa Fe P.R. Co.*, 329 U.S. 591, 597.

[49] *Knauer v. United States*, 328 U.S. 654.

[50] 320 U.S. 118.

[51] 322 U.S. 665.

consequence, it was decided to argue fraud in the oath of allegiance first, as follows:

I. The evidence establishes beyond a troubling doubt that in 1937, when petitioner renounced allegiance to the German Reich and took an oath of allegiance to the United States, he committed conscious and deliberate fraud.

II. Fraud in the oath of allegiance is a proper ground for cancellation of a certificate of naturalization.

III. The evidence likewise establishes beyond a troubling doubt that petitioner's representation at the time of his naturalization that he was attached to the principles of the Constitution of the United States was consciously and deliberately false; and this is an additional ground for cancelling his certificate of naturalization.

The case was decided in the Government's favor on the ground that Knauer's oath of allegiance had been shown to be fraudulent, and the Court thus did not reach the question of attachment.[52]

(iii) It may happen on occasion that correct analysis and effective presentation require the broader and more difficult proposition to be argued first. A striking illustration of such an instance was the case that involved the refusal of the Rhode Island courts to enforce treble-damage actions for overcharges in violation of OPA ceilings, on the ground that these were actions for penalties based on the statute of a foreign sovereign![53]

Two questions were involved, one being whether such a proceeding was really an action for a penalty, and the other whether, even if it was, it could be maintained nonetheless. The argument for the plaintiff (joined by the Price Administrator as intervenor) was that, under the federal rule, the action was not one for a penalty, but that, even so, the state courts were bound to enforce it. Which point should be argued first? The quotation is from the first argument paragraph of the prevailing brief:

We assume *arguendo* at the outset that the present action—a consumer's action for treble damages under Section 205(e) of the Emergency Price Control Act as amended—is an action for a penalty even though the actual recovery here was limited to the amount of the overcharge plus an attorney's fee. We make that assumption in order to bring more sharply into focus our contention that, since the courts of Rhode Island are open to actions for

---

[52] "Since fraud in the oath of allegiance which Knauer took is sufficient to sustain the judgment below, we do not reach the other questions which have been argued." *Knauer v. United States,* 328 U.S. at 674.

[53] *Testa v. Katt,* 330 U.S. 386.

penalties founded upon state law, they cannot consistently with the Supremacy Clause of the Constitution refuse to take jurisdiction of similar actions founded on federal law. Thereafter, once the basic question of discrimination against a federal cause of action is disposed of, we proceed to show that, since the consumer's action under the Emergency Price Control Act is a federal right, its nature must be judged by federal standards, and that, under the decisions of this Court, it is clearly a remedial action and not one for a penalty, even though multiple damages plus an attorney's fee may be recovered. That being so, *a fortiori* the Rhode Island courts cannot refuse to entertain such actions.

The Court followed this approach, assumed without deciding that the section in question was a penal statute, and then held that the state courts were not free under Article VI of the Constitution to refuse enforcement of the claim.[54]

(iv) The advocate's problem is underscored by the comparison of example (iii), above, with examples (i) and (ii): When is it appropriate to argue the easier point first and when the harder one? The only honest answer, of course, is "it all depends"— because there just isn't any ironclad rule that will fit every case. Normally it is sound technique to start on the line of least resistance, but occasionally a situation will call for grasping the nettle firmly, for arguing the really difficult point at the outset. The last example discussed illustrates such a situation—and it's simply up to the lawyer handling the case to decide which approach is more likely to succeed. There is no ready-made rule of thumb to save you from the pain of choosing which course to pursue—but once you decide, adhere to the approach you have selected, and don't wobble back and forth as though you still couldn't decide.

Section 35. Legal arguments that had better be avoided.—

(a) *Weak Propositions.* Perhaps the most important admonition under this heading is to avoid arguing weak questions or any in which you have no faith; their inclusion only serves to weaken the rest of your argument, and may well result in serious prejudice to your case.

Indeed, critics of outstanding competence have emphasized that it is the ability to discern weak points, and the willingness to discard weak points, that constitute the mark of a really able lawyer.

For example, Judge Learned Hand, in his tribute to one of America's greatest patent lawyers, the late Charles Neave, said:

> With the courage which only comes of justified self-confidence, he dared to rest his case upon its strongest point, and so avoided that appearance of

---

[54] *Testa v. Katt,* 330 U.S. at 389.

weakness and uncertainty which comes of a clutter of argument. Few lawyers are willing to do this; it is the mark of the most distinguished talent.[55]

And the late William D. Mitchell, one-time Attorney General of the United States, and one of the ablest of Solicitors General, wrote:

Some lawyers, of course, do not have enough confidence in their own judgment or are not competent to select weak points, but the most effective advocate is one who has the courage to eliminate such arguments.[56]

Indeed, it may safely be laid down as a proposition of general application that to include a weak point is virtually certain to dilute every strong one.

I have had in my own experience an object lesson in this proposition, in the *Di Re* case.[57] There the question, stated most favorably for the prosecution, was, "Whether, when officers have been informed that contraband is to be transferred at a certain place, and their observations reasonably justify the conclusion that a transfer has taken place in an automobile at such place, they are justified in searching and arresting a third person present in the automobile about whom they had no previous information." In the petition for certiorari it was urged that Di Re's search could be justified without regard to the validity of his arrest—first, under the principle that a vehicle may be searched by officers having reasonable cause to believe that it is being used to carry contraband;[58] and, second, on the ground that, in any event, probable cause existed for the arrest.[59]

After the petition was granted, and in the course of writing the brief on the merits, I was beset with doubts as to the soundness of the first proposition, because after all it is quite a step from searching the automobile to searching the people who ride in it. In the end, we reversed the order of the points in the brief, arguing first, that "the search of respondent was justified as incident to a lawful arrest," and second, that "alternatively the search of respondent was

---

[55] Hand, *In Memory of Charles Neave*, in *The Spirit of Liberty* (Dilliard's 2d ed. 1951), 127–128.

[56] Book Review (1950), 64 Harv. L. Rev. 350, 351.

[57] *United States v. Di Re*, 332 U.S. 581.

[58] See *Carroll v. United States*, 267 U.S. 132; *Husty v. United States*, 282 U.S. 694; *Scher v. United States*, 305 U.S. 251; compare, for a decision after the *Di Re* case, *Brinegar v. United States*, 338 U.S. 160.

[59] Judge Clark had said, dissenting below, "Police officers cannot be held unreasonable in declining to view as a mere bystander one who accompanies a criminal to a crime rendezvous." *United States v. Di Re*, 159 F.2d 818, 820 (C.C.A. 2).

justified as incident to the search of a moving vehicle reasonably believed to be carrying contraband." At the oral argument I simply stated the alternative point, and did not in any sense bear down on it. But my real mistake was in leaving it in at all. It was a weak point, I had no faith in it, and yet it colored the entire case. We lost, and the Court's opinion took up and demolished our weak ground first. By the time that was disposed of, the Court was in a fine frame of mind to do execution on our strong point—and it did just that.

The weak point, then, didn't help; it only undermined the good point. I don't mean that we would necessarily have prevailed on the stronger point, but at least it would have been considered and disposed of in a more favorable setting. So I learned, and, with the conviction derived of painful experience, I urge avoid arguing questions in which you have no faith.

(b) *Hornbook Generalizations.* Another sound caution is to avoid emphasizing or relying upon elementary, or hornbook, propositions. Any time, for instance, that a lawyer goes all out on the presumption of constitutionality, it all but indicates that he very much doubts the validity of the statute on which he is relying. Similarly, any time a brief dealing with a question of statutory construction cites *Holy Trinity Church v. United States,*[60] an astute court at once recognizes that it is being asked to rewrite a law in the way the legislature should have done but didn't. (This is not to suggest that the days of judicial tinkering with statutes are over, by any means, but a decent regard to current techniques of the *elegantia juris* as applied to the pretzel bending of statutory provisions (compare Section 56, below) precludes resort to anything as bald as the *Holy Trinity Church* case, which in consequence had better not be cited.)

(c) *Arguments of Last Resort.* There are other indicia of last resort arguments also, points that should simply not be made because to make them amounts to giving the court a signal that your case is hopeless—and that you know it is hopeless.

Indeed, the advance sheets over the last few years indicate that the frequency with which trifling points are presented on appeal on the view that they are somehow "arguable"[61] is itself so serious an appellate problem that it warrants discussion.

---

[60] 143 U.S. 457.

[61] "Some lawyers are willing to take a case, if it presents what they describe as an 'arguable' position, on the theory that every man is entitled to have a lawyer present his case." William D. Mitchell in 64 Harv. L. Rev. at 352.

We can put to one side the phenomenon of the "great case," so called. Centuries ago, Lord Coke noted that "many questions are raised rather out of the weight of the matter than the difficulty of the case."[62] Mr. Justice Holmes made the same point, saying, "But cost and importance, while they add to the solemnity of our duty, do not increase the difficulty of decision except as they induce argument upon matters that, with less mighty interests, no one would venture to dispute."[63]

The problem here considered is the tendency, in wholly run-of-the-mill cases, to magnify trivia. Judges have characterized this tendency in various ways, all essentially similar, none complimentary. Here are some examples: "piddling quibbling";[64] "a worship of the inconsequential"; "a contention * * * made for good measure rather than for good reason";[65] "the remaining miscellany of minor contentions."[66] One court has made the obvious comment that "It is familiar technique for an appellant to seize upon every peccadillo committed by the lower court and magnify it until it becomes a blunder of major proportions,"[67] another the remark, which should be equally obvious, that "We do not clutch at gossamers."[68]

Those quotations are not taken exclusively from criminal cases, nor even from appellate opinions; had they been so restricted there would at least be this excuse, that some convicted person with the means to retain counsel wants desperately to stay out of jail, and accordingly grasps at any straw that comes to hand—the doctrine of *tabula in naufragio* (or, freely translated, any port in a storm) did, after all, have some currency in English equity for

---

[62] Preface to 10 Co. Rep. (1826 ed.) xxi.

[63] *Sanitary District v. United States,* 266 U.S. 405, 425.

See also Holmes, J., dissenting in *Northern Securities Co. v. United States,* 193 U.S. 197, 400–401: "Great cases, like hard cases, make bad law. For great cases are called great, not by reason of their real importance in shaping the law of the future, but because of some accident or immediate overwhelming interest which appeals to the feelings and distorts the judgment. These immediate interests exercise a kind of hydraulic pressure which makes what was previously clear seem doubtful, and before which even well settled principles of law will bend."

[64] Clark, J., in *Republic of Italy v. De Angelis,* 206 F.2d 121, 124 (C.A.2).

[65] Murphy, Jr., in *Application of House,* 144 F.Supp. 95, 99 (N.D. Calif.).

[66] Medina, Jr., in *Dictograph Products v. Federal Trade Commission,* 217 F.2d 821, 829 (C.A.2).

[67] Lemmon, Jr., in *Mitchell v. United States,* 213 F.2d 951, 953 (C.A.9).

[68] *Rotundo v. Isthmian Steamship Co.,* 243 F.2d 581, 584 (C.A.2) (*Per curiam*; L. Hand, J., presiding).

many years.[69] Insofar as counsel in a criminal appeal has a choice between weak points and strong ones, he owes it to his client to abandon those that are weak lest he dilute those that are strong. Insofar as such counsel has no strong points—and in some criminal trials, even when they extended over many days and even weeks, there will not be a single good point for an appeal, much less for certiorari—then there is ultimately involved a conflict of interest between attorney and client, between the client who risks his liberty, and the lawyer who stands to injure his professional reputation.[70] That conflict, necessarily, is one that every lawyer must resolve for himself. But there is hardly the same dramatic conflict when counsel seizes on and makes picayunish contentions in a civil case at the trial level.

Just to complete the discussion, two special situations with respect to weak points should be noted: Appointed counsel owe an affirmative duty to present points on appeal, regardless of the prospects of success, just so long as those points are substantial.[71] And Government counsel on occasion are under a duty to confess error. The appellate court is not bound by any such action,[72] but if reversal follows the appellate court's acceptance of a confession of error, it is hardly appropriate for the trial judge then to complain that he was "sold short."[73]

(d) *Evasion of Issues.* At first blush it would appear not only unnecessary but indeed presumptuous to remind lawyers that their briefs must meet the other side's arguments. But a number of documents which have passed over my desk indicate that such an obvious admonition still needs to be emphasized. Unless both

---

[69] See 3 Scott, *The Law of Trusts* (2d ed. 1956), § 311.1.

[70] See Mr. Mitchell's comment, quoted *supra*, note 61; the passage then continues: "Other lawyers decline cases which they consider are without merit, because they take no professional satisfaction in arguing them; and because the litigant deserves to have his case presented by a lawyer (if one is available) who believes in it and who, therefore, can argue it more persuasively. It also is true that a lawyer who becomes known as one who does not make a practice of accepting cases in which he does not believe has a long start in the confidence of the courts and on the road to victory."

[71] *Ellis v. United States,* 356 U.S. 674, reversing 249 F.2d 478 (D.C. Cir.); *Cash v. United States,* 357 U.S. 219, reversing 261 F.2d 731 (D.C. Cir.). See also *Hansford v. United States,* 357 U.S. 578, and *Kitchens v. United States,* 358 U.S. 42.

[72] *Young v. United States,* 315 U.S. 257; compare *Cases v. United States,* 343 U.S. 808; *Orloff v. Willoughby,* 345 U.S. 83, 87-88.

[73] See *Petition of Plywacki,* 115 F. Supp. 613, 615 (D. Haw.).

the opposition and the court are hopelessly obtuse—an unlikely coincidence—it is never safe for a lawyer to write his brief on the wishful assumption that out-of-sight is equivalent to out-of-mind, or that the difficult points of a case can somehow be disposed of by being swept under the rug, as it were, either by not deigning to mention them at all, or else by relegating them to footnotes.

Here are two actual examples:

(i) In *Williams v. Lee*,[74] the petitioning Indians urged that under the doctrine of *Worcester v. Georgia*[75] there was no jurisdiction in the State courts to entertain actions against them in respect of transactions taking place on their Reservation. In respect of that basic doctrine, petitioners relied, as had the State court in a previous decision,[76] on a presidential veto of a bill that had proposed to extend State jurisdiction over this particular tribe and on a repassage by Congress of the same bill minus those jurisdictional features,[77] and also on a subsequent Act which had conditionally conferred jurisdiction over Indians on a number of States on condition that those States would take certain steps[78]—which in fact had not been taken in the instant case.

The Government argued that in the veto "there is no indication that jurisdiction already possessed by the respective states should be withdrawn or that no such preexisting jurisdiction was thought to exist"; and that the subsequent Act "did not deal with the reserved jurisdiction which the states already possessed." Both statements appeared—in a footnote![79]

Petitioners accordingly replied,

What 'reserved jurisdiction'? What 'preexisting or reserved state power'?

Such expressions have a nostalgic pre-Appomattox flavor, but that is assuredly their only distinction. For under the Constitution, there is no reserved state power or jurisdiction over Indians, and there never has been, as anyone who troubles to read *Worcester v. Georgia*, 6 Pet. 515, will soon learn. Indeed, only this year both the court below as well as the Supreme Court of the neighboring State of New Mexico held that state courts had no criminal jurisdiction over Navajo Indians committing within the Navajo Reservation acts which if done by non-Indians would have violated the criminal laws of the

---

[74] 358 U.S. 217.

[75] 6 Pet. 515.

[76] See *Begay v. Miller*, 70 Ariz. 380, 385, 222 P.2d 624, 627–628.

[77] See Sen. Doc. 119, 81st Cong., 1st sess., and 95 Cong. Rec. 14784–14785. The modified bill became the Act of April 19, 1950, c. 92, 64 Stat. 44, 25 U.S.C. §§ 631–640.

[78] Sections 6 and 7 of the Act of August 15, 1953, c. 505, 67 stat. 588, 590.

[79] Brief for the United States as *Amicus Curiae*, No. 39, Oct. T. 1958, p. 7, note 4.

states concerned. *Application of Denetclaw*, 83 Ariz. 299, 320 P. 2d 697; *State v. Begay*, 63 N.M. 409, 320 P.2d 1017, certiorari denied, 357 U.S. 918.

The Supreme Court mentioned the veto and the repassage of the bill less its objectionable features, pointed out that the State had not accepted jurisdiction under the later Act—and reaffirmed *Worcester v. Georgia* in ringing terms.[80]

The question which the student of advocacy may well ask himself is: How can any lawyer worthy of the name really expect to dispose of the central issue of a case by such glancing (and obviously questionable) references in a footnote? And how can a lawyer expect that a court will pay attention to him when he does?

(ii) *United States v. Greenberg*[81] was a case turning on the scope of the Fifth Amendment's protection against self-incrimination, with particular reference to the showing of hazard that the witness was required to make before his claim of privilege would be allowed. Adverse rulings below were followed by a petition for certiorari, which was "held" during the pendency of the very similar case of *Hoffman v. United States*.[82] In the opinion thereafter handed down in the latter case, the prerequisites for claiming the privilege were set forth in detail; a week later, the judgment in *Greenberg* was vacated, and the case remanded for reconsideration in the light of *Hoffman*.[83]

On such reconsideration, the Court of Appeals (which had also decided *Hoffman*),[84] adhered to its prior ruling,[85] and when Greenberg then sought certiorari a second time, his petition was granted.[86]

The Government filed an 80-page brief on the merits, the thrust of which is perhaps best portrayed reflexly[87] by the following excerpt from petitioner's reply:

---

[80] 358 U.S. at 222-223.

[81] 187 F.2d 35 (C.A.3).

[82] 341 U.S. 479.

[83] 341 U.S. 944.

[84] 185 F.2d 617 (C.A.3).

[85] *United States v. Greenberg*, 192 F.2d 201 (C.A.3).

[86] 342 U.S. 917.

[87] I am indebted to the late Mr. Ernest Knaebel, Reporter of Decisions of the United States Supreme Court for more than 27 years, for this expression. See *Selective Draft Law Cases*, 245 U.S. 366, 368: "As it is manifestly impracticable to restate these arguments [against the constitutionality of the Selective Draft Law of 1917] separately, perhaps the best recourse available is to exhibit their leading features reflexly, by summarizing the answers to them contained in the single brief of the United States, viz. * * *."

A. The Government starts its argument (U.S. Br. 21) by quoting that portion of the opinion in *Hoffman v. United States*, 341 U.S. 479, 486, which commences by saying that

> The privilege afforded not only extends to answers that would in themselves support a conviction under a federal criminal statute but likewise embraces those which would furnish a link in the chain of evidence needed to prosecute the claimant for a federal crime.

But the Government's brief, though it extends over 80 pages, never goes on to quote the last portion of the paragraph in question, *viz.*,

> However, if the witness, upon interposing his claim, were required to prove the hazard in the sense in which a claim is usually required to be established in court, he would be compelled to surrender the very protection which the privilege is designed to guarantee. To sustain the privilege, it need only be evident from the implications of the question, in the setting in which it is asked, that a responsive answer to the question or an explanation of why it cannot be answered *might* be dangerous because injurious disclosure *could* result.

(We have italicized the conditional words to emphasize that certainty of incrimination is not a prerequisite to successful invocation of the constitutional privilege.)

Nor does the Government at any point quote the further portion of the *Hoffman* opinion, *id.* at 488, where the Court said that

> Petitioner could reasonably have sensed the period of prosecution for federal offenses ranging from obstruction to conspiracy.

The omitted portions of the *Hoffman* opinion necessarily undercut all of the Government's obviously labored endeavors (U.S. Br. 14-18, 21-55) to whittle down the privilege against self-incrimination to the point where it would be available only in circumstances where the assertion that an answer would be incriminating would in and of itself incriminate the witness.

Five days after argument, the Supreme Court reversed *per curiam*—on the authority of *Hoffman*.[88]

The case may not have been as open-and-shut as counsel for petitioner ultimately brought themselves to think—two justices dissented—but how could any lawyer have thought for a moment that he could overcome the recently decided *Hoffman* opinion by simply ignoring those portions thereof that were unfavorable to him?

In short, "Grasp your nettles firmly" is an admonition fully as applicable to unfavorable points of law as it is to unfavorable facts.

---

[88] 343 U.S. 918.

(e) *Requests to Overrule Cases.* Another line of argument that it is usually desirable to avoid is the out-and-out request that a governing precedent be squarely overruled. Lower courts can't overrule cases (although, believe it or not, they are on occasion asked to do so),[89] and the courts of last resort are reluctant to do so. This is true even in that most open-minded of tribunals, the United States Supreme Court.

There is always a basic reluctance to overturn what was once decided, for a number of reasons. First, no one likes to admit that he was once wrong, particularly in the recent past, and judges who have once decided a point after full consideration are certainly no exception to that very human reaction. Second, even judges who most ardently desire to effect new departures strive to maintain at least the appearance of continuity. Indeed, a distinguished legal historian has pointed out that the way to spot Lord Coke's innovations is to look for a sentence beginning "for it is an ancient maxim of the common law."[90]

Consequently, particularly when the precedent in the way is of fairly recent vintage, it is far easier for the advocate to suggest distinctions and differentiations. Frequently an effective technique is to talk around the offending case and give it a form of silent treatment, by emphasizing the principles that lead to a different conclusion. At the very least, this technique may result in a favorable decision on another ground.

---

[89] This is perhaps subject to the qualification that on occasion lower courts or lower court judges correctly divine that a decision of a court of last resort is about to be overruled. See *Barnette v. Nest Virginia State Board of Ed.,* 47 F. Supp. 251 (S.D.W.Va.), affirmed, 319 U.S. 624, where the court, *per* Parker, Circ. J., correctly foretold the impending demise of *Minersville School Dist. v. Gobitis,* 310 U.S. 586; and *United States v. Girouard,* 149 F.2d 760, 764-767 (C.C.A. 1), reversed 328 U.S. 61, where Woodbury, Circ. J., dissenting, accurately predicted the early end of the *Schwimmer* (279 U.S. 644) and *Macintosh* (283 U.S. 605) cases.

[90] "As a rule of thumb it is well to remember that sentences beginning 'For it is an ancient maxim of the common law,' followed by one of Coke's spurious Latin maxims, which he could manufacture to fit any occasion and provide with an air of authentic antiquity, are apt to introduce a new departure. Sentences such as 'And by these differences and reasons you will better understand your books,' or 'and so the doubts and diversities in the books well resolved,' likewise indicate new law. If I may formulate a theory of my own, I advance this—the longer the list of authorities reconciled, the greater the divergence from the cases cited." Thorne, *Sir Edward Coke 1552–1952* (Selden Society Lecture), 7.

Thus, in the *Knauer* case,[91] the Government's brief dealt with the attachment to the principles of the Constitution point of the *Schneiderman* case[92] largely by rearguing that question *de novo*, as an original proposition. As indicated above, Section 34 (b), the Court decided the *Knauer* case on the other ground, though I had the impression at the oral argument that at least some members of the *Schneiderman* majority were seeing the attachment point in a new light. Similarly, in the *Haupt* treason case,[93] it was necessary to undermine the apparent rationale of the but recently decided *Cramer* case.[94] Again, the brief dealt with many of the Cramer premises *sub silentio* in preference to making an all-out assault upon them. In both instances, questions from the bench emphasized the points of similarity with the earlier decisions, and in both instances the replies to those questions stressed what appeared to us to be the determinative differences.

As a matter of advocacy—i.e., persuasion, because it is impossible to stress too much the proposition that advocacy is persuasion—the oblique approach undoubtedly contributed to the successful outcome of the later cases. In law, as in war or football or even love, the direct frontal assault on a prepared and fortified position is only rarely a successful maneuver.

Of course there will be instances when a lawyer must ask for a case to be overruled. The progress of federal constitutional and statutory law is full of instances where old precedents were squarely overruled, generally at the request of counsel. But the basic reluctance to overturn what was once decided is still present, so that it is well, when the request must be made, to make it at the end of the brief after a full demonstration that logical consistency requires such a step.

Section 36. Convincing presentation of the evidence in argument on the facts.—The problem of effectively arguing facts boils down to one of so marshalling your evidence as to make it thoroughly convincing to the judicial reader. Basically, three steps are necessary: assertion, presentation, and conclusion. First you state what you intend to show. Next you set forth the evidence, using pertinent quotations from documents and testimony, stressing any inconsistencies in the case against you, and making full use of that

---

[91] *Knauer v. United States*, 328 U.S. 654.

[92] *Schneiderman v. United States*, 320 U.S. 118.

[93] *Haupt v. United States*, 330 U.S. 631.

[94] *Cramer v. United States*, 325 U.S. 1.

most deadly of all comparisons, the parallel column technique. Finally you conclude, generally by restating your original assertion.

Whenever the case is at all complicated, it is well to divide up the several points you are making, and to make liberal use of argumentative subheadings, so that the direction of your thought is clear. Remember that what you are aiming at is to leave conviction in the minds of your readers, and remember also that no characterization, however apt, ever has the stark impressiveness of verbatim extracts from damaging testimony or from letters that the writer later wishes he had never written. And I repeat: Stress the inconsistencies in your opponent's documents and testimony, bear down on every self-contradiction in the record. For although of course it is the law that a very bad man may have a very good case, nonetheless courts are human and nobody loves a liar.

Bear in mind, however, that the technique of *arguing* facts is very different from that appropriate for *stating* facts. In writing the Statement of Facts (see Sections 23 to 28), the aim is to state the facts appealingly but straightforwardly, so that the effect derives from the selection and juxtaposition of the facts. Once the Argument is reached, however, the facts should be frankly argued, commented on, and editorialized. The only limitations are those dictated by good taste and professional standards (see Sections 28 and 79), and by the caution that on occasion a restrained argument may be more effective than one that seems to shout too much.

In the Statement of Facts, you get your color from the facts themselves; in the Argument, you get your effect either from arguing inferences from the undisputed facts or from frankly arguing to a conclusion from disputed facts. You do not add comments of your own in the first instance; you do in the second. The foregoing principles can perhaps not be profitably illustrated except by taking actual briefs involving questions of fact, and comparing the way the evidence is simply set out in the Statement of Facts with the way that same evidence is later argued in the Argument.

Frequently, however, the carefully prepared factual argument in a brief appears to be love's labor lost, because the case goes off on a point of substantive law or on a question of jurisdiction. Whether one's labor is actually lost depends on an intangible of the judicial process that cannot be stated in statistical terms, viz., on how far a court deciding a problem of jurisdiction is really affected or influenced by the circumstance that one of the parties is shown by the record to have been an arrant cheat. Does a good brief arguing facts really help the jurisdictional argument in such a situation? All that can be said with assurance is this—it certainly doesn't do any harm.

It should be added, though perhaps only by way of reminder, that the rule that the Statement of Facts should be free of editorial comments and argumentative matter by no means dispenses with the necessity that it set forth the facts as effectively and appealingly as the record will permit. The examples discussed in Section 27, above, show how a case frequently turns, not so much on how the facts are argued in the Argument, as on how they are arranged in the Statement of Facts.

Section 37. Careful attention to all portions of the brief.—Just as it is a mistake to toss in a dry statement of facts on top of a good argument on the law, and thus to mar the finished product, perhaps with irreparable injury to the case, so also it is a mistake to neglect any other portion of the brief. The circumstance that these other portions are easier to write or may be less important still does not warrant giving them so little attention that they depreciate the quality of the whole. Three parts of a brief, too frequently given but little care, are considered here.

(a) *Summary of argument.* The rules of many courts require that all briefs, or all except the very shortest ones, contain a summary of the argument. Some courts prescribe in detail just how such a summary is to be constructed, and require that it contain a citation to every authority relied upon in the argument proper. What follows is addressed only to the usual situation, not to the specially prescribed forms.

First of all, consider the importance of the summary. It is required in order that the court may have a bird's-eye view of your argument, in somewhat more elaborate form than that available from the index (which, of course, simply sets forth your headings). And, mark this, the summary is one of the portions of the brief read at the outset. You will in consequence be well advised to make your summary as appealing as possible, rather than dry as dust, and, generally, to expand it substantially over a mere repetition of your headings.

Therefore, within the space at your disposal, don't be afraid to make it long enough to be effective. The real secret of a good summary is to go beyond mere assertion, because the further you get beyond that, the more convincing the summary will be to the reader. And, although a summary normally should not cite many cases (except when specifically required by rule of court), it is a very good idea to sprinkle your summary with a few of the leading authorities on which you rely.

One caution to be added is that the summary should not deviate from the Argument proper; it should be a synopsis of the Argument, not a novel or different train of thought.

(b) *Conclusion.* Generally the conclusion should be pretty formal, as for example:

"The judgment below should be affirmed."

"For the foregoing reasons, the judgment below should be reversed, with directions to dismiss the petition."

Or, in a supplemental brief:

"For the foregoing additional reasons, the judgment of the district court should be reversed, with directions to enter a judgment granting appropriate relief to the United States."

On occasion, it is helpful to expand the conclusion somewhat, and to summarize the nub of the argument. Thus, in the case that involved the refusal of a state court to entertain an action based on a federal statute,[95] the conclusion of the petitioner's brief read:

> The decision below is based upon a misconception of the nature of the federal system. The judgment should therefore be reversed with instructions to enter judgment on the verdict.

And, in the *Haupt* treason case,[96] a long brief was concluded as follows:

> Petitioner was convicted of treason after a sober, careful, and eminently fair trial, on the basis of evidence clearly establishing by the required two witnesses a number of legally sufficient overt acts of aid and comfort to the enemy, and clearly showing intent to betray. Reversal of the judgment below can be supported only by artificial refinements and technicalities which find no support in the treason clause of the Constitution. We therefore respectfully submit that the judgment below should be affirmed.

It is not generally profitable to extend a conclusion further; it loses its effectiveness if made too long or it is turned into a peroration.

One caution: Never fail to indicate just what kind of relief you want in addition to reversal, e.g., reinstatement of the judgment of the trial court, or release of the appellant from custody, or dismissal of the indictment. Be specific so that the court's order will likewise be specific, and be sure to ask for the relief to which you

---

[95] *Testa v. Katt*, 330 U.S. 386.

[96] *Haupt v. United States*, 330 U.S. 631.

are really entitled, else there will be mistakes and a lot of very red faces all around.[97]

(c) *Appendix.* The Appendix in this connection is not the so-called Appendix Record required by the rules of many courts, pursuant to which counsel print as pertinent portions of the record (which is not separately printed), but is the Appendix to the brief that contains the collection of statutes involved and similar materials, whenever such matter is too long to be set out in the brief proper.

The basic cautions, so far as statutes are concerned, are to quote from the original statute, and, whenever amendments are pertinent, to show clearly and unmistakably the development of the statute through successive amendments.

Remember, with reference to federal statutes, that the United States Code is only *prima facie* evidence of the law, except where particular titles have been enacted into positive law. In the absence of such enactment, you will frequently do better to rely on the Statutes at Large.

I know that when I was primarily a state practitioner, I felt that the Code was all that counted, but I soon found out, after beginning to feed at the public trough, that the experts in the various federal specialties never used Code citations except for purposes of parallel reference; they always talked about section so-and-so of the National Defense Act, or of the Mineral Leasing Act, or of the Puerto Rican Organic Act, or of sections thus-and-so of the Revised Statutes. Consequently, I learned, or thought I did, to use the Code

---

[97] In a case some years ago, the Court of Claims entered judgment in favor of the plaintiff in the sum of $3,227.93, and the Government petitioned for certiorari, assigning as error the entry of judgment for $1,877.93 in respect of a particular item, as to which it was contended that the contracting officer's determination was final. *John McShain, Inc. v. United States*, 88 C. Cls. 284, certiorari granted, 307 U.S. 619. The single item was the only one in issue, but the Government concluded by saying, "It is respectfully submitted that the judgment of the Court of Claims should be reversed, and the cause remanded with instructions to enter judgment in favor of the United States." Less than three weeks after argument the Supreme Court entered a memorandum *Per Curiam* in the precise language of the conclusion in the brief, viz., "The judgment is reversed, and the cause is remanded to the Court of Claims with instructions to enter judgment in favor of the United States. [Citing cases.]" *United States v. John McShain, Inc.*, 308 U.S. 512. This deprived the respondent of the sums admittedly due, with the result that, four weeks later, the Court had to amend its order to read: "The judgment is reversed to the extent that it includes the $1,877.93 alleged to be due from the United States in paragraphs XIV through XXIV of the petition to the Court of Claims, and the cause is remanded to the Court of Claims with instructions to enter judgment in favor of the United States with regard to this item. [Citing cases.]" *United States v. John McShain, Inc.*, 308 U.S. 520.

primarily as a secondary and parenthetical citation, citing the statute in the first instance as it appeared in the Statutes at Large.

I say "or thought I did" because in one case I didn't check the Appendix carefully, and the statutes involved were printed there as they appeared in the Code, namely, amended up to date. The case involved the effect of successive amendments to the governing statute, and while I was up on my feet, Chief Justice Stone complained in open court that he didn't like the Appendix because it didn't show him the statute before and after. There are, I can assure you, more comfortable courtroom experiences than that one. So—

(i) Always show the statute before and after, whenever something turns on the amendment.

(ii) If the statute has been amended from time to time, but the case isn't affected thereby, print the statute as it was at the time in question, e.g., when the offense was committed, and indicate that fact.

(iii) Use any available typographical aid to point up the amendments—italics for the new portions, brackets for the old ones, explanatory footnotes, and so forth. And—

(iv) Check your Appendix carefully; you just can't afford to let it go with a once-over-lightly. (I know!)

Of course, an Appendix to a brief is not necessarily restricted to statutes. In appropriate cases, it should set out executive regulations; texts of administrative rulings; legislative materials, whether excerpts from debates or from committee reports; opinions in cases either unreported or not yet reported; forms of conveyances or of relevant documents; explanation of related proceedings; identification, by way of dramatis personae, of the individuals involved in the case (as for instance in complicated antitrust proceedings involving many corporate defendants, each having many individual officers who are referred to in the brief); lists of exhibits; and the like. Include whatever is relevant or whatever may be of assistance to the court in understanding the case and its background.

In this connection it is appropriate to point out the advisability, when listing appendices in the index at the beginning of the brief, to indicate what each contains. "Appendix A, Appendix B, and Appendix C," showing where each may be found, does nothing to whet a judicial reader's curiosity; whereas setting forth the subject matter on the index page, as "Appendix A—Statutory provisions; Appendix B—Summary of Land Court proceedings;

Appendix C—Form of territorial conveyance," does, at the very least, indicate the scope of the Appendix materials.

Section 38. Leaving an impression of conviction with the reader and satisfying his curiosity.—If a case is a close one, even the most experienced and learned judges will be in doubt after having read the briefs on both sides. But no one should be left either in doubt or with curiosity unsatisfied after reading the brief on only one side. If anyone is, then that particular lawyer hasn't written an effective appellate brief.

I have left this element for the end, not because it is the least important but because it is really the sum total of what you are driving at when you sit down to write a brief. At the very least, the brief must be convincing by itself. At the very least, your brief should be in such shape that, if the other side filed nothing, a judge reading your brief would understand the case and be persuaded that you should prevail.

Of course, there isn't any magic talisman for that. All the other items that have been discussed contribute to it, yes, but every case differs from every other case, and so the techniques that carry conviction to the reader in one situation will fail to do so in another.

Perhaps I can best explain what I am driving at under this heading by recalling the circumstances that gave rise to its formulation:

Government briefs for Supreme Court cases are prepared either by the agency concerned (the Securities and Exchange Commission, the Interstate Commerce Commission, and so forth) or by the appropriate division of the Department of Justice—Tax, Criminal, Claims, Antitrust, Lands, and so forth. Those briefs are then reviewed by an attorney on the staff of the Solicitor General, who makes whatever revisions he deems necessary before submitting them to the Solicitor General for final approval. The revisions are often extensive, and on occasion amount to a complete rewriting. The revising process is frequently a painful one, either to the rough-drafter, whose beloved brain children are ruthlessly carved up and irreparably maimed, or to the reviewing lawyer, who is struggling under pressure to supply the analysis or the research or the literary quality that should have been contributed earlier, or to both. I have been in both positions, so I think I can discuss the business dispassionately.

At the reviewing level, my normal inclination was to pass an adequate job, add a few commas or a citation or two, and then let it go on—not because I was more tolerant of other people's sensibilities, but essentially I suppose because I was more indolent. Yet, every once in a while, I would get a draft brief over my desk that I couldn't pass, that I simply had to rewrite despite my basic disinclination to do so—because it wasn't adequate, i.e., it didn't convince me when I read it through but instead left me with a host of bothersome and unanswered questions. So, with (at least) a sigh, I would dig in, and start reading cases, and think about the problem, and reanalyze it, and by the time a week or so had elapsed, the brief would have been rewritten and recast.

If it left me, who was sympathetically inclined, unconvinced and curious, you can imagine how a judge lacking such an inclination would have reacted to it. A brief just hasn't done its job when it leaves that kind of impression.

Analytically, here are some of the elements that contribute to such a brief's unsatisfactory character:

(a) Inadequate analysis—problem not thought through.

(b) Discussion of a tangential question, as a main point, which was not really reached on the record.

(c) Extensive discussion of a prior decision, urging that it be not extended, without fully stating its facts or holding.

The last is what I have in mind when I speak of unsatisfied curiosity: in order to understand the discussion, it was necessary to get the volume down from the shelf and read the case. But it shouldn't be; a brief should give the reader enough of any case it discusses at length to enable him to know what that case holds and why it is either applicable or inapplicable, without having to look it up in the library. I don't mean for a moment that a judge can escape reading the case when he sits down to write the opinion, but I do insist that he shouldn't have to do so when he first reads the party's brief in order to be convinced by that brief.

Any tangential thoughts that a reasonably learned lawyer may have as he reads a particular brief should likewise be satisfactorily answered, *in the brief,* as he reads along—why, for instance, the case isn't governed by *Schmaltz v. Commissioner,* just recently decided, or why it isn't affected by the statute passed last year, or why the claim in question isn't barred by limitations. The brief-writer must be sufficiently aware of all such potential questions, not only to be able to answer them, but also to make sure that they are answered in the brief he is writing.

This is particularly true when he writes a brief for an appellee or a respondent. When judges read the briefs, whether before or after argument, it may be assumed that they will follow the logical course of reading the appellant's or petitioner's brief first. If, then, appellant or petitioner makes what at first blush appears to be a strong, persuasive, and controlling point, and the brief on the other side was written on the hopeful but wholly mistaken assumption that silence is somehow as effective as on occasion it may be dignified (compare some of the examples noted in Section 35(d), *supra*), then the latter brief will not carry conviction to the judicial reader.

It is highly desirable to ignore any personalities that may have crept into the brief filed first (compare Section 79(d), *infra*); name-calling is a contest no one can win. It is well not to pay too much attention to trifles or to arguments that verge on quibbling. Those can usually be disposed of in a sentence or two at the most. But when the other side makes a real, thumping argument, or digs up a citation that really undercuts the judgment you are engaged in defending, you *must* reply. If you do not, your brief will generate doubts in the judges' minds, doubts that a little reflection will only serve to intensify. On an appeal as in a trial, even a poor answer is frequently better than a studied refusal to answer at all.

Section 39. The final accolade.—The real test of whether a brief has been effective—the ordeal by fire—is whether it wins the case. True, there are many good briefs that don't win cases, and assuredly there are poor ones (including some exceptionally poor ones) that do. But a brief that didn't win, however close to perfection it may have come, just wasn't an effective brief; it didn't persuade the court, so it lapses into the realm of "fine try" and "well played." The lawyer needn't be ashamed of it, but the client lost the case, and fees are normally paid with an eye to the final result. The pat story in this connection concerns the Northern gambler who cleaned out all the local talent in a little Southern town, after which the hometown boys gathered round in a somewhat menacing manner and insisted that he tell them whether in his opinion Grant or Lee was the better general. The slick Yankee thoughtfully considered the question, gave even more thoughtful consideration to the group around him, and then answered, "Well, gentlemen—they paid off on Grant." So here: clients don't pay off on good losing briefs.

However, when the winning brief is inadequate, and forces the court to do a lot of independent research, and the opinion relies on cases not discussed or even cited by counsel and flatly rejects the proposition advanced by the prevailing side, then that wasn't a very effective brief either: it didn't persuade.

So I conclude with this proposition: that a really effective brief is one that (a) wins your case, and (b) persuades the court to follow your analysis of the problem and to rely on your authorities.

It may reflect an inadequate or erroneous set of values, but I never get the same pleasure out of winning a case when the court goes off on a tack of its own as when it follows the analysis I have labored over and set out in the brief. And I must confess to feeling the ultimate in forensic satisfaction when the opinion uses an analogy I invoked[98] or incorporates into the final text one of my own pet phrases from the brief.[99] Those are the trifles I regard, rightly or wrongly, as the final accolade for the brief-writer.

---

[98] "The analogy suggested by counsel for the appellant seems apposite: namely, that of a defendant who commits a crime in Canada, escapes to the United States, and then returns to Canada; he cannot defend on the ground that between the offense and the trial he was beyond the jurisdiction of the Canadian court." *United States v. Malanaphy,* 168 F.2d 503, 507 (C.C.A. 2), reversed sub. *nom. Hirshberg v. Cooke,* 336 U.S. 210.

[99] (a) "Congress understood that it was writing finis to a long chapter in the Nation's history, and that conditions had entirely changed from the days when truly imperial grants had been deemed necessary to induce entrepreneurs to build the lines of steel without which the West could not have been opened to settlement. Now it was time to close the books, to balance the accounts, to end the further disposal of public lands in aid of construction to which the United States was obligated." Brief for the Petitioners in *Krug v. Santa Fe P. R.* Co., at pp. 37–38. "We think Congress wrote finis to all these claims for all railroads which accepted the Act by executing releases." *Krug v. Santa Fe P. R. Co.,* 329 U.S. 591, 598.

(b) "The necessary consequence would be that the writ of habeas corpus would thereby be perverted into what is simply a delayed motion for a new trial, available long out of time, which will forever keep open the prospect that on some later and, it may be, brighter day, the record of trial can be once more reviewed in a more favorable legal climate. and the defendant released from custody for what is then shown to be an error of law on the part of the trial judge." Brief for the Petitioner in *Alexander v. U.S. ex rel. Kulick,* p. 27.

"If in such circumstances, *habeas corpus* could be used to correct the error, the writ would become a delayed motion for a new trial, renewed from time to time as the legal climate changed." *Sunal v. Large* (and *Alexander v. U.S. ex rel. Kulick),* 332 U.S. 174, 182.

CHAPTER 4

Hints on the Process of Brief-Writing and Research

Section 40. Introductory.—This chapter will include a few suggestions designed to facilitate the process of writing an appellate brief. I have found them helpful in my own practice—after learning each the hard way. I pass them on here, not with any thought that what follows is either the "approved solution" or the last word on the subject, but solely with the view that what has helped one lawyer may similarly help other lawyers.

Section 41. The basic precepts.—My principal suggestions under the present heading can be very simply stated:

(a) Write the Statement of Facts before you write the Argument.

(b) Finish your analytical thinking and complete your basic research before you start to write the Argument.

(c) Write the Argument consecutively.

(d) Write the Summary of Argument last of all.

(e) Check (or, preferably, have someone else check) every citation and record reference.

Section 42. Write the Statement of Facts first.—The importance of the Statement of Facts (compare Section 23, *supra*) really demands that this portion of the brief be written first. A lot of lawyers don't do it that way, preferring to toss in a casual or cursory Statement of Facts after they have labored long and lovingly on the intricate learning of their legal argument. I used to do it that way myself on occasion—when I was new at the game. But, for reasons that would simply repeat what is set out at length in Sections 23 to 28, above, I don't do it that way any more: I invariably write the Statement of Facts first, regardless of the nature of the brief, because a substantial experience has convinced me that this is the order that results in the most effective product.

It results in a more effective product for two reasons. First (see Sections 23 to 27, above), the facts are frequently, perhaps usually, the most important element in every case, and so they deserve and should receive primary attention. Second, once your Statement of Facts is completed, it will help you in the writing of your argument—new legal arguments are bound to suggest themselves to you once your Statement of Facts has been properly done.

Sometimes a Statement of Facts can be very short, reflecting the thinness of the record. On other occasions, when the case has a record running to thousands of printed pages, the Statement of Facts is necessarily more voluminous. But it does not follow that the length of the Statement of Facts should increase in direct proportion to the length of the record—although it is true that the longer the record, the longer the labors of the really able lawyer. The remark, variously attributed to Cicero and to Pascal—"If I had had more time, I would have written you a shorter letter"—is apposite here in full measure.

Section 43. How to go about writing the Statement of Facts.— The painful but inescapable preliminary to writing the Statement of Facts is reading the record; there just isn't any shortcut or labor-saving gadget to spare the lawyer who actually pushes the pen. If you are unwilling or simply not in a position to take the time to read the record, you must get someone else to write the Statement of Facts.

Assuming that you are at the rough-drafting level of the working staff (i.e., junior partner or law clerk or P-4 in the Government service), the best way to start is to take a deep breath and simply plunge in, taking more or less complete notes as you go along. Ideally, if time permits, you should make a complete index of the testimony and of the exhibits, preferably with a carbon copy. In well-regulated law offices, this is done by the young men during the trial, generally at night and over week-ends, while the seniors in charge of the litigation are regaining their strength and, generally, keeping their minds open for the larger aspects of the controversy. At any rate, before the appellate brief is about to be written, someone will have to make a workable guide to the transcript.

One copy is the consecutive index; the second becomes the cross-index. The latter is thereafter marked to show division into topics, after which the index as to each topic is reassembled, either by pasting or copying; this enables you to compress all the testimony on a particular topic into convenient compass without having to run through the entire index anew each time that you pass to a new topic. If the index is not too bulky, you can get the same effect with marginal notes in colored inks or pencils for each particular topic—i.e., red for the merger negotiations, green for the threat of patent litigation, blue for the accounting system, and so on.

Under ideal conditions, with a maximum of clerical help, the easiest and the best way is to dictate the index directly to a stenographer or Dictaphone as you go along. It should look something like this:

OATMEAL-DIRECT

674–675–Is V.P. of Schmaltz Mfg. Co.; has been for 16 years; knows D intimately, socially as well as in business.

676   –Was present at June 5 directors' meeting; D made the bond issue proposal, unanimously approved.

677–679–Also present at July 10 directors' meeting; D made report re progress of loan; no one objected.

680–683–Also present at August 11 directors' meeting; D made further progress report; details re that report.

683–687–Long colloquy re admissibility of draft minutes; admitted as DX 43.

With someone to take your dictation it isn't nearly so difficult as pushing a pen late at night. When your dictation has been typed up, mark up the carbon by topics in the margin, and let the stenographer collect in a single sequence all the testimony under the particular topic, always indicating whose testimony is referred to. E.g.:

H-JUNE 5 DIRECTORS' MEETING

OATMEAL-DIRECT

676   –Was present at June 5 directors' meeting; D made the bond issue proposal; unanimously approved.

OATMEAL-CROSS

732–733–Doesn't recall extent of discussion of bond issue proposal at June 5 meeting; only certain there was no objection.

734   –Positive that was the first time D mentioned it.

735–736–Never had had earlier talks with him concerning it, either privately or in the office.

737   –Pl X 73 doesn't change recollection re that. 738–740–Long colloquy re PI X 73.

741   –Adhere to statement, bond issue first broached at June 5 dir. meeting.

OATMEAL-REDIRECT

789   –Pl X 73 referred to Schmaltz Mfg. Co.'s subsidiary.

OVERSHOE-DIRECT

973–974–Remembers June 5 directors' meeting vividly; was his wedding anniversary and Mrs. O. was put out over his attending it.

974   –D made some sort of bond issue suggestion; sounded O.K. and D was financial man.

975   –Possibly D mentioned it before; can't recall.

OVERSHOE-CROSS

1001   –Never saw Pl. X 73 before coming to court just now.

And so on, for every witness whose testimony bears on this particular topic. When you are all through, you have a workable key to the record, which will instantly locate for you what everyone said on every point; and you will need to refer to the actual record only for exact quotations and, where your index covers two or more pages (i.e., 973–974), for the precise page reference.

As I say, this is the ideal; with less, or less efficient, help, you will have to curtail your indexing. And of course the time factor cannot be ignored. But it may be stated with some considerable assurance that the better the index, the less the time that is later used up in hunting for an elusive but important bit of testimony not reflected therein. Time spent in constructing an effective index to the record is time well invested.

Section 44. Steps after completing the index of testimony.— Having completed your index of the testimony, you will have a fairly good idea of the scope and extent of the record in your case and of the major topics it involves. The next step, then, is to block out the order in which you will set forth those topics in the Statement of Facts. Having done that, you are ready to write: your outline is your guide, your topical index gives you the key to the materials, and you can fill in the record references as you go along. You will frequently need to refer to the actual transcript, either to get the exact page reference whenever the index notes refer to several consecutive pages lumped together, or whenever you deem it helpful to quote exactly from a witness or a document. But, given outline and index, you have control of your materials, no matter how bulky they are, and you should therefore be able to make very satisfactory progress.

It is well to pause at this point to stress the absolute necessity for having record references to every portion of the Statement of Facts. That need simply cannot be overemphasized. For one thing, a Statement of Facts buttressed by record references carries a kind of reassuring conviction to the reader. For another, when the reader (i.e., specifically, the judge who is going to pass on your case) turns to the record, his curiosity whetted, and finds that what you have said is true, he gains confidence in the accuracy and veracity of what you have written.

Contrariwise, if long passages of assertive prose are devoid of record references, the sophisticated judge is at once beset by doubts. "Where does this fellow get this stuff from?" "Is this just a free-wheeling opening to a jury, or are we here on appeal?" Doubts are immediately generated by any Statement of Facts not supported by page references to the record. And if a record reference duly included turns out not to support the text—look out! *Falsus in uno, falsus in omnibus* is a standard applied not only to witnesses by lawyers and juries, it is a standard applied to lawyers by appellate judges.

To resume: Once a fair first draft is ready, you will want to read it over for verbal revisions. When those are made, put your corrected Statement of Facts to one side—on ice, as it were.

(Some folks have the verbal fluency, as well as a sufficient number of competent stenographers, to be able to dictate a brief. I just can't; I have to push the pen, and as each portion is finished and revised, I send it off for typing in draft—triple-spaced, in order to leave plenty of room for later corrections and additions.)

This seems as good a place as any to mention the desirability of referring to the parties by some designation that will make for understanding and clarity. To call the parties "appellant" and "appellee" throughout in a civil appellate brief is bound to confuse; mistaken references are inevitable; and the designations simply reflect the happenstance of the outcome below and do not characterize the parties' positions in the context of the controversy on appeal.

The object should be to use a characterization conducive to understanding. In a negligence case, it is perfectly adequate to refer to the parties as they were below, as "plaintiff" and "defendant," because the plaintiff is always the injured party. But in a domestic relations controversy the terms "plaintiff" and "defendant" only show who brought suit, which is not very illuminating. Hence, in that situation the parties should be referred to as "husband" and "wife."

Use shorthand terms that assist understanding: e.g., "the corporation," "the minority stockholders," "the Commission." Similarly, where long corporate names are involved, use a compressed shorthand designation, just as courts do in their opinions; e.g., "Allied Chemical and Reagent Co., Inc., hereinafter called simply 'Allied.'"

There is one apparent exception to the basic precept: in a criminal appeal involving only a single defendant, you are perfectly safe in calling the convicted person "appellant" or "petitioner." In that instance the docket designation cannot possibly confuse. But where there are several appellants or petitioners, the rule just discussed should once more be followed.

A very simple test will solve your problem. Just ask yourself these questions: Will the terms in which your brief refers to the parties enlighten the judge who reads it? Or will your designation simply confuse him?

Section 45. Final revision of the Statement of Facts.—Later, when the rest of the brief is also finished, it is a very good idea to reread the record, taking notes then of only those items of testimony you think you missed earlier. Insert those additional references, or additional topics, in the revised draft Statement of Facts that you had earlier put to one side.

There are bound to be some you have missed, and you will regret every last one of those if you permit the brief to go into final print before you catch them. There are bound to be others you may have thought you missed that turn up, duly included in your draft. To the extent that such references are included after all, it shows that your system is working—fine! But when you get to the final showdown, it is those you have missed that annoy and cause pain, and it is for this reason that the rereading should not be omitted.

So much for the working level, for the pencil-pusher echelon. Now suppose that you are somewhat higher in the hierarchy, that you are the senior partner who will argue the case, or the Government lawyer who will actually wear the striped pants and emit the sound effects. In that event you should still read the record before the brief goes into final and irrevocable print. (No lawyer, and I will say it dogmatically, here and now and many times again, should ever risk his reputation by arguing a case on a record he has not read. And since you should read it anyway, the time for that reading is when the process can still influence the brief.)

At the nonwriting level it is not necessary to take very copious notes, but you should note the bits of testimony that, as you read, seem most significant. If the brief has been well written by an able lawyer, most of those items will have been included. But there will always be a few whose significance the man actually arguing the case will more keenly appreciate, and it is the inclusion of those select and significant few that often makes the difference between a good brief and a very good one. So, I repeat, reading the record at this point, when the results of your own analysis can still be added, is time well spent.

One of the most difficult—and unsatisfactory—situations in which an advocate can find himself is to be retained or assigned to argue a case where the brief is already filed. He can then hardly abandon points whose value he doubts, nor can he effectively add new contentions that he regards as substantially stronger. Even if the lawyer who is to argue the case was for one reason or another unable to follow the wise counsel that he should actually have written the final form of his own brief, at the very least he should have been able to make his own decisions as to the points that it should have included.

Finally—and now I am back at the working level—be sure that every record reference and every quotation you have included in the Statement has been meticulously checked; see Section 64, below.

Section 46. Think before you write the argument.—The basic admonition to the lawyer who is sitting down to write the Argument is simply this: Never start to write until you have thought the case through and have completed your basic research. That doesn't mean every citation or every footnote, but it does include a reading, and, whenever required, a rereading, of all the important cases— because the basic authorities are always full of suggestive leads for further development. And be certain that you have really thought your argument through and outlined it, before you put pen to paper (or lips to dictograph). If it doesn't outline properly, it hasn't been properly analyzed—another point on which one may safely be dogmatic. And, even with an apparently satisfactory outline, a brief that hasn't been properly thought through or researched just doesn't turn out well. Frequently, of course, your writing is done under the pressure of deadlines; you must begin, even though you feel unready. But in that event, your original indirection and unreadiness are almost certain to be reflected in your final work.

The question will naturally arise, how does one know when "the case has been thought through" or when "the basic research has been completed"? The only answer is, you come to sense it. There isn't any gauge or instrument; it is just a feeling. How do you know when you have had enough to eat? It's the same sort of thing, an instinctive reaction that develops after a time. You will recognize it, never fear, and when you do, then you can safely start writing—but not before!

Section 47. Never let the other side write your brief.—Always write your brief in such a way as to set out and make the most of your affirmative case. This admonition is perhaps most to be borne in mind when you are appellee or respondent; don't content yourself, in that situation, with a point-by-point reply to appellant or petitioner. Accentuate the affirmative features of *your* case, don't let the other side write your brief or even shape it.

I can illustrate this approach first with an anecdote and then with actual and specific instances. The anecdote concerns one of the ablest of Solicitors General, who was asking when the Government's brief in *Oatmeal v. United States* would be ready. He was told that it had not yet been started since the petitioner's brief had not yet come in. "What's the matter?" he asked. "Haven't we got a case?"

So, don't follow the appellant's outline of points, even when you must reply to all of them. Put your own strongest point first, because what may be strongest for him may not be so for you.

The actual instances illustrate different applications of the principle.

(a) Thus, in the *Douglas Chandler* radio broadcasting treason case,[1] the appellant opened his written argument with an attack on the jurisdictional basis of the prosecution. Here was his order of points:

    I. The court should not have exercised jurisdiction over the person of the defendant.

    II. The court lacked jurisdiction of the crime alleged, for

        1. Congress has not by law directed the place of trial of crimes committed within the territorial jurisdiction of a foreign government.

        2. If Judicial Code, Section 41, is construed as applicable, the District of Massachusetts was not that into which the defendant was first brought.

    III. The indictment is duplicitous.

    IV. Treason against the United States is not committed by adherence to the enemy by one residing in enemy territory.

    V. The overt acts alleged in the indictment are insufficient to establish the offense of treason, for

        1. They do not in themselves and in their setting manifest any criminal intention.

---

[1] *Chandler v. United States*, 171 F.2d 921 (C.A. 1), certiorari denied, 336 U.S. 918.

2. They are manifestly merely preparatory parts of acts not treasonable unless completed and not set forth in the indictment.

VI. The proof of the overt acts submitted to the jury was insufficient to establish the offense of treason.

VII. The court erroneously admitted evidence upon the issue of the defendant's intent to betray the United States and erroneously instructed the jury upon that issue.

VIII. The court erroneously instructed the jury with respect to the weight to be given the defendant's motives in determining whether he had a specific intent to betray.

I am not suggesting for a moment that this was not an effective presentation for appellant's purpose, and certainly Chandler's defense, ably conducted by appointed counsel,[2] reflected the finest traditions of the American bar. But the foregoing order of points did not center attention on what the prosecution deemed to be the controlling legal questions. Consequently, rather than answering Chandler's contentions seriatim, the Government rearranged the points at issue in an entirely different order, and concentrated on the core of the substantive offense:

I. The indictment charged and the evidence established the crime of treason.

A. Broadcasting propaganda on behalf of an enemy is a treasonable act.

B. The overt acts were acts which gave the enemy aid and comfort.

C. All of the overt acts were supported by the testimony of two witnesses within the meaning of the Constitution.

D. The judgment below must be sustained so long as there is a single sufficient overt act.

E. Appellant's treasonable intent was not nullified by his belief that what he did was in the interests of the United States.

F. The recordings were properly received in evidence on the issue of appellant's intent.

G. The indictment is not duplicitous.

II. Congress has made treason committed abroad an offense and Congress had constitutional power to do so.

III. Appellant was lawfully apprehended and lawfully brought within the jurisdiction of the district court.

IV. The District of Massachusetts was the proper forum for appellant's trial.

A. Congress has made specific provision for the trial of offenses against the United States committed abroad.

B. The District of Massachusetts was the district into which appellant was first brought.

---

[2] Messrs. Claude B. Cross and Edward C. Park of the Boston Bar.

Chandler's conviction was sustained. But the real proof of the pudding, so far as the prosecution's order of points was concerned, was this: First, the court had this to say concerning the arguments that did not go to the merits:

Counsel for appellant have not suggested any alternative procedure which in their view properly could have been employed to bring Chandler to trial; in fact, all their arguments involve the conclusion, which we deem unacceptable, that there was no way in which a court of the United States could obtain lawful jurisdiction over Chandler unless he should choose to relinquish his asylum in Germany and voluntarily return to the United States.[3]

Second, the court dealt with the question of the proper district, which the prosecution had relegated to the end of its brief, with the remark, "It would indeed be unfortunate if we were compelled to hold, on such a highly technical ground, that this elaborate trial has gone for naught."[4]

The prosecution's order of points, therefore, was vindicated in the result.[5]

(b) In other cases, it may not even be necessary to join issue with the appellant or petitioner. If his strongest point, legally speaking, is not really raised on the facts, you may safely reject his chosen battleground, and stand on your own strong points.

So, write your brief affirmatively. Put your own strong points forward. Don't be content with simply a point-by-point denial of what the other side has said, and don't go all out demolishing a point that the other side vainly hopes will seem to be in the case. Any time you simply follow such a course, you are letting the opposition write your brief.

Section 48. Research; Some general considerations.—This chapter is emphatically not a rehash of the several excellent works now in print on "How to Find the Law." It is written for the reader who already knows the use of every bibliographical tool, and who, with the aid of digests, encyclopedias, textbooks, sets of annotated cases, citators, collections of judicial definitions, and miscellaneous indices, is able to chart a workable path through the morass of current case law. It seeks rather to assist in the evaluation of noncase material, the proper use of which is increasingly significant in appellate practice.

---

[3] 171 F.2d at 936.

[4] 171 F.2d at 933.

[5] Counsel for the petitioner were gracious enough to say in their reply brief, "* * * The arrangement of the points discussed, in what may be thought the order of their importance, seems to us impressive and one which we perhaps should have adopted."

Section 49. The case in point.—In an intermediate appellate court, the citation of a decision from the court of last resort that is on all fours with the case at bar generally suffices for all purposes— except only in the extraordinary situation when the intermediate court feels that the cited decision is about to be overruled. The same condition likewise obtains in any court of last resort that considers itself bound by the principle of *stare decisis*, and gives that approach more than lip service. But in the Supreme Court of the United States, certainly as that august tribunal has recently been constituted, citation of the case in point is by no means the last word.

A striking example from my own experience was *Girouard v. United States*,[6] the case which held that a conscientious objector was eligible for citizenship. The petitioner, a Seventh Day Adventist, had expressed himself as willing to serve in the armed forces but unwilling to bear arms. As a matter of precedent, his case was ruled, not by that of Rosika *Schwimmer*,[7] who was a fairly fuzzy-minded, world-brotherhood, there-is-no-sovereignty brand of pacifist; nor by that of Douglas *Macintosh*,[8] who desired to pass judgment on the justness or unjustness of each particular war as it arose, so that he could determine for himself whether to participate; but by that of Marie *Bland*[9] (argued and decided together with the last preceding), the Canadian nurse who did not object to war but only to bearing arms.

But—the authority of the *Bland* case, notwithstanding the then recently decided case of the conscientious objector who was denied admission to the bar,[10] would not have won a single vote in the *Girouard* case; no justice was willing to support *Schwimmer, Macintosh,* or *Bland* as a matter of judicial decision.[11] The Government had therefore to establish a legislative ratification of the earlier decisions. Even that did not convince a majority of the Court,

---

[6] 328 U.S. 61.

[7] 279 U.S. 644.

[8] 283 U.S. 605.

[9] 283 U.S. 636.

[10] *In re Summers,* 325 U.S. 561.

[11] "With three other justices of the Court I dissented in the *Macintosh* and *Bland* cases, for reasons which the Court now adopts as ground for overruling them. Since this Court in three considered earlier opinions has rejected the construction of the statute for which the dissenting justices contended, the question, which for me is decisive of the present case, is whether Congress has likewise rejected that construction by its subsequent legislative action, and has adopted and confirmed the Court's earlier construction

(continued)

although it did persuade Chief Justice Stone, who had joined in the *Macintosh* and *Bland* dissents, as well as Mr. Justice Frankfurter, who, while still on the Harvard Law School faculty, had been active in sponsoring a legislative repeal of the earlier cases.[12]

In short, in this particular instance the case in point, without more, did not get a single vote.

Section 50. When there is no case in point.—When there is no case in point, either in the court of last resort or in an intermediate appellate court or in some neighboring jurisdiction, you must draw on other resources. You must have recourse, first of all, to analysis. If you have nothing but logic and reasoning to support and sustain your analysis, by all means use logic. But usually there is available something more than simply your own process of reasoning. There are almost always analogies to which you can profitably turn. Frequently you can make effective use of legislative materials and legislative history. Not infrequently, you will find helpful noncase materials for the asking. But, above all, you must never let a good argument die for want of a case.

This admonition is fully documented in the sections that follow, which discuss the technique of using analogies, the problems involved in statutory analysis and the ascertainment of legislative history, the complexities of distinguishing cases that at first blush appear to be against you, and the use, citation, and reliance upon noncase materials.

Section 51. Use of analogies.—The use of apt analogies, I am more and more coming to believe, is the mark of a really good lawyer. Any clerk can look up cases in the digests, but it takes an actively trained legal mind to search for and find persuasive analogies.

Two fine lawyerlike examples that remain vividly in mind are Mr. Justice Cardozo's analogies in the Social Security cases,[13] and Alfred Bettman's article on the *Constitutionality of Zoning*[14] (which antedated and forecast the Supreme Court's decision on the

---

of the statutes in question. A study of Congressional action taken with respect to proposals for amendment of the naturalization laws since the decision in the *Schwimmer* case leads me to conclude that Congress has adopted and confirmed this Court's earlier construction of the naturalization laws. For that reason alone I think that the judgment should be affirmed." Stone, C. J., dissenting. 328 U.S. at 72–73.

[12] See Hearings before the House Committee on Immigration and Naturalization on H.R. 297, 72d Cong., 1st sess., p. 68; and see 75 Cong. Rec. 15356.

[13] *Steward Machine Co. v. Davis*, 301 U.S. 548; *Helvering v. Davis*, 301 U.S. 619.

[14] 37 Harv. L. Rev. 834 (May 1924).

question).[15] Examine those, study the technique of comparison there employed, and you will begin to appreciate the essential difference between a lawyer on the one hand and a mere attorney at law on the other.

Of course analogies must be accurate, and they must not be carried too far. Two of our greatest judges have left us warnings on that score. Mr. Justice Holmes said: "As long as the matter to be considered is debated in artificial terms there is a danger of being led by a technical definition to apply a certain name, and then to deduce consequences which have no relation to the grounds on which the name was applied."[16] And thirty years later Mr. Justice Cardozo remarked that "When things are called by the same name it is easy for the mind to slide into an assumption that the verbal identity is accompanied in all its sequences by identity by meaning."[17]

But, more frequently than otherwise, the real difficulty is not that the analogy used is doubtful or that it is sought to be extended too far; the trouble is that the lawyer never invokes any analogy at all. The corpus is now so large that, with the inevitable specialization which follows, the current thinking of many if not most practitioners is marked by too much compartmentalization, and far too little cross-fertilization. Not infrequently, judges are apt to think that their colleagues share the bar's shortcomings in this respect in not paying adequate heed to analogous situations.[18] Unfortunately, all too often, the best analogies occur to the brief-writer after the case is over.

Section 52. Handling authorities apparently against you.—One of the most difficult problems for the brief-writer is how to deal with decisions that appear to be against you—and that quite frequently live fully up to their appearances.

Some approaches to this problem have already been discussed in the preceding chapter; see Sections 34 and 35, above.

One solution is to ignore the offending precedent—always provided, of course, that it is not a square holding—and to deal with it *sub silentio*. In the *Haupt* treason case,[19] we—that is to say,

---

[15] *Euclid v. Ambler Co.*, 272 U.S. 365 (November 1926).

[16] *Guy v. Donald*, 203 U.S. 399, 406.

[17] *Lowden v. Northwestern National Bank*, 298 U.S. 160, 165.

[18] Cf. *United States v. Atlantic Mut. Ins. Co.*, 343 U.S. 236, 242–243 (Frankfurter and Burton, JJ., dissenting); *Pennsylvania Coal Co. v. Mahon*, 260 U.S. 393, 416–422, especially at 422 (Brandeis, J., dissenting).

[19] *Haupt v. United States*, 330 U.S. 631.

Government counsel—were faced with some very strong and, as we believed, very wrong language from the recently decided *Cramer* treason case.[20] See Section 35(e), *supra.* We felt that we had a winning case on the facts, that *Haupt* was strong in every respect where *Cramer* had been weak. So we undertook to chart an independent course through the historical and judicial materials, which would show beyond peradventure that the language of the *Cramer* case was wrong but which carefully avoided saying so directly. For the text of the result, see the opinion of the Court,[21] and see particularly the concurring opinion of Mr. Justice Douglas,[22] who had earlier written the dissent in the *Cramer* case.[23]

(I should say parenthetically here that, although I fully appreciate the reluctance of any reader to haul down numerous volumes from library shelves, there is really no way of learning the techniques of advocacy other than the detailed examination of briefs and opinions, plus—ideally—actually hearing the cases argued. The older reporters knew this, and so set down the points of counsel as well as the opinion of the court.)

Another solution is to attack the offending precedent boldly and frontally. As has been indicated above, Section 35(e), this is an operation that engenders much resistance. It is really successful only when the precedent is generally acknowledged to be on its last legs.

The third way is to distinguish it, and that poses the real problem: How can a lawyer most effectively distinguish a case apparently against him?

The soundest advice on this score is to distinguish the offending precedent boldly: Go on a broad ground, don't get bogged down in finicky details, and don't go in for overrefined analysis.

On this point also I found the *Haupt* case[24] most instructive—in teaching me what not to do in the future.

In that case, twelve overt acts of treason had been submitted to the jury, which returned a general verdict of guilty. We argued first that each of the twelve overt acts was supported by the evidence of the required two witnesses. We then went on to argue that, even if some of the overt acts should be deemed not to have been proved by two sufficient witnesses, the judgment of conviction must still be affirmed.

---

[20] *Cramer v. United States,* 325 U.S. 1.
[21] 330 U.S. 631.
[22] 330 U.S. at 644.
[23] 325 U.S. at 48.
[24] *Haupt v. United States,* 330 U.S. 631.

That argument was primarily based on the proposition that, as a matter of the substantive law of treason, it was sufficient to sustain a conviction if, on review subsequent to trial, one overt act charged had been proved by two witnesses, even though additional overt acts alleged in the indictment were not so proved. That had been the English law since 1660;[25] the earliest American decision was the same;[26] and every modern American jury considering a case of treason had uniformly been charged to the same effect.[27] An unbroken rule of law from 1660 to 1943, continuous over a period of 283 years, should have been fairly persuasive. But the point was not briefed in the *Cramer* case, which came to the Supreme Court in 1945. There the Court held that two of the three overt acts submitted to the jury had been insufficient, after which it went on to hold, *in a footnote*:

> The verdict in this case was a general one of guilty, without special findings as to the acts on which it rests. Since it is not possible to identify the grounds on which Cramer was convicted, the verdict must be set aside if any of the separable acts submitted was insufficient. *Stromberg v. California, 283 U.S. 359, 368; Williams v. North Carolina, 317 U.S. 287, 292.* * * *[28]

The way that this footnote should have been dealt with in the *Haupt* case was as follows: First, the prosecution should have pointed out that for 283 years the rule of substantive law in treason cases had been to the contrary; that in the fairly recent *Stephan* case[29] the conviction was sustained on appeal notwithstanding the Circuit Court of Appeals' determination of the insufficiency, as a matter of two-witness proof, of four of the ten overt acts submitted to the jury, and that none of these authorities had been brought to the Supreme Court's attention in the *Cramer* case in any of the voluminous briefs there filed. (In view of the disposition made of the *Cramer* case, the way was probably not open for an argument

---

[25] *Trial of the Regicides*, 5 How. St. Tr. 947, 1033; *Trial of Robert Lowick*, 13 How. St. Tr. 267, 277; *Trial of Christopher Layer*, 16 How. St. Tr. 94, 313-314; s.c., *sub nom. The King v. Layer*, 8 Mod. 82, 93; 1 Hale, *History of the Pleas of the Crown* *122; Foster, *Crown Law* (1st ed. 1762) 194; 2 Hawkins, *Pleas of the Crown* (4th ed. 1762), 436.

[26] *Case of Fries*, Fed. Case No. 5127, 9 Fed. Cas. at 932 (C.C.D. Pa. 1800).

[27] *United States v. Fricke*, 259 Fed. 673, 677 (S.D.N.Y.); *Stephan v. United States*, 133 F.2d 87, 92 (C.C.A. 6), certiorari denied, 318 U.S. 781 (see R. 326, 339-341, No. 792, Oct. T. 1942); *United States v. Haupt*, 47 F. Supp. 836, 839 (N.D. Ill.), reversed on other grounds, 136 F.2d 661 (C.C.A. 7); *Cramer v. United States*, 325 U.S. 1 (R. 442, 446, No. 13, Oct. T. 1944); *Haupt v. United States*, 330 U.S. 631 (R. 39, No. 49, Oct. T. 1946).

[28] 325 U.S. at 36, n. 45.

[29] *Stephan v. United States* 133 F.2d 87 (C.C.A. 6), certiorari denied, 318 U.S. 781.

that the holding, having been contained in a footnote, was not to be regarded as a precedent.[30])

Second, and here is the nub of the matter, the *Stromberg* and *Williams* cases, cited in the *Cramer* footnote, should have been distinguished on a broad ground, viz., that they dealt with the Supreme Court's review of federal questions coming up from state courts, whereas what was here presented was appellate review of the sufficiency of a conviction for treason, which involved a well-settled rule of substantive criminal law.

I say, that is the way the *Cramer* footnote should have been dealt with. Unfortunately, I went into far more detail. After stating the rule in the treason cases, I went on to discuss some general rules, viz., that, in mail fraud and conspiracy cases, a verdict stands if a single overt act has been proved, even though the others may be bad; that, in any kind of case, a general verdict on an indictment containing many counts is supported by a single good count; and, similarly, with a general sentence. I argued that, since special verdicts are not generally employed in criminal cases, a contrary rule would mean that a defendant could never be charged with more than one overt act of treason except at the risk of acquittal if a single additional overt act submitted to the jury failed of proof; "that is to say, the more active the traitor and the more complex his treason, the better his chances of escaping the noose." Then I went on to a detailed analysis of the *Stromberg* and *Williams* cases—without stressing the real distinction mentioned above. Finally, I urged that since the doing of the overt acts was not disputed, the jury could not have been misled by an insufficiency of proof as to any overt act.

The result? A reaffirmance of the rule of the *Cramer* footnote—in another footnote! The Court said:

When, speaking of a general verdict of guilty in *Cramer v. United States*, 325 U.S. 1, 36, n. 45, we said "Since it is not possible to identify the grounds on which Cramer was convicted, the verdict must be set aside if any of the separable acts submitted was insufficient," of course we did not hold that one

---

[30] There is a remark attributed to Chief Justice Hughes to the effect that "I will not be bound by a footnote," but unfortunately it is not to be found in any opinion. Indeed, the footnote in the first *Carolene* case, to the effect that "There may be narrower scope for operation of the presumption of constitutionality when legislation appears on its face to be within a specific prohibition of the Constitution, such as those of the first ten amendments, which are deemed equally specific when held to be embraced within the Fourteenth" (*United States v. Carolene Products Co.*, 304 U.S. 144, 152, n. 4), foreshadowed much that, for better or worse, is now current constitutional doctrine. For a comment on the *Carolene* footnote, see Frankfurter, J., concurring, in *Kovacs v. Cooper*, 336 U.S. 77, 90–92.

overt act properly proved and submitted would not sustain a conviction if the proof of other overt acts was insufficient. One such act may prove treason, and on review the conviction would be sustained, provided the record makes clear that the jury convicted on that overt act. But where several acts are pleaded in a single count and submitted to the jury, under instructions which allow a verdict of guilty on any one or more of such acts, a reviewing court has no way of knowing that any wrongly submitted act was not the one convicted upon. If acts were pleaded in separate counts, or a special verdict were required as to each overt act of a single count, the conviction could be sustained on a single well-proved act.[31]

In consequence, prosecutors now ask for special verdicts on the overt acts submitted to the jury in treason cases.[32] Possibly the result might have been the same if the *Stromberg* and *Williams* cases had been properly distinguished on broad grounds. At any rate, I am now convinced that it was poor argumentation and presentation to spin the matter out in such great detail, and that the proper way to have handled the apparently adverse decisions would have been the broad distinction suggested above.

Section 53. Use of dissenting and concurring opinions.—When you are not counsel in a case, but are above the conflict, writing for a non-judicial audience on what the law should be, you are of course perfectly free to quote from dissenting opinions, and to indicate why you prefer the reasoning these set out. As the old professor put it, "What the court says carries no mandate to the logical faculty." But when you are counsel seeking to win an appeal for your client, you need the votes of a majority of the court in which the case is pending, and consequently you will not help to persuade the judges by quoting from dissents that failed to persuade them, particularly from recent dissents. If the court in question currently follows *stare decisis*, this point would appear to be almost too obvious to require mention.

We have, however, experienced something of a bloodless constitutional revolution since the late 1930s, in which some notable earlier dissents, by judges of the stature of Holmes, Hughes, Brandeis, Cardozo, and Stone, have become law. So there has developed, especially in some law schools, a veritable cult of dissent, to such an extent that the lads in their moot court cases will frequently cite the dissenting opinions of a judge whom they like in preference to the majority opinions written by a judge whom they hold in disesteem.

---

[31] *Haupt v. United States*, 330 U.S. at 641, n. 1.

[32] As in the *Chandler, Best,* and *Axis Sally* cases.

Some carry that habit with them after admission to the bar—where it can only hurt their clients' causes.

Just ask yourself this question: If there was a strong dissent in a 7–2 case, and five of the original seven are still on the bench, do you really think you can persuade any of them by quoting the views with which they disagreed, views that expressed in forceful language their own error? Of course not; your task is to persuade three additional judges, and to rely on the old dissent is just the way to fail in that endeavor.

Much the same principle applies to concurring opinions. Those are very helpful to the advocate in any situation where he needs to pick up votes, because they show how the concurring judges feel about the problem, and thus they enable him to shape his arguments in an effort to persuade those judges in the next case. But don't quote from the concurring opinions in the hope that somehow the passage in the brief will prove more persuasive with the other judges now than it was in conference when it was first considered by them.

Reliance on, and quotations from, concurring opinions in a brief are justified only where a court was so divided that no single opinion expressed the views of a majority. In that currently not at all unusual situation, it is perfectly proper—indeed it is often necessary—to urge the concurring views. But don't quote a single judge's views too obviously; he will think you are just trying to curry favor, even to fawn, while the others whom he failed to persuade in the first instance are not likely to be persuaded by you at second hand.

Indeed, it is of the essence of advocacy that one endeavors to avoid stirring up opposition on non-essential or collateral matters. Some judges, once they have been outvoted, put the matter to one side, filing it mentally under "finished business." With others, however, a sharp difference of opinion leaves a mark, so that the feelings it engendered are apt to rankle, and for a much longer time than many outsiders would suppose.

Therefore, skirt around the differences disclosed in the reports, if at all possible, and, when you can, use a formula substantially like this: "The issue that divided the Court in *Doe v. United States* is not present here." Narrow the area of disagreement as far as feasible—and don't, *don't*, DON'T cite recent dissenting opinions if your objective is victory on appeal.

Section 54. Briefs filed in earlier cases involving the same or related questions.—Not only does the examination of briefs aid the lawyer who is studying the techniques of advocacy, but, if the case in which they were filed is related to the one presently before him, he is bound to find therein, at the very least, a good deal of suggestive material. Any lawyer who has access to collections of briefs is therefore very fortunate. The fact that more and more libraries now have microfilm collections of Supreme Court briefs testifies to a growing recognition of the importance of those documents.

First of all, if some other lawyer has written a winning brief on the point on which your case will turn, you may save yourself untold preliminary labor by starting your research there. (I say "may," because on occasion examination discloses that it was the court and not the lawyer whose argument won the case.) Once a brief has been filed, of course, it becomes a public document; there is no copyright and hence no infringement; this is therefore a field, preeminently, for the cynical advice to "plagiarize, plagiarize, plagiarize—but remember, please, always to call it 'research.'"

But there is a second and frequently even more compelling reason for examining briefs filed in earlier cases that involved questions similar to or identical with those in your own case.

It is written in the Bible, "behold, my desire is, * * * that mine adversary had written a book."[33] Well, if mine adversary had written a brief, the chances are that he wrote something very different the last time, particularly if he represents the Government, which, more frequently than not, takes inconsistent litigating positions, sometimes (as in tax matters) because it must.

Mere inconsistency, of course, proves nothing; you are not going to win any appeal simply by making debating points, and of course it is not necessary to cite authority for the proposition that the United States is not subject to estoppel. But if you can establish, through indisputable references, that the other side has made a complete about-face on an issue of substance, or on any proposition that was never fairly debatable, it puts at least a crimp into that party's arguments, and it may well enable you to advance your own presentation right at the outset.

Section 55. Statutory analysis.—Sometimes the answer to a given problem is found, not in judicial decisions, but in painstaking analysis of the controlling statute. In such a situation, a lawyer's normal reaction is to look to see how the statute has been construed, to analyze the decisions construing it, and then to write his brief accordingly. That is always, quite properly, the first approach,

---

[33] Job xxxi. 35.

but too often the tendency is to stop there and to rely solely on the decided cases.

The difficulty with not going further is that all too often the court which first construed the statute did not have all the relevant statutory materials before it; that it proceeded to determine the legislative intent without examining the expressions from which that intent could be ascertained; and that subsequent decisions merely interpreted the first case and ceased to attempt to interpret the statute. The consequence of this technique is a stab at statutory analysis that did not analyze the statute but only undertook to reconcile decisions that had similarly failed to analyze it. Accordingly, the ultimate result has frequently been very far from what the legislature really had in mind when it passed the act.

So—when you deal with a problem of statutory analysis, start by analyzing the statute. Look at the section that is in question in your case, not only as it stands, but in relation to the act of which it was first a part. In this connection, it is well to bear in mind that annotated codes may be somewhat of a hindrance, for by their very wealth of annotation they render more difficult your bird's-eye survey of the relevant provisions. Therefore it is very frequently helpful to get the feel of the related sections as they appear consecutively in the official edition of the U.S. Code, or of the state statute book, in such a way as to understand the statute as a whole, before turning to the annotations to the separate sections of the law in the USCA or in similar annotated editions of state statutes.

Remember that, certainly so far as federal statutes are concerned, you are not bound by your provision's present position in the U.S. Code or in the Revised Statutes, nor, generally, by minor changes in phraseology. The *Nye*[34] and *Williams*[35] cases hold that it is proper to go back to the law as originally enacted to ascertain the Congressional intent.[36] One final (and perhaps unsettling) word: Don't overlook *Erie R. Co. v. Tompkins*,[37] which stands as authority for the proposition that even long-continued construction of a statutory provision will not be followed when further research shows that construction to be erroneous.

---

[34] *Nye v. United States*, 313 U.S. 33.

[35] *Williams v. United States*, 327 U.S. 711.

[36] Of course the statutory revision may have been so far-reaching as to change the meaning of the original provision. See ex parte *Collett*, 337 U.S. 55; *Kilpatrick v. Texas & Pacific R. Co.*, 337 U.S. 75; *United States v. National City Lines*, 337 U.S. 78.

[37] 304 U.S. 64.

Section 56. Legislative history.—After the statute has been analyzed in its setting, the lawyer should routinely check the legislative history: successive drafts, committee reports, and the debates on the floor of the legislature. Such material is most complete for federal legislation, and is now more generally accessible to the bar through publication in a number of legislative services. In the libraries, research is facilitated through reference to the "History of Bills and Resolutions" index of the Congressional Record, and by the fact that the later volumes of the Statutes at Large, beginning with volume 33, show the bill number of each act.

The foregoing, however, is only the beginning of one's legislative history troubles. At times it is difficult to escape the conviction that perhaps the English courts are on firmer ground than we are in their view that it is not permissible to look to what was said in the legislature in ascertaining the meaning of a statute.[38] Certainly adherence to that view and to the (delusively) simple ten canons of Blackstone[39] would save American lawyers—and American courts—infinite grief.

At first, the relaxation of the rule in the United States, which came rather later in the day than most lawyers realize, was sensible enough: where the language of a statute was doubtful, resort might be had to the committee reports and to the debates.[40] There were qualifications, to the effect that little if any weight would be given to the remarks of members not in charge of the legislation.[41] In a sense, these were conventions, like all rules of statutory construction; the task was to ascertain the "intent" of the legislature in a situation that the legislature obviously did not have in mind when the act was passed. A court construing the statute was frequently in the position of the English judge in the not so apocryphal probate proceeding: "This will has no meaning but it is my duty to give it one."

Nonetheless, the conventions were observed, so that courts would be aloof from the conflicts of the political arena, and free

---

[38] See Holdsworth, *Some Makers of English Law* (Cambridge Univ. Press), pp. 294–296.

[39] 1 Bl. Comm.* 87–91.

[40] E.g., among the earlier cases, which consider committee reports, *Holy Trinity Church v. United States*, 143 U.S. 457, 464–465; *The Delaware*, 161 U.S. 459, 472; *Buttfield v. Stranahan*, 192 U.S. 470, 495; *Binns v. United States*, 194 U.S. 486, 495–496. One of the first cases to rely upon proceedings on the floor was *United States v. St. Paul, M. & M. Ry. Co.*, 247 U.S. 310, 316–318; but see the qualifications noted at p. 318.

[41] E.g., *McCaughn v. Hershey Chocolate Co.*, 283 U.S. 488, 493–494, and cases there cited; *United States v. Wrightwood Dairy Co.*, 315 U.S. 110, 125.

from the cynical approach of "The purpose of the statute? Why, to gain votes, of course!"

In time, however, the emphasis came to be less and less on the language of the statute, and more and more on the legislative materials, in order to give effect to the "intent" of the legislature. "When aid to construction of the meaning of words, as used in the statute, is available, there certainly can be no 'rule of law' which forbids its use, however clear the words may appear on 'superficial examination.'"[42] "The meaning to be ascribed to an Act of Congress can only be derived from a considered weighing of every relevant aid to construction."[43]

It is significant that both quotations are from cases decided on the same day by five-to-four votes. With the adoption of such a technique, of course, the floodgates were open, for the "considered weighing of every relevant aid" necessarily shifts the emphasis from "construction" to a consideration of desirability and social and economic values. Preoccupation with legislative history and with the legislative debates inevitably draws courts into an evaluation of legislative, i.e., purely political, factors. The rules or conventions of ascertaining legislative intent are in consequence given less and less weight today. Sometimes a decision all but exemplifies the waggish remark that the language of a statute is never to be looked at unless the legislative history is doubtful.[44] All too often, legislative history is, after the manner of Caesar's wife, all things to all men.

Nonetheless, an advocate in the federal courts, or one arguing federal questions in a state court, cannot afford to ignore legislative history. Of course, his technique will necessarily vary from case to case. When the language of the statute is your way and the legislative history is opposed, stress the statute; when the situation is reversed, stress the legislative history; when both are favorable, bear down on both—and when both are against you, talk about the "essential purpose" of the legislation, or stress whatever helpful tidbits you may have found in the hearings on the bill.

---

[42] *United States v. American Trucking Ass'ns*, 310 U.S. 534, 543–544.

[43] *United States v. Dickerson*, 310 U.S. 554, 562.

[44] Cf. *United States v. Carbone*, 327 U.S. 633. And see the reference in the opinion in *Aetna Casualty & Surety Co. v. United States*, 170 F.2d 469, 471 (C.A. 2), "in the light of the language and purpose of the statute," to which is appended a footnote: "We consider both, of course; for we do not proceed on the principle that a court is to look at the statute only if its legislative history is ambiguous." (Affirmed, *United States v. Aetna Casualty Co.*, 338 U.S. 366.)

Two additional suggestions may be made for cases susceptible to the more orthodox approach: (a) On particular occasions, the committee reports will be valueless—because later disavowed on the floor of Congress.[45] (b) Sometimes the pay dirt is in the reports that preceded the initiation of the legislation.

Section 57. Use of essentially historical materials.—Mr. Justice Holmes, who more than most judges before or since understood both the value and the limitations of historical learning, remarked on different occasions that "historic continuity with the past is not a duty, it is only a necessity,"[46] and that "It is revolting to have no better reason for a rule than that it was so laid down in the time of Henry IV."[47]

Legal history in its purely antiquarian aspects will have but few uses for the lawyer. But since there are so many terms in the Constitution of the United States that would be meaningless without a thorough grounding in the common law,[48] and since constitutional law accordingly presupposes an understanding of the common law,[49] historical materials, including the earliest cases, may sometimes be controlling, will generally be helpful—and will always be suggestive.

A number of instances of effective use of such materials come to mind. Undoubtedly a classic instance of a change of decision in consequence of more accurate historical knowledge appeared long ago in *Vidal v. Girard's Executors*,[50] where the Supreme Court modified its earlier decision in *Baptist Ass'n v. Hart's Executors*[51] and upheld the charitable trust established by Stephen Girard's will, on the strength of then recent publications of the Records Commissioners of England which demonstrated that the English Court of

---

[45] *Chicago etc. R. Co. v. Acme Freight*, 336 U.S. 465.

[46] Holmes, *Learning and Science*, in *Collected Legal Papers*, 138, 139. See also *Law in Science and Science in Law, id.* 210, 211: "* * * continuity with the past is only a necessity and not a duty."

[47] Holmes, *The Path of the Law*, in *Collected Legal Papers*, 187. See *United States v. Dege*, 364 U.S. 51, which turned on the applicability of the quotation in the text.

[48] See, in this connection, as required reading, the illuminating comments of Jackson, J., concurring in *D'Oench, Duhme & Co. v. Federal Deposition Ins. Corp.*, 315 U.S. 447, 465, 470–471.

[49] "* * * the provisions of the Constitution are not mathematical formulas having their essence in their form; they are organic living institutions transplanted from English soil. Their significance is vital not formal; it is to be gathered not simply by taking the words and a dictionary, but by considering their origin and the line of their growth." *Gompers v. United States*, 233 U.S. 604, 610 (*per* Holmes, J.).

[50] How. St. Tr. 127.

[51] 4 Wheat. 1.

Chancery had entertained jurisdiction over charitable trusts long before the Statute of 43 Elizabeth I.

But there are modern examples also. In *United States v. Wood*,[52] the question was whether Congress could constitutionally provide, consistently with the Sixth Amendment's guaranty of trial "by an impartial jury," that Government employees not shown to be actually biased might sit on juries in criminal cases in the District of Columbia. An earlier case in point apparently barred the way.[53] But the Government's brief, which collected and discussed all the early English authorities on the point, some of them from the era of black-letter folios,[54] demonstrated that King's servants were not ineligible per se as a matter of common law. The Supreme Court was persuaded by these authorities, and disapproved its earlier decision.

In the *Haupt* treason case,[55] the basic question was whether the constitutional command that "No Person shall be convicted of Treason unless on the Testimony of two Witnesses to the same overt Act"[56] required that "Testimony" to be eyewitness testimony, or "direct testimony," or whether, if the latter, it excluded any testimony that as a matter of ordinary speech might be considered circumstantial. In order to resolve this question, the Government's brief traced the two-witness requirement in treason cases back to the Statute of 7 & 8 Will. III, c. 3, which settled that requirement in the English law for 250 years,[57] and took up and discussed, from the proceedings set forth in Howell's State Trials, the rulings under that statute in English treason trials antedating the American Revolution. It then turned to the earliest American trials on the same point. The Government argued, on the basis of these historical

---

[52] 299 U.S. 123.

[53] *Crawford v. United States*, 212 U.S. 183.

[54] All the matter in Law French was, however, duly translated into English in the Government's brief. See Brief for the United States, No. 34, Oct. T. 1936. For cases where the opinion of a Twentieth Century court relies upon and quotes from the Year Books in the original black-letter law French, see *Dyson v. Rhode Island Company*, 25 R. I. 600, 57 Atl. 771, and *Stevens v. Union Railroad Company*, 26 R. I. 90, 58 Atl. 492. The Rhode Island reports, according to local tradition, had to have a new font of type set on this occasion; the National Reporter System compromised on plain roman, plus some typographical dashes and flourishes.

[55] *Haupt v. United States*, 330 U.S. 631.

[56] U.S. Const., Art. III, Sec. 3.

[57] The two witness requirement was repealed by the St. 8 & 9 Geo. VI, c. 44 (The Treason Act, 1945), which seems to have been passed to reach the case of Lord Haw Haw. See J. W. Hall, ed., *Trial of William Joyce*, pp. 12–14, 16. Joyce was brought to England from Germany the day after the Treason Act, 1945, received the Royal assent. Cf. *Joyce v. Director of Public Prosecutions* [1946] A. C. 347.

materials, that the constitutional requirement did not render insufficient testimony that required some interpretation; and the Supreme Court agreed.

Resort to the reports in Howell's State Trials was likewise had in the *Harris* search and seizure case,[58] to show that a search of premises incident to an arrest represented an existing and widespread practice in England that was unaffected by Lord Camden's ruling in *Entick v. Carrington*[59]—and reference was made to reports in the *American State Trials* to show that the practice had never theretofore been deemed affected by American constitutional provisions.[60] The Supreme Court agreed, though assuredly later decisions have undermined the authority of the *Harris* case. Indeed, the trend since the date of that decision strongly suggests that the very concept of Due Process of Law is now deemed to include a constitutional guaranty of privacy.[61]

However, even when they do not find their way into the decision or even into the *ratio decidendi* of the decision, historical materials are at least suggestive and hence helpful to the advocate. I found this to be so in the case of *Wade v. Hunter*,[62] which involved the right of the Army to try a soldier by a second court-martial after the case had been withdrawn from the first court-martial when the tactical situation—in this instance the final advance into Germany in the spring of 1945—made it impracticable to continue the first trial.

The question was whether the second trial improperly subjected Wade to double jeopardy, and the case turned largely on the difference between the provisions of the Fifth Amendment, "nor shall any person be subject for the same offence to be twice put in jeopardy of life or limb," and those of the 40th Article of War,[63] "No person shall, without his consent, be tried a second time for the same offense * * *." Clearly, under the remaining portions of Article of War 40, Wade had not been "tried";[64] had he, however, been "put in jeopardy"?

---

[58] *Harris v. United States*, 331 U.S. 145.

[59] 19 How. St. Tr. 1029.

[60] *Trial of Patrick Hart*, 26 How. St. Tr. 388, 396; *Trial of Henry and John Sheares*, 27 How. St. Tr. 255, 321; *Trial of Arthur Thistlewood*, 33 How. St. Tr. 682, 811–812; *Trial of James Ings*, 33 How. St. Tr. 957, 1047; *Trial of Levi and Laban Kenniston*, 14 Am. St. Tr. 237, 244 (Mass.).... For the modern English law on the point, see *Dillon v. O'Brien*, 20 L.R. Ir. 300, 16 Cox C.C. 245; *Elias v. Pasmore*, [1934] 2 K.B. 164.

[61] *McDonald v. United States*, 335 U.S. 451, 453, *Wolf v. Colorado*, 338 U.S. 25, 27–28.

[62] 336 U.S. 684, affirming 169 F.2d 973 (C.A. 10).

[63] 10 U.S.C. 1511.

[64] "* * * but no proceeding in which an accused has been found guilty by a court-martial upon any charge or specification shall be held to be a trial in the sense of this

(continued)

The Supreme Court had early ruled that the Fifth Amendment did not preclude a second trial in a criminal case after the first trial had terminated in a disagreement by the jury.[65] But the lower courts in more recent cases had been applying a rather mechanical rule, to the effect that "jeopardy" attached once evidence was heard,[66] or even after the jury had been sworn, in a situation where the prosecutor failed to have his witnesses present.[67] An early case was most helpful in resolving this apparent conflict. Mr. Justice Washington, who had been a contemporary of the framers, had said:

> * * * we are clearly of opinion, that the *jeopardy* spoken of in this article [Fifth Amendment] can be interpreted to mean nothing short of the acquittal or conviction of the prisoner, and the judgment of the court thereupon. This was the meaning affixed to the expression by the common law. * * * the moment it is admitted that in cases of necessity the court is authorized to discharge the jury, the whole argument for applying this article of the constitution to a discharge of the jury before conviction and judgment is abandoned, because the exception of necessity is not to be found in any part of the constitution; and I should consider this court as stepping beyond its duty in interpolating it into that instrument, if the article of the constitution is applicable to a case of this kind. We admit the exception, but we do it because that article does not apply to a jeopardy short of conviction.[68]

The *Wade* case was decided, both in the Tenth Circuit and by the Supreme Court, on the scope of the necessity exception and not on any interpretation of "jeopardy," but I found the early decisions extremely suggestive and helpful when I briefed and argued the case in the intermediate court.

Right here I will digress to draw the attention of brief-writers to the mine of material available in the *Federal Cases*—the old circuit court decisions that antedate the Federal Reporter. Many of them, of course, are of only antiquarian interest today. But others are highly authoritative, for two reasons. First, they reflect the constitutional views of judges whose lives, frequently, were contemporaneous with

---

article until the reviewing and, if there be one, the confirming authority shall have taken final action upon the case."

[65] *United States v. Perez*, 9 Wheat. 579.

[66] *Clawans v. Rives*, 104 F.2d 240 (App. D.C.); *McCarthy v. Zerbst*, 85 F.2d 640 (C.C.A. 10). See, however, for a broader view, *Pratt v. United States*, 102 F.2d 275 (App. D.C.).

[67] *Cornero v. United States*, 48 F.2d 69 (C.C.A. 9).

[68] *United States v. Haskell*, 4 Wash. C.C. 402, 410–411, Fed. Case No. 15321, 26 Fed. Cas. at 212 (C.C.E.D. Pa.). See also *United States v. Watkins*, 3 Cranch C.C. 441, 570, Fed. Case No. 16649, 28 Fed. Cas. at 479 (C.C.D.C.).

the framing and ratification of the Constitution. Second, they were in large measure the work of the Supreme Court justices riding circuit, and so are regarded as more authoritative than the run of what today one finds in F.2d. To a surprising degree cases in the Supreme Court rely or even can turn on what one of the worthies of old decided while circuit riding.[69]

Section 58. Use of noncase materials.—The successful advocate is not limited to decisions and statutes, the latest case turned up in the digests, the most recent regulation spawned by a restless bureaucracy, or the last amendment adopted by the legislature. He is free to turn to other materials to buttress his arguments, and will frequently find it helpful to do so. There will be discussed below, not at all exhaustively, the employment of noncase materials as authorities.

(a) *Economic and sociological materials.* The classic example of the use of economic and sociological materials in constitutional litigation, over eighty years ago, was in *Muller v. Oregon,*[70] which sustained the validity of a state statute limiting the hours of labor for women. There Mr. Louis D. Brandeis, as he then was, filed a brief in which he collected a list of similar state and foreign statutes; "extracts from over ninety reports of committees, bureaus of statistics, commissioners of hygiene, inspectors of factories, both in this country and in Europe, to the effect that long hours of labor are dangerous for women, primarily because of their special physical organization"; and "extracts from similar reports discussing the general benefits of short hours from an economic aspect of the question,"[71] all in support of the proposition that the legislation in question bore a reasonable relationship to the public health and safety—admittedly valid exercises of the police power. His success in that case, and the approbation that the brief received in the unanimous opinion written by that rugged apostle of *laissez faire*, Brewer, J., led to increasing use of the same technique in other cases.[72]

Perhaps the most expert development of what accordingly came to be known as the Brandeis brief was presented in *Adkins v.*

---

[69] E.g., *United States v. Summerlin*, 310 U.S. 414, 417–418; *Farrell v. United States*, 336 U.S. 511, 513, 522, 523; cf. *Wheeling Steel Corp. v. Glander*, 337 U.S. 562, 577.

[70] 208 U.S. 412.

[71] 208 U.S. at 420, note.

[72] E.g., *Bunting v. Oregon*, 243 U.S. 426; *Stettler v. O'Hara*, 243 U.S. 629; *Adkins v. Children's Hospital*, 261 U.S. 525; see Bikle, *Judicial Determination of Questions of Fact Affecting the Constitutional Validity of Legislative Action*, 38 Harv. L. Rev. 6; Freund, *On Understanding the Supreme Court* (1949), pp. 86–92.

Children's Hospital[73] and in the *Gold Clause*[74] and AAA cases,[75] though it may well be that those decisions, equally with the later ones in *West Coast Hotel Co. v. Parrish*,[76] and the several decisions upholding the National Labor Relations Act[77] and the Social Security Act,[78] were influenced less by what was collected in the winning briefs than by other and less strictly scientific considerations. As one of losing counsel in the 1936 New York minimum wage cases[79] remarked in 1937, after the *West Coast Hotel* decision had been announced, "Better a poor argument after election than a good one before it." Nonetheless, the Brandeis brief still has a considerable scope of usefulness.

One caution, however, should be noted. The function of the Brandeis type of brief is to collect and marshal facts that show the reasonable basis of and hence support the legislation in question. Briefs that assemble data showing that the law under consideration is unwise or unsound are more appropriately addressed to the legislature.[80]

(b) *Scientific materials.* On occasion there arises a point that is susceptible of effective treatment with the use of strictly scientific, nonlegal materials. The *Anne Johnson* case[81] is an apt illustration.

---

[73] 261 U.S. 525. In this instance, the brief was notably unsuccessful. "It is said that great benefits have resulted from the operation of such statutes, not alone in the District of Columbia but in the several States, where they have been in force. A mass of reports, opinions of special observers and students of the subject, and the like, has been brought before us in support of this statement, all of which we have found interesting but only mildly persuasive." 261 U.S. at 560, *per* Sutherland, J.

[74] *Norman v. Baltimore & O. R. Co.* and *United States v. Bankers Trust Co.*, 294 U.S. 240; *Norts v. United States*, 294 U.S. 317; *Perry v. United States*, 294 U.S. 330; dissenting opinion, *sub nom. Gold Clause Cases*, 294 U.S. at 361.

[75] *United States v. Butler*, 297 U.S. 1.

[76] 300 U.S. 379.

[77] *Labor Board v. Jones & Laughlin*, 301 U.S. 1; *Labor Board v. Fruehauf Co.*, 301 U.S. 49; *Labor Board v. Clothing Co.*, 301 U.S. 58; dissenting opinion, sub *nom. Labor Board Cases*, 301 U.S. at 76; *Associated Press v. Labor Board*, 301 U.S. 103; *Washington Coach Co. v. Labor Board*, 301 U.S. 142.

[78] *Carmichael v. Southern Coal Co.*, 301 U.S. 495; *Steward Machine Co. v. Davis*, 301 U.S. 548; *Helvering v. Davis*, 301 U.S. 619.

[79] *Morehead v. New York ex rel. Tipaldo*, 298 U.S. 587.

[80] "If the proponents of union-security agreements have confidence in the arguments addressed to the Court in their 'economic brief,' they should address those arguments to the electorate. Its endorsement would be a vindication that the mandate of this Court could never give." Frankfurter, J., concurring, in *A. F. of L. v. American Sash Co.*, 335 U.S. 538, 553.

[81] *Johnson v. United States*, 333 U.S. 10.

There narcotic agents, attracted by the smell of burning opium, entered petitioner's room without a warrant. She was subsequently indicted and convicted for violations of the narcotic laws. She argued that odors alone, uncorroborated by other information, could not be evidence sufficient to constitute probable ground for any search; and she cited numerous cases in support of that contention.[82] The Government urged that smoking opium had a distinctive and unmistakably identifiable odor, quoting not only from the testimony in the case but also from encyclopedias, pharmacopoeias, and similar disinterested sources of information. The Court held that odors alone might well constitute probable cause,[83] but went on to decide, four justices dissenting, that in the circumstances the officers were not entitled to proceed without a warrant.

The same sort of technique will be helpful in any situation where a rule of law has become crystallized but can be shown by scientific data to be not in accord with the factual basis on which it purports to rely. However, when the case is going to turn on scientific facts, it is preferable—and safer—to lay the foundation at the trial, through live witnesses subject to cross-examination (as was done in *Anne Johnson*), and then to use the materials cited in the brief by way of supplement.

Section 59. Encyclopedias; Collections of annotated cases.—It is not belittling the value of encyclopedias or of the several collections of annotated cases to urge that they should be used primarily to orient the lawyer in unfamiliar fields of law, or to supply him with citations to cases and with leads for further research—but that they should not generally be relied upon or cited as authorities. Normally—and certainly before the Supreme Court of the United States and the more learned state and federal courts of appeal— the careful advocate will never refer to such publications in his briefs except to write, "The cases are collected in. . . ."

Some readers will ask, why this insistence on such a limited use, in the face of the undoubted fact that some courts of last resort cite these works in their opinions? The real reason, basically, is this: Encyclopedias and annotations are written by lawyers who, though honest and diligent, are neither in practice nor in law teaching.

---

[82] *Taylor v. United States*, 286 U.S. 1; *United States v. Kronenberg*, 134 F.2d 483 (C.C.A. 2); *Cheng Wai v. United States*, 125 F.2d 915 (C.C.A. 2); *United States v. Kaplan*, 89 F.2d 869 (C.C.A. 2); *United States v. Lee*, 83 F.2d 195 (C.C.A. 2); *United States v. Schultz*, 3 F. Supp. 273 (D. Ariz.); *United States v. Tom Yu*, 1 F. Supp. 357 (D. Ariz.).

[83] 333 U.S. at 13.

Some are undoubtedly able, others are little better than legal hacks. For myself, I admire their industry, and I value it highly, as witness the price law offices pay for the fruits thereof. But I do not regard their analysis of the cases as *authority*, and certainly a survey of the reports indicates that courts of the highest standing do not do so either. I regard any competent lawyer's signature on a brief as being at least as authoritative as these gentlemen's own frequently anonymous say-so.

Consequently, I profit by their labors, which shorten my own correspondingly. But having been fortunate enough always to have access to excellent library facilities, I do not and never have cited these works to any court, save always as a reasonably reliable compilation of the decisions.

Section 60. Use of law review materials.—In 1915, Dean Wigmore, in the preface to the second edition of the then Supplement to his monumental—and immortal—treatise on *Evidence*, deplored the prevailing tendency of courts to overlook the treasures locked in the pages of legal periodicals, and to cite a second- or third-rate textbook in preference to a first-rate article in a law review.[84] His strictures were not repeated in the second edition of the Treatise, published in 1923, and by 1930 or thereabouts "the conspiracy of silence" had pretty well been dissolved,[85] and today the pendulum has swung far in the opposite direction, and lawyers who would not

---

[84] "* * * What are some of the shortcomings of the usual opinions rendering justice in the usual State Supreme Court?

"(c) There is no *discrimination* in the use of the expository authorities. Such a discrimination is the mark of a sound legal education and a correct scholarly standard. But, in the judicial opinions, the superficial products of hasty hack-writers, callow compilers, and anonymous editors are given equal consideration with the weightiest names of true science. Obviously, any printed pages bound in law-buckram and well advertised or gratuitously presented constitute authority fit to guide the Courts.

"Note, however, that it must be *bound*: for if it is in periodical form, it is ignored. For ten to twenty years past there have been at the service of the profession some half a dozen legal periodicals, publishing the weightiest critiques of current legal problems. There is nothing in judicial opinions to show that these articles have ever been read; apparently their great labor and acute skill have been wasted on the judges. The article by Louis Brandeis and S. D. Warren on 'The Right of Privacy' (published in the Harvard Law Review some twenty-five years ago) is the most notable of the rare exceptions discoverable." Pp. v, vi.

[85] See Maggs, *Concerning the Extent to Which the Law Review Contributes to the Development of the Law* (1930) 3 So. Cal. L. Rev. 181; Cardozo, *Introduction to Selected Readings on the Law of Contracts* (1930), pp. vii, ix: "Certain, in any event, it is that the old prejudice is vanishing. Within the last ten or fifteen years the conspiracy of silence has been dissolving, with defections every year more numerous and notable."

dream of citing encyclopedias or annotated reports or third-rate textbooks in their briefs seem to think that they are pretty learned fellows when they refer to and rely upon expressions of opinion in the law reviews.

Law review materials fall into two groups: the leading articles, invariably signed, and the student notes and comments, which are frequently and perhaps generally unsigned.

So far as the student notes are concerned, the brief-writer will, by and large, be well advised to use them as case-finders and as sources for his own ideas, rather than as expressions of authority to be cited to the courts. A little reflection will show the reason why. After all, your task as an advocate is to persuade a court of more or less learned and more rather than less elderly judges to decide your case in your favor. They are not likely to be persuaded by what some lads on a law review have said. Sometimes the judicial reaction to a law review citation is essentially one of amusement, as for example the remark (probably not wholly apocryphal) attributed to Mr. Justice Holmes: "I don't mind when the lads on the Law Review say I'm wrong, what I object to is when they say I'm right." Sometimes the reaction is one of impatient annoyance; I have heard just precisely that kind of comment, in open court, from some of our most distinguished federal judges (directed, I should hasten to add, at my opposition). And on occasion the matter goes beyond that, as witness the testy comments in one of the late Mr. Justice Butler's last dissents:

> The opinion also cites, footnote 7, selected gainsaying writings of professors—some are lawyers and some are not—but without specification of or reference to the reasons upon which their views rest. And in addition it cites notes published in law reviews, some signed and some not; presumably the latter were prepared by law students.[86]

True, student notes are nowadays frequently cited by the courts, and the views expressed above are not in any sense the consequence of sour grapes. I too have tooted on The Bugle, and one note that I committed while in school, which criticized two Supreme Court decisions,[87] was twice cited by that Court—as it qualified the one[88] and overruled the other.[89] I strongly suspect,

---

[86] *O'Malley v. Woodrough*, 307 U.S. 277, 298.

[87] Note. *Aftermath of the Supreme Court's Stop, Look, and Listen Rule* (1930) 43 Harv. L. Rev. 926.

[88] *Pokora v. Wabash Ry. Co.*, 292 U.S. 98, 106 n. 4, limiting *Baltimore & O. R. R. v. Goodman*, 275 U.S. 66.

[89] *Erie R. Co. v. Tompkins*, 304 U.S. 64, 74 n. 7, overruling *Swift v. Tyson*, 16 Pet. 1.

however, that in those instances as in the others, the student note citations were added by the justices' law clerks, by way of encouragement to their former colleagues still at the school.

At any rate, I would urge that, except in rare instances, student notes should not be cited as authority. They should be used, however, for the ideas they reflect, and as case-finders.[90] Such use will save the brief-writer a lot of labor at the research stage, since law review notes and comments are very apt to contain references to cases that simply do not turn up in the digests.

Leading articles, on the other hand, stand on a different footing. At worst, they represent the opinions of individual lawyers, and hence should have, for purposes of citation, at least the same value as an ephemeral textbook written by some hack in a law publisher's stable and duly bound in buckram or fabrikoid. And, at best, depending in each instance on the stature and reputation of the author, they may well be authoritative.

Thus, Mr. Charles Warren's article, *New Light on the History of the Federal Judiciary Act of 1789,*[91] undermined the authority of *Swift v. Tyson,*[92] and was in large measure responsible for *Erie R. Co. v. Tompkins.*[93] Rarely has a single bit of historical research so significantly influenced our law. Another classic example of a bit of original legal thinking, one that opened up a new field of law, was the celebrated Warren and Brandeis article on *The Right to Privacy.*[94] Those are perhaps the two most striking examples, though there have been other instances of substantial judicial reliance placed on the reasoning and the research set forth in law review articles.[95] It is

---

[90] I am not ashamed to acknowledge that, on numerous occasions, referring to law review notes has saved me much work in collecting cases, and has turned up worthwhile ideas that advanced my own arguments.

[91] 37 Harv. L. Rev. 49.

[92] 16 Pet. 1.

[93] 304 U.S. 64.

[94] 4 Harv. L. Rev. 193 (1890). See Nizer, *The Right of Privacy: A Half Century's Developments* (1941) 39 Mich. L. Rev. 526.

[95] See, for example, Frankfurter and Landis, *Power of Congress over Procedure in Criminal Contempts in "Inferior" Federal Courts—A Study in Separation of Powers,* 37 Harv. L. Rev. 1010. This article, sharply critical of the decision in *Toledo Newspaper Co. v. United States,* 247 U.S. 402, was cited by and certainly influenced the Court in *Nye v. United States,* 313 U.S. 33, 47, when it overruled the *Toledo* case. See also the effect of Hale, *Conflicting Judicial Criteria of Utility Rates,* 38 Col. L. Rev. 959, and Hale, *The Fair Value Merry-Go-Round,* 33 Ill. L. Rev. 517, on the concurring opinion in *Power Comm'n v. Pipeline Co.,* 315 U.S. 575, 599, 603, the views in which thereafter shaped the majority opinion in *Power Comm'n v. Hope Gas Co.,* 320 U.S. 591.

proper to add, however, that leading articles in law reviews are more respected as authority when they reflect the results of scholarly researches or the views of members of rule-making committees than when they simply set forth the opinions of individual lawyers, frequently with a client's axe to grind or else rearguing in professional publications the cases they have lost in court.

Section 61. The next step in brief-writing.—I shall assume, at this point, that your basic research has been completed, and that you have made useful notes covering your materials.

I will not undertake to make suggestions for note-taking; that is a matter which depends entirely on individual habits and temperament. The standards that follow, however, are universally applicable.

(a) Be accurate; you will waste a great deal of time and effort if you have to go back to get the exact wording of a title or citation that you took down in sloppy fashion the first time.

(b) Make your notes complete enough so that they will be helpful to you, but don't waste your time in doing mere copywork.

(c) Don't jot down on the same sheet of paper references to unrelated matters; to do that means an infinite amount of shuffling through papers to find a single citation. Your time is more valuable than scratch-paper, even at today's inflated prices for office supplies.

(d) Don't rely on your notes to the exclusion of the reports, particularly as to the leading cases cited. You will have to read and reread those, no matter how extensive your notes may be.

Next, having gone over your notes, and having already analyzed your case thoroughly, it is time to outline your argument. This involves, among other things, a resolution of the problem of which points to argue first; see Section 34, above. It involves also a formulation of the argumentative headings for the several points in your argument; see Section 30, above. And it involves also, very definitely, a breaking down of your main points into their supporting subsidiary points.

The only general rule that is universally applicable at this juncture is the warning that, if the outline is faulty, then the thinking is faulty. Consequently, if the draft outline won't wash, your case needs further and clearer analysis, and you will have to labor over it some more. Work over it, slave over it if need be, turn to other matters to clear your head if the deadline allows you that luxury. But keep at it until the outline is sound. Then—and only then—are you ready to write.

Section 62. Write consecutively.—There is always a strong temptation to leave the difficult or the less important point for the end—to toss in the jurisdictional argument later, or to do the easy points first and to reserve the difficult one until you get into the swing of writing. That is the easy way, no doubt about it—and a very natural one; years ago I frequently succumbed to it. But I found that when I did, my briefs would acquire a lopsided twist that no amount of future editing would ever quite eradicate.

So, having learned this also, again the hard way, I pass it on: Always write consecutively. Start with Point One and follow through to the conclusion. Go cross-country, as it were, over the easy terrain as well as over the rocky ground. And keep right on going.

I don't mean that it is necessary to stop and interrupt the train of your thought while looking up some largely ornamental citation, or to compose a long but somewhat tangential footnote, or even to fill in a little paragraph of text that is going to involve a lot of additional research. Those are the little fringes and tassels, the buttons and bows of brief-writing, which can safely be postponed. They can wait, provided they are not basic. As to the basic argument, however, you must go straight ahead, and with as much steam as you can muster.

Later, after the basic text has been written, and, after submission to partners or colleagues for comment or criticism, it has been revised and where necessary rewritten, you can relax and proceed to fill in the holes and supply the additional citations that, had you stopped for them earlier, would have distracted you and disturbed the continuity of your writing.

Inevitably, though, it is just those last little trifles that are bound to—and do—take a disproportionate amount of time. It has been my experience that the last few citations and the last few footnotes always keep me running breathlessly around the library, fighting the deadline—and delay my meeting it.

Section 63. Write the Summary of Argument last of all.—After the Argument proper has been written and revised, and not before, is the time to write the Summary of Argument. See Section 37 (a), above, for suggestions as to what the Summary should contain. It is well, also, to cite therein a few of the leading cases discussed and relied upon in the body of your Argument, to serve as shorthand guideposts and landmarks for the court. (It was Mr. Justice Reed, when Solicitor General of the United States, who insisted that the Summary of Argument in Government briefs should do so.) And, I repeat, the Summary should summarize; it should not go off on a tack—or a frolic—of its own.

As a practical matter, the normal procedure under the pressure of deadlines is to let the Argument go to the printer, and later, when it comes back in galley proof, to insert the Summary before the entire brief is returned to the press for paging.

Section 64. Finally, check!—Check every citation, quotation, and record reference. *Check every citation, quotation, and record reference!* CHECK EVERY CITATION, QUOTATION, AND RECORD REFERENCE! Regardless of your own intrinsic accuracy, errors are bound to creep into your manuscript. Sometimes it is your fault, and at other times it is a clerical problem, but the slips will slip in either way. The name of a case will be incorrectly rendered, digits in a citation will become transposed, a word in a quotation will be garbled, a line will be left out of a quotation, a record reference or two or three will be completely wrong. Most usually the final typed manuscript will contain a combination of these common errors.

So—when you get the first set of printer's proofs, whether galley or page, check each citation (and every part of it), every record reference, and every quotation whether from record or from decision, *against the original reports and the original record!* That is a must. It is standard operating procedure in the U.S. Solicitor General's Office and on the better law reviews. (The former employs full-time checkers who do nothing else.) You, as a private practitioner—or as a prosecutor in the District Attorney's or State Attorney General's office—cannot afford to do less.

It should be noted parenthetically that the most effective checking is that done by someone other than the brief-writer, not because checking is a chore to be passed down the line, but because of the demonstrable psychological fact that the author's eye will reflect the author's thought rather than the error on the page. That is why most people are better proofreaders on the other fellow's stuff. Consequently, the admonition here set down—"check"—means, preferably, "have someone else check."

To continue: Whenever there have been corrections made in any set of proofs, be sure to check the next succeeding set of proofs, not only to see whether the first corrections have been made, but also to ascertain whether any additional errors have crept in. (They generally have.)

Finally, when you receive the completed briefs from the printer, all clean and nicely bound, don't rush the required number over to the clerk of court in the same happy mood of creative pride with which you distribute cigars to your friends consequent upon the birth of issue. Curb your impulse; sit down and read one copy consecutively. ("Read" here, pre-eminently, means "have someone else read.") Why? Because, almost inevitably, in the process of correcting the errors noted on the final proofs, new errors will have been made. A most annoying kind of new error, and unfortunately a not too uncommon one, is the transposition of entire lines of type. The fact of the matter is that typographical errors are an unavoidable form of human fallibility, which simply cannot be entirely stamped out, regardless of efforts made.[96] That being so, it is incumbent on every lawyer to have his finished briefs read carefully, very carefully, before he files them with the court. On the strength of a long and frequently sad experience, I emphasize this final caution; indeed, I cannot emphasize it too strongly.

And if you find slips? Correct them with pen or pencil, and file as corrected. And, of course, when the final copy is way off, the printer is bound to correct his own slips; the customer pays only for proof changes that he makes himself.

At any rate, after the completed briefs have been checked, corrected if necessary, and finally filed, you can relax. If you have been working really hard on the case, you will undoubtedly feel a tremendous letdown at that point. What you do thereafter, before it is time to prepare for the oral argument, will depend largely on such otherwise irrelevant matters as your temperament, your state of health, your doctor's orders, and the local option situation [as to alcohol sales] in the particular jurisdiction.

---

[96] "The most baffling device of the imp [of the perverse] is to cause a new error in the process of correcting an old one. This residuary misprint is one against which there is no complete protection. When General Pillow returned from Mexico he was hailed by a Southern editor as a 'battle-scarred veteran.' The next day the veteran called upon him to demand an apology for the epithet actually printed, 'battle-scared.' What was the horror of the editor, on the following day, to see the expression reappear in his apology as 'bottle-scarred.'" Koopman, *The Perversities of Type,* in *The Booklover and His Books,* 152, 157.

CHAPTER 5

The Finer Points of Brief-Writing

Section 65. Introductory.—This chapter deals with the minutiae of brief-writing, with those details wherein a good brief differs from one not so good. The discussion of some of these details may appear to pertain to trifles, but, as has aptly been remarked, it is the trifles that make perfection—and perfection is no trifle.

There will also be included in this chapter a discussion of the problems peculiar to reply briefs and to petitions for rehearing; and I shall once more stress, from still another approach, the need for absolute accuracy in citations and record references.

Section 66. Citations; Number of citations.—One of the best, if not the best, single article on appellate arguments was (and remains) Mr. John W. Davis's *The Argument of an Appeal.*[1] In one of the introductory paragraphs of that paper, there appears the following:

> I assume also that the briefs are not overlarded with long quotations from the reported opinions, no matter how pat they seem; nor overcrowded with citations designed it would seem to certify to the industry of the brief-maker rather than to fortify the argument. A horrible example of this latter fault crossed my desk within the month in a brief which, in addition to many statutes and text-writers, cited by volume and page no less than 304 decided cases, a number calculated to discourage if not to disgust the most industrious judge.

I happened to be present in the audience when the foregoing was first delivered, at the Association of the Bar of the City of New York—and, as it happened, the "horrible example" referred to was the Government's brief in the *Northern Pacific* reargument,[2] a case I had argued against Mr. Davis just a week or so previously. Together with Judge E. E. Danly and some others, I had sweated over that brief all summer long. At any rate, when I saw the speaker

---

[1] Davis, *The Argument of an Appeal,* 26 A.B.A. J. 895.

[2] *United States v. Northern Pacific Ry. Co.*, 311 U.S. 317.

127

immediately after his lecture, he seemed nonplussed, and the following conversation took place:

W: I'm sorry you didn't like our brief.

D: Well, I did think you cited too many cases.

W: If I were inclined to be critical of your production, I should
    say that you cited too few cases.

D: Had it occurred to you that we had too few cases which we
    could cite?

All of which passed off very pleasantly and amiably. I was never
too much concerned about the criticism, because after all—as a
friend of mine noted when he first saw the paper in print—the
reargument was decided in my favor! And the Foreword to the first
version of the present work bears witness to the fact that Mr. Davis
has not been too seriously upset by my counter criticism.

As a general proposition, of course, it goes almost without saying
that it is better to cite and discuss a few leading and controlling
decisions than to construct an encyclopedic footnote. But there are
cases and cases, and what may be an excess of citations in one situation may be far too few in another. The matter is entirely relative,
and one cannot safely be dogmatic about absolute numbers.

Consider the *Northern Pacific* case: It involved the final adjust-
ment of the land grant to the Northern Pacific Railway and its
predecessors, a grant of some forty million acres of land—almost
equal to the aggregate area of the six New England states. The litigation in question had been specifically directed by Congress, after
an investigation that had lasted five years.[3] Some nine years more
elapsed before the U.S. District Court entered an interlocutory
decree. Meanwhile Congress had authorized an appeal from that
decree, direct to the Supreme Court,[4] because the litigation was
simply too complex for ordinary appellate procedures. The case
was first argued in the Supreme Court in the spring of 1940, some
ten years after the proceeding had been brought. Three hours
were allowed on each side for oral argument instead of the usual
one hour.[5] After that, the Court set the case down for reargument

---

[3] Act of June 25, 1929, c. 41, 46 Stat. 41. The investigation was authorized by the Joint
Resolution of June 5, 1924, c. 267, 43 Stat. 461; the report of the Joint Committee of
Congress that conducted the investigation appears in S. Rep. 5, 71st Cong., 2d sess.

[4] Act of May 22, 1936, c. 444, 49 Stat. 1369.

[5] Journal, U.S. Sup. Ct., Oct. T. 1939, p. 177.

on its own motion, and asked for argument on questions that had not been taken up and on assignments of error that had not been urged on the original argument.[6]

On reargument, the Government filed a brief extending to 295 pages. The brief argued the questions involved by invoking analogies that seemed apposite, and stressed what Government counsel felt was the disregard of settled rules of law on the part of the master and of the District Court. It was necessary to buttress the analogies with citations so that they would not appear to be mere assertions, and in order to show the number of decisions that, it was believed, the decree below had ignored. Having regard to all of these factors—the complexity of the issues, the circumstance that the Court was obviously in doubt and frankly seeking guidance, and the number of subsidiary points and principles that needed to be explored and developed—I still think, as I thought in 1940, that the number of citations was not excessive, and that, notwithstanding the acknowledged eminence of the critic, the stricture quoted above was not justified in the particular instance, particularly since the Court ultimately reserved decision on some of the fundamental issues as to which there was an equal division of opinion. (Any reader of the foregoing is, of course, free to disagree with me—provided he will first read the 848 pages of the printed record, the numerous bulky exhibits that were not printed, the 460 pages of briefs filed on the original argument, the appendix of relevant statutes running to 156 pages, the 397 pages of briefs filed at the reargument, and the 53-page opinion at 311 U.S. 317.)

Section 67. More about the number of citations.—The normal or usual case, of course, does not require nearly so detailed a documentation, and the brief-writer should adapt his citations to the problem he is facing.

The following standards will cover the usual situations, but they are standards only, not ironclad rules.

(a) It is, by and large, unwise to overload one's brief with citations. In this connection it is well for the brief-writer to keep in mind a question I once heard a Supreme Court justice ask counsel during argument: "Mr. X, I see that on page *ab* of your brief you cite a lot of cases for that proposition. Give me the two most important ones that you want me to read."

---

[6] 310 U.S. 615. Six additional hours were allowed for the reargument. Journal, U.S. Sup. Ct., Oct. T. 1940, p. 29.

(b) Don't weaken a really pat citation that is on all fours by including a lot that bear only tangentially on the issue; and if you have a square holding, don't add the stray dicta from other cases. Possible exception: when the holding is an old one, it may be helpful to add a modern or fairly recent reaffirmation, even though dictum in the later case—to show that the proposition on which you are relying is still recognized as law.

(c) Generally, the higher the court in which you are, the fewer the citations you will need—because the higher the court, the less the judges deem themselves bound by what is decided below—and the more they conceive of themselves as making the law.

(d) Always adapt your citations to the court and to the question involved. For instance, when you are dealing with federal questions, statutory or constitutional, your citations may well be restricted to decisions of the Supreme Court of the United States. Certainly when that tribunal has passed squarely on the point involved, you add very little by going on to cite cases from the lower federal courts. Furthermore, on federal questions, state court cases are never authoritative, and indeed are frequently not even illuminating. But occasions might arise when such citations would be thoroughly appropriate, as for instance where there is a uniform interpretation in the state courts and the federal rule is still unsettled. Moreover, as has already been indicated, always cite freely from your own court, to show its own application of the governing principles.

(e) In state courts, there always arises the question whether and how far it is desirable to look for and cite decisions from other jurisdictions. If your state has a solid body of law, and an established practice, there is no sense at all in citing outside cases. On the other hand, if your state has only a limited number of reports, you are practically forced to cite from other jurisdictions. (When I commenced practice, in Rhode Island, which had then attained to 51 R.I., the usual result in looking up a point of law was, "There are no Rhode Island cases, and there is a split of authority elsewhere.") In between those two extremes, the safest course, when you are relying on persuasive authorities from other jurisdictions, is to cite those that will most readily persuade your court. Time was when Massachusetts decisions were most frequently cited by other courts, with New York next; I suspect that, since the days of Cardozo, Ch. J., and his successors in New York, that order would now be reversed. At any rate, study the recent cases in your court to see which outside tribunal is currently most authoritative there.

(f) Where sheer weight of numbers is a point in itself, all that weight should be used. For instance, whenever it is appropriate to emphasize the settled nature of the rule relied upon, it is entirely in order to cite more cases than when the particular settled rule was questioned neither by the court below nor by your adversary.

Thus, in the *Petrillo* case,[7] the Government's brief dealt with the proposition that in the absence of a separability clause there would be a presumption of inseparability.[8] The brief pointed out that such a presumption was by no means conclusive—and went on to cite in a footnote 47 cases in which the Supreme Court had held statutes severable despite the absence of a separability clause!

So, where it is considered necessary to show not just that the rule in the federal courts is such-and-such but that, in fact, every circuit so holds, it is well that every one of the eleven circuits be represented.

(g) You will need more citations where the question is one of first impression or where you are undertaking to tidy up a confused field of law or where the court below has disregarded settled law, than in a situation where you are dealing only with the application of an earlier decision or with a variant on a well-established rule.

Thus, in *Williams v. Fanning*,[9] where the Supreme Court undertook to settle the question whether, in injunction proceedings against a public officer, the officer's official superior was an indispensable party—a matter that, because of the apparent conflict between *Gnerich v. Rutted*[10] and *Webster v. Fall*[11] on the one hand, and *Colorado v. Toll*[12] on the other, had been in hopeless confusion in the several circuits[13]—the Government's brief cited and classified all the decisions on the question. And in the *Douglas Chandler* treason case,[14] which came before a court that had never in its history had occasion to consider that particular offense, both sides presented voluminous authorities, the object being—in my judgment properly so—to lay before the tribunal every decision and

---

[7] *United States v. Petrillo*, 332 U.S. 1.

[8] E.g., *Williams v. Standard Oil Co.*, 278 U.S. 235; *Electric Bond & Share Co. v. Securities & Exchange Commission*, 303 U.S. 419.

[9] 332 U.S. 490.

[10] 265 U.S. 388.

[11] 266 U.S. 507.

[12] 268 U.S. 228.

[13] Most of the cases are collected in 158 A.L.R. 1126. As there appears, some circuits with a fine impartiality decided the point both ways.

[14] *Chandler v. United States*, 171 F.2d 921 (C.A. 1), certiorari denied, 336 U.S. 918.

every bit of historical material that would assist in deciding the case. Thorough research in such a situation lightens the court's labors rather than otherwise.[15]

The question of how many cases to cite is an entirely relative one; it is all a matter of proportion and emphasis. There is no one single "approved solution" that can be laid down to fit every situation. The experienced brief-writer soon senses when to cite many cases and when only a few. Like Grandmother's famous recipe, you take a little of this and a pinch of that and add enough of the other until the mixture seems just right.

One final observation: I always consider it a reflection on my brief when the court's opinion cites a case in point that I did not cite to them.[16] After all, one purpose of any brief is to assist the appellate court by pointing out the actual state of the decisional law.[17] On occasion, judges are sufficiently annoyed, when counsel neglect their homework, to make pointed references to controlling decisions "apparently overlooked by counsel,"[18] or the lack of essential allegations that both sides have failed to notice in an indictment.[19]

The discussion just above sufficiently demonstrates the vice of overloading a brief with too many citations, but it is surely a more serious criticism of counsel when the appellate court says in its published opinion that "The so-called briefs, of two pages and one page respectively, * * * have been of no help to us at all,"[20] or when

---

[15] "We have been much aided by the industry and thoroughness of Government counsel and of court-appointed counsel for the defendant in their researches on the case, and by the distinguished ability with which they have marshaled their respective arguments." *Id.*, 171 F.2d at 924.

And see *Cramer v. United States*, 325 U.S. 1, 8, n. 9: "Counsel have lightened our burden of examination of the considerable accumulation of historical materials."

[16] In *Henry v. Hodges*, 171 F.2d 401 (C.A. 2), certiorari denied sub nom. *Henry v. Smith*, 336 U.S. 968, I cited three cases for the proposition that, where statutory direction was qualified by words such as "if available," "when it can be avoided," and the like, it was to be construed as directory rather than mandatory, so that failure to comply with the direction did not invalidate the proceedings. *Martin v. Mott*, 12 Wheat. 19; *Mullan v. United States*, 140 U.S. 240; *Swaim v. United States*, 165 U.S. 553. The Second Circuit added two additional citations, precisely in point, viz., *Bishop v. United States*, 197 U.S. 334, and *Kahn v. Anderson*, 255 U.S. 1—which I took, then as now, as bespeaking inadequate research on my part.

[17] See the thoroughly unpleasant comments made in *Thys Company v. Anglo California National Bank*, 219 F.2d 131 (C.A. 9) at 133 and *passim.*

[18] *Yee Si v. Boyd*, 243 F.2d 203, 208 (C.A. 9); *Phillips v. United States*, 243 F.2d 1, 7 (C.A. 9).

[19] *United States v. Deutsch*, 243 F.2d 435 (C.A. 3).

[20] *Boufford v. United States*, 239 F.2d 841, 842 (C.A. 1).

it remarks that "The defendant's brief is unique in that it does not cite a single authority in support of the contentions made."[21]

Section 68. The ornamental citation.—The temptation to toss in a bit of tangential learning or to button up a train of thought with a pat quotation is frequently a very strong one. I know it is that way in my own case, and I note below some instances of that tendency—simply by way of illustration, and not at all, I should hasten to add, to show what a very learned fellow I can be at times.

To the extent that the inclusion of an ornamental citation (or even a few of them) does not interfere with or detract from the mainstream of the argument, indulgence in this particular form of vanity can do no harm; it may even give one's brief an appealing overtone of erudition that a court will respect. The first two examples noted below may qualify as illustrations.

On occasion, too, the quest for the ornamental citation turns up either the winning case in point, or at least one that will really harry the opposition; see example (c), below. And finally there is the ornamental citation or ornamental discussion that leads nowhere and adds nothing, and is therefore bad. See almost any volume of the Federal Reporter for examples; further identification would be both invidious and unnecessary.

(a) In the *Girouard* case,[22] already discussed in Section 49, above, the Government brief stressed that, in view of the legislative history, adoption of petitioner's view would involve the rewriting of an Act of Congress. By way of sharpening the issue, the brief went on:

> In view of this compelling legislative history, of Congressional action and of highly significant Congressional inaction, the rule of the *Schwimmer, Macintosh,* and *Bland* cases has become a statutory rule, having an independent legislative basis, which, we submit, can be reconsidered only by Congress, and which is not open for reconsideration or reexamination here.

> We need not stop now to inquire when and to what extent adherence to the precept of *stare decisis* is either necessary or desirable. There is here no question of common law, requiring resolution of the paradox that "law must be stable and yet it cannot stand still," Pound, *Interpretations of Legal History,* 1; cf. Cardozo, *The Growth of the Law,* passim. There is before this Court no problem of reconciling situations which involve similar factual patterns embroidered with varying niceties of legal expression, such as this Court considered against an equivocal background of legislative history in *Helvering v. Hallock,* 309 U.S. 106. The present case does not require a reexamination of

---

[21] *Bell v. United States,* 251 F.2d 490, 494 (C.A. 8).
[22] *Girouard v. United States,* 328 U.S. 61.

constitutional doctrine in the light of legislative reenactments which necessarily question earlier judgments or decisions on constitutional issues. See *Helvering v. Griffiths*, 318 U.S. 371, 400-401, discussed in Petitioner's Brief, pp. 33–34. Nor is there here any question of either the power or the propriety of this Court's reexamination and reconsideration of its prior constitutional determinations; we have ourselves, *supra*, pp. 39–42, invited a reexamination of the constitutional aspect of the *Macintosh* decision.

The proposition here is broader and bolder: It is that this Court rewrite an Act of Congress. It is that this Court, by reconsidering the steps which led to a result which Congress has since independently adopted, arrive at a new result which Congress advisedly refused to adopt.

In that context, Pound and Cardozo were unquestionably ornamental citations, but their inclusion did serve to add support to one of the steps in the argument.

(b) A soldier who had been badly wounded in the war sought to sue the United States to recover just compensation for the use of his body.[23] The case is set out in the following excerpt from the Government's brief in opposition to the petition for certiorari:

STATEMENT

Petitioner, Edward C. Commers, was inducted into the military service on October 19, 1942, pursuant to the provisions of the Selective Training and Service Act of 1940, c. 720, 54 Stat. 885 (50 U.S.C. App. 301 *et seq.*) (R. 4). Prior to that time he was earning, as a manual laborer, at least $200 per month (R. 8). After receiving his basic training he was assigned to the 6th Infantry Division of the United States Army and served with that Division in various campaigns in New Guinea and the Philippine Islands (R. 4–6). In these campaigns he received severe injuries and was afflicted with malaria and other diseases and tropical maladies (R. 5–7). During his service in the Army, from which he was discharged on August 6, 1945, he was awarded two Silver Stars,* one Bronze Star Medal,† three Purple Hearts,‡ and a Good Conduct Medal§ (R. 4, 6, 16).

---

* Awarded for gallantry in action. See Army Regulations 600-45, 22 September 1943, par. 13.

† Awarded for gallantry in action, to recognize minor acts of heroism in actual combat. Army Regulations 600-45, 22 September 1943, as changed by Changes No. 3, 25 April 1944, par. 15 1/2.

‡ Awarded for wounds received in action. Army Regulations 600-45, 22 September 1943, as changed by Changes No. 7, 14 July 1945, par. 16.

§ Awarded for exemplary behavior, efficiency, and fidelity. Army Regulations 600-68, May 4, 1943.

---

[23] *Commers v. United States*, 66 F. Supp. 943 (D. Mont.), affirmed, 159 F.2d 248 (C.C.A. 9), certiorari denied, 331 U.S. 807.

On March 26, 1946, petitioner filed an amended complaint in the District Court of the United States for the District of Montana alleging that because of the injuries and sicknesses which he had suffered during his Army service he is unable to follow any substantial gainful occupation as a manual laborer, and that it is reasonably certain that his disabilities will continue in a totally disabling degree throughout his life (R. 7). He is now receiving from the Veterans' Administration of the United States for his disabilities the sum of $34.50 a month when he is not hospitalized and $20 a month when he is in a hospital (R. 8).

The petitioner prayed for a declaratory judgment holding in substance, (1) that the taking of his body and earning power for use in the military forces of the United States was a taking of private property for a public use; (2) that the United States is obligated not only under the Fifth Amendment, but as a matter of natural right, to make just compensation to petitioner and all other veterans disabled in World War II; (3) that petitioner and all other disabled war veterans are constitutionally entitled to try their claims for bodily impairment in the district courts of the United States and to have the jury trial guaranteed by the Seventh Amendment; (4) that the consent of the United States to be sued upon the claims of its war disabled is implied from the Fifth Amendment (R. 15–16).

The United States filed a motion to dismiss the complaint on the grounds that it did not state a claim upon which relief could be granted and that the court was without jurisdiction as the United States had not consented to be sued in this manner (R. 17). The judgment of the District Court (R. 35) granting the motion to dismiss was affirmed by the court below without opinion (R. 48).

ARGUMENT

Petitioner contends that the admitted power of the United States to raise armies by conscription (Pet. 21) is subject to the provision of the Fifth Amendment that "private property" shall not be taken for public use without just compensation, that any soldier whose "bodily integrity and earning power have been consumed in the common defense" is entitled to compensation therefor, and that such soldier may have the existence and extent of his disabilities determined in the courts of the United States and be "justly compensated therefor as a matter of constitutional right" (Pet. 7, 8).

Petitioner's contentions have a certain philosophical appeal, but that is their only merit. Whatever may be the scope of the Fifth Amendment with respect to property destroyed in the course of actual military operations (*United States v. Pacific Railroad*, 120 U.S. 227), the short and conclusive answer to petitioner's argument is that, since the ratification of the Thirteenth Amendment, there has been no property right in a living human body. And, while that Amendment ended slavery and all other forms of *involuntary* servitude (*Clyatt v. United States*, 197 U.S. 207; *Bailey v. Alabama*, 219 U.S. 219; *United States v. Reynolds*, 235 U.S. 133), it did not terminate the numerous civic duties which require the citizen to devote his labor and if need be, his life, to the service of the community. In those categories are included the duty to render military service (*Selective Draft Law Cases*, 245 U.S. 366), the duty to labor for a reasonable time on public roads near his residence without direct compensation (*Butler v. Perry*, 240 U.S. 328), and the duty to assist the police to enforce the justice of the state (*Matter of Babington v. Yellow Taxi Corp.*, 250 N.Y. 14, *per* Cardozo, Ch. J.).

This Court has several times pointed out the nature of the obligation of military service. *Jacobson v. Massachusetts*, 197 U.S. 11, 29; *Selective Draft Law Cases*, 245 U.S. 366, 378. In the latter case, Chief Justice White said, in words which have frequently been quoted:

"It may not be doubted that the very conception of a just government and its duty to the citizen includes the reciprocal obligation of the citizen to render military service in case of need and the right to compel it."

The same thought is expressed in the Congressional declaration contained in Section 1 (b) of the Selective Training and Service Act of 1940, 54 Stat. 885, 50 U.S.C. App. 301 (b):

"that in a free society the obligations and privileges of military training and service should be shared generally in accordance with a fair and just system of selective compulsory military training and service."

The basic fallacy of petitioner's view is that he confounds the nation's right to compel the citizen's obligation to render military service with a taking of property. Once that distinction is recognized, his entire case falls. It may be a distinction which is historical rather than logical, but it is well settled; and, here also, "Upon this point a page of history is worth a volume of logic." *New York Trust Co. v. Eisner*, 256 U.S. 345, 349. Consequently we do not deem it necessary to discuss the technical jurisdictional infirmities of the present complaint, which are adequately disposed of in the opinion of the District Court (R. 30-39).

The citations to the Army Regulations governing the awards of the lad's decorations were ornamental in the dragged-in-by-the-ears sense, but the citations to the several instances of legally compelled services were necessary to the argument. As to the final Holmes quotation—well, that was just too pat to be omitted.

(c) Perhaps in some of the examples just cited the ornamental citations were merely reflections of the brief-writer's more or less angular personality; I must leave that to more objective judges than myself. But every once in a while the search for the ornamental citation pays off, and then it compensates for and outweighs a good deal of what might otherwise be simply a somewhat vulgarly ostentatious display of learning.

An example in my practice was the *Hackfeld* alien property case,[24] in which a vital question, and, in the end, the controlling one, was

---

[24] *United States v. Rodiek*, 117 F.2d 588 (C.C.A. 2), rehearing denied with opinion, 120 F.2d 760, affirmed by equally divided court, 315 U.S. 783. See also *Rodiek v. United States*, 100 C. Cls. 267.

whether Hackfeld had acquired citizenship in the then Republic of Hawaii through the receipt of a Certificate of Special Rights of Citizenship issued under Article 17 of the Constitution of that Republic.[25] There were no reported cases on the point, argument based on the constitutional provision itself had ranged far and wide, and the Government was faced with an adverse ruling of the Secretary of State that the Certificate did confer citizenship.[26]

While in Hawaii taking depositions in the case in 1938, I had occasion to discuss the matter with a number of eminent local practitioners, now unfortunately all deceased, who assured me that the Hawaiian bar all considered the Secretary's ruling clearly erroneous. These gentlemen had been contemporaries of the Republic of Hawaii: Judge A. G. M. Robertson was then the sole survivor of the Convention that had framed the Constitution of that Republic, judge W. L. Stanley had served on the bench shortly thereafter, and Governor W. F. Frear had been a judge under Monarchy, Provisional Government, and Republic alike and had moreover been a member of the Commission that had drafted the Hawaiian Organic Act.[27] Surely the unanimous opinion of men such as these, to the effect that the receipt of a Certificate of Special Rights of Citizenship did not confer Hawaiian nationality, was weighty indeed—but how to bring their views before the U.S. District Court for the Southern District of New York?

---

[25] Art. 17, Sec. 2: "Any person not a Hawaiian citizen, who took active part, or otherwise rendered substantial service in the formation of, and has since supported the Provisional Government of Hawaii, who shall within six months from the promulgation of this Constitution procure from the Minister of the Interior a certificate of such service, as herein set forth; and who shall take an oath to support this Constitution and the laws of the Republic so long as he shall remain domiciled in the Republic, shall be entitled to all the privileges of citizenship without thereby prejudicing his native citizenship or allegiance."

Art. 17, Sec. 5: "Any person to whom such certificate shall be granted shall be admitted, upon application, to naturalization, without showing any further qualifications."

[26] See 3 Hackworth, *Digest of International Law*, 125. The State Department had gone astray because it blindly followed the ruling in *Bowler's Case*, 2 For. Rel. of the U.S. (1895) 853; see also *Godfrey's Case*, id. at 867, without observing the complete change in the Hawaiian naturalization laws effected by the Constitution of the Republic. Bowler had been naturalized under the laws of the Monarchy, and although Godfrey had become a denizen under the Republic, the real question before the U.S. State Department was not whether he had acquired Hawaiian nationality but whether he had forfeited American diplomatic protection. The moral of these rulings in the light of the *Hackfeld* case is, I submit, that when a lawyer deals with foreign law, he is well advised to approach that subject with a high degree of intellectual humility.

[27] Provided for in the Joint Resolution of Annexation, 30 Stat. 750, 751.

I worked out a somewhat labored syllogism while in the Islands: (1) A U.S. Court would judicially notice the foreign law of an antecedent sovereignty on U.S. soil. (2) However, judicial notice is not judicial knowledge. *Shapleigh v. Mier.*[28] (3) Foreign systems of law are, to us, "like a wall of stone"; one has to be brought up within the system to understand it. *Diaz v. Gonzales.*[29] (4) Hawaiian law is to be regarded as foreign, equally with Puerto Rican law. *Waialua Agricultural Co. v. Christian.*[30] Therefore, (5) it is proper to look to the views of those brought up within the system.

Fortified by this self-constructed theory, I duly asked these witnesses (plus two others), "Were persons who received such special rights of citizenship considered by the bar of Hawaii to be Hawaiian citizens?" My opponent screamed that I was asking for the witnesses' opinions on a point of law, as indeed I was; but I got the expected helpful answers, and then took the depositions back to the mainland and prepared for the trial.

In the course of expanding the foregoing syllogism for the trial brief on the law, I looked for a suitable ornamental citation to document the first and undisputed proposition that a United States court would judicially notice the foreign law of an earlier sovereign on American soil. A quick check in Wigmore turned up *Fremont v. United States,*[31] where Chief Justice Taney had said:

And when there are no published reports of judicial decisions which show the received construction of a statute, and the powers exercised under it by the tribunals or officers of the government, it is often necessary to seek information from other authentic sources, such as the records of official acts, and the practice of the different tribunals and public authorities. *And it may sometimes be necessary to seek information from individuals whose official position or pursuits have given them opportunities of acquiring knowledge.* [Italics added.]

---

[28] 299 U.S. 468.

[29] 261 U.S. 102, 105–106, per Holmes, J.: "This Court has stated many times the deference due to the understanding of the local courts upon matters of purely local concern. * * * This is especially true in dealing with the decisions of a Court inheriting and brought up in a different system from that which prevails here. When we contemplate such a system from the outside it seems like a wall of stone, every part even with all the others, except so far as our own local education may lead us to see subordinations to which we are accustomed. But to one brought up within it, varying emphasis, tacit assumptions, unwritten practices, a thousand influences gained only from life, may give to the different parts wholly new values that logic and grammar never could have got from the books."

[30] 305 U.S. 91.

[31] 17 How. St. Tr. 542, 557.

This of course made the Hawaiian lawyers' opinions admissible; the quest for the ornamental citation had paid off in jackpot fashion. At the trial, the testimony in question went in with the mere citation of the *Fremont* case, and both the District Court and the Circuit Court of Appeals placed reliance on that testimony in ruling that receipt of the Certificate of Special Rights had not made Hackfeld (who had been born in Germany) a citizen of the Republic of Hawaii.[32]

Section 69. Citations; Manner of citation; In general.—Legal citations are abbreviations designed to identify the location, the source, and hence *prima facie* the weight, of the authorities relied upon by the brief-writer. Citations must be short enough to save the reader's time, and yet long enough to preclude the slightest possibility of confusion by reason of over-compression. Like any other kind of abbreviation constantly in use, legal citations reflect the conventions and usages of the profession that employs them. Consequently, while in many instances there is a wide range of variant citation forms that are equally correct and hence equally acceptable, in other instances there is a sharp, clear line between correct and incorrect usage, a line that sets off the well-educated lawyer who is steeped in the traditions of a learned profession from his less privileged brethren to whom the practice of law is simply a more or less remunerative trade.

Like all professional conventions, fashions in citation forms change with the times. It was formerly customary to insert a comma between the volume and the page of the report being cited, as for instance, "10 Modern, 138."[33] Similarly, when the Federal Reporter was first published, it was only partially abbreviated; the usual citation was, e.g., "14 Fed. Rep. 682."[34] And, when the United States Code was still a novelty, one of the most meticulous of Supreme Court Justices cited it simply as "C.," followed by title and section

---

[32] "That the mere acceptance of one of these special rights certificates did not entitle the holder to citizenship in the Republic was further shown by a great mass of evidence introduced by the Government, as follows: * * * (2) Five distinguished Honolulu lawyers testified that it was the general understanding of the bar of Hawaii that the mere acceptance of such a special rights certificate had no such effect as Hackfeld claimed." Oral opinion of Coxe, D.J., directing a verdict for the United States, C.C.A. record, pp. 745–46.

"The testimony of five distinguished members of the Hawaiian bar accords with our interpretation of the Hawaiian law." *United States v. Rodiek, supra,* 117 F.2d at 594.

[33] Wallace, *The Reporters* (Heard's 4th ed. 1882) 274.

[34] E.g., 120 U.S. at 111.

numbers.[35] Other examples of changing citation conventions will readily occur to the reader.

The number of persons doing legal writing and thus employing citations grew markedly as more and more legal journals came to be published. In time, the editors of those publications—like editors everywhere—prescribed style manuals to which all contributors were required to conform. At first such formbooks were simply drawn from the citation usages met with in the older series of reports. Later, refinements and innovations were introduced, such as, in Federal citations, an indication of the court deciding the case. Inasmuch as the Federal Reporter for its first 50 years or so reported the decisions of all the lower Federal courts—the Circuit Courts as long as they existed, the Circuit Courts of Appeals from the time of their creation, and the District Courts until the Federal Supplement began publication—it was obviously most helpful to a reader to have some indication of the authority of a given "Fed." citation.

But along with such useful additions, which were varied in minor details over the years—so that, in the larger law offices, one could tell from a particular lawyer's citation forms just what volumes of the law review he had helped to edit—the law school journals invented and began to use a virtually cryptographic code to signal the weight to be accorded a particular citation appearing in their pages. Along with *accord* and *semble*, which had the support of legal tradition, they introduced the use of "see," "cf.," "but see" and "but cf." Each of these prefixes had a value—in the minds of the editors—as precise as those attaching to algebraic symbols. At this juncture, the path of the law reviews on the one hand, and that of practitioners and judges on the other, diverged sharply; such "introductory signals" carried as little meaning to the profession as, for example, a localized and topical classroom pleasantry. And, ultimately, with the appearance of the 9th edition of *A Uniform System of Citation*, published in 1954, the law reviews in important respects turned their backs on professional tradition, and marked off in a different direction all their own.

The nature of their more important departures from accepted lawyer usage will be pointed out in the sections that follow. At this juncture it will suffice simply to set forth some general observations to guide the lawyer who undertakes to write briefs for real courts (i.e., other than moot courts).

---

[35] Holmes, J., in *Mitchel v. Hampel*, 276 U.S. 299, 302.

First of all, follow a system of citation that is clear, that is simple, and with which the judicial reader will feel comfortable. The practitioner in the Federal courts is in consequence well advised to adopt—at least as a starting point—the citation form employed in the official U.S. Reports.

Second, be consistent—or at least reasonably so. (A former colleague always insisted that the only real essential was to avoid inconsistency on the same page.)

Third, be sufficiently flexible to eliminate even an appearance of pedantry. Thus, while it is generally desirable to add the designation of the court in parentheses, as for instance *Parsons v. Smith*, 255 F.2d 595 (C.A. 3), there is no need to do so when you have already indicated the court in your text—e.g., "as held by the Third Circuit in *Parsons v. Smith*, 255 F.2d 595."

Fourth, use *A Uniform System of Citation* with caution. It is full of useful suggestions, but the practitioner will be well advised not to follow it blindly.

Section 70. Citations; Manner of citation; Titles of cases.—Very frequently the title of a case is extremely long as it appears at the commencement of the report. Thus, a recent Supreme Court case bears the title, *Daniel, Attorney General, et al. v. Family Security Life Insurance Co. et al.*[36] How much of the foregoing should go into the brief?

The rule of thumb used in the U.S. Solicitor General's Office is to cite the case as it appears in the running head of the report, except that the first word will not be abbreviated. In the instance stated, the citation would be *Daniel v. Family Ins. Co.*

Where the first word is abbreviated in the running head, it is spelled out in the brief. E.g., *International Union, U.A.W.A., A.F. of L., Local 232, et al. v. Wisconsin Employment Relations Board et al.*[37] has the running head *Auto. Workers v. Wis. Board.* The first word of petitioner and respondent is abbreviated; hence the case would be cited in a brief as *Automobile Workers v. Wisconsin Board.*

Similarly, *United States v. B. & O.R. Co.*[38] in the running head becomes *United States v. Baltimore & O.R. Co.* in the brief; *U.S. v. Capital Transit Co.*[39] becomes *United States v. Capital Transit Co.;* and

---

[36] 336 U.S. 220.
[37] 336 U.S. 245.
[38] 333 U.S. 169.
[39] 325 U.S. 357.

American Power Co. v. S.E.C.[40] appears as *American Power Co. v. Securities & Exchange Comm.*

The same rules are universally applicable to any reports, federal, state, or English.

Section 71. Supras and infras.—Use these sparingly; it is very annoying for any reader to have to hunt for the original citation, and it isn't going to make the judge who reads your brief any more sympathetic toward your point of view if he has to grope through pages he has already read in order to locate the citation that now for the first time interests him. (Frequently, in the haste of meeting deadlines, the original citation is apt to drop out somewhere along the way, and then the case on which you are relying will be utterly lost.)

The best solution is to use both the *supra* and the original citation; the first indicates that you have already cited the case before, the second makes the citation immediately available. And do the same thing when you are using a page reference later on: e.g., "*Cramer v. United States*, 325 U.S. 1, *supra*"; "Or, as the Court said in the *Cramer* case, *supra*, 325 U.S. at 35."

There is really nothing more irritating than to read, time and time again, "See *Wilson v. United States, supra*, at 743"—and then to have to try to find the volume from somewhere on up the line.

Section 72. Citations; Accuracy of citations.—As has been noted (Section 64, above), the only safe way is to check your proof against the original reports—not against your original notes! It is very easy indeed for a judge to lose interest in your brief if he can't find the case you cite because of a mistake in the citation. He may take a keen interest in you after such an experience, i.e., to see what manner of would-be lawyer this is who writes such sloppy briefs, but he probably won't concentrate very hard on your brief after that.

Similarly, misspelling the name of a well-known case marks you as a lawyer distinctly under par. When the case is a leading one in its field, and one of the parties thereto a person of some prominence, as for instance the case of *Philadelphia Co. v. Stimson*, 223 U.S. 605, which was brought against Mr. Henry L. Stimson during his first tour of duty as Secretary of War and which was a leading authority in the area of suits-against-the-United States, then, if you cite it as *Philadelphia Co. v. Stimpson*, it marks you as distinctly under par professionally. (I should add that this is not an imaginary illustration.)

---

[40] 325 U.S. 385.

And finally, if you fail to use that indispensable tool of legal research, *Shepard's Citations*, you are apt to commit the unpardonable legal sin of citing an overruled case. Your face will then be as red as *Shepard's Citations'* own scarlet covers, any court is bound to mistrust anything you say thereafter, and certainly the incident will not help your case.[41]

So—check citations, check names of cases, and Shepardize everything in the brief. Any time you think these steps aren't necessary, some avoidable mistake will happen along and prove that they are!

Section 73. Use of quotations.—It is a good, sound rule of thumb that quotations from opinions should be included only when they add something, and that, whenever possible, they should be short rather than long. But I cannot at all agree that they should invariably be omitted. (Compare the excerpt from Mr. Davis's paper quoted in Section 66, above.)

After all, a good many judges read briefs while sitting in easy chairs, and it is therefore going to advance your case if you quote enough pat matter to satisfy their curiosity without discommoding them and making them get up—particularly if their reading takes place where they do not have ready access to the law library.

Sometimes limitations of space will automatically curb the number and extent of your quotations. But, even in the rare cases when the length of a brief is unlimited, I think that the question "To quote or not to quote" is essentially a matter of judgment and proportion, not susceptible of being reduced to fixed rules (compare Sections 66 and 67, above, as to number of citations), and that all one can do is to formulate some standards. I venture the following:

(a) Quote only when the quotation adds something. A good standard to follow is to use a quotation whenever a court has said something as well or better than you are able to do on your own, or, preeminently, when some judge of acknowledged authority says what you are trying to say in language more striking or more dramatic than a journeyman lawyer writing a brief would feel free to use. A good illustration, for the first instance, is the quotation from Chief Justice Taney in Section 68 at p. 138, above; and, for the second, the Holmes quotation at p. 138, n. 29.

---

[41] Compare the Supreme Court's opinion in *Oklahoma Packing Co. v. Gas Co.*, 309 U.S. 4, especially at 7–8, with its earlier opinion in the same case, 309 U.S. 703, 705–709. The difference was due to a later state case, decided after the decree below, that had not been originally called to the attention of the Supreme Court; accordingly the earlier opinion was ordered withdrawn. See 308 U.S. 530.

(b) Always quote when the mere statement of the case's holding whets but does not satisfy the reader's curiosity.

(c) Never quote hornbook propositions.

(d) Never, *Never*, NEVER, quote sentences out of context. To do so is an unpardonable professional sin, besides which it leaves you wide open to being shown up by the opposition.

(e) In at least three instances, or so it seems to me, fairly extensive quotations are justified in any court:

First, when you are relying on temporarily unfamiliar decisions, and you need to recall the exact *ratio decidendi* to the court's mind. Thus, in *Testa v. Katt*,[42] the question was whether a state could refuse to enforce in its courts a cause of action arising under a federal statute where that cause of action was in conflict with the public policy of the state. The point had not arisen for thirty years, and so it was considered helpful to include in the Government's brief rather long quotations from the opinions in the two leading cases, *Second Employers Liability Cases*,[43] and *Minneapolis & St. Louis R.R. v. Bombolis*.[44] Those quotations served to bring the reasoning of those decisions to the judges' attention, without unduly taxing either their memories or their comfort. Omission of the quotations, in the circumstances, would have made the brief much harder to follow—and of course Chief Justice White's rolling periods in the *Bombolis* case could not have been either profitably or intelligibly rendered in small compass.

Second, when you are relying on materials not readily accessible. For instance, in the *Haupt* treason case,[45] the Government quoted extensively from Howell's *State Trials;* no library has more than one set, and it was necessary to bring the cases to the attention of nine judges. Similarly, Government briefs in a number of military law cases have quoted extensively from the opinions of the Boards of Review established in the Office of the Judge Advocate General of the Army.[46] Those opinions were multigraphed in such unhappily limited quantities that they are not available in even the largest law

---

[42] 330 U.S. 386.

[43] 223 U.S. 1.

[44] 241 U.S. 211.

[45] *Haupt v. United States*, 330 U.S. 631.

[46] E.g., *Humphrey v. Smith*, 336 U.S. 695; *Henry v. Hodges*, 171 F.2d 401 (M. A. 2), certiorari denied *sub nom. Henry v. Smith*, 336 U.S. 968; *DeWar v. Hunter*, 170 F.2d 993 (C.A. 10), certiorari denied, 337 U.S. 908.

libraries; in order to bring them fairly to the attention of the courts, therefore, it was necessary to set them out at length in the briefs.

Third, when you are dealing with documents or exhibits in a long record—papers that cannot fairly be summarized. Thus, in the Government's brief in the *Line Material* reargument,[47] the memoranda and documents leading up to the cross-license agreements there considered were very fully set out. It was difficult, perhaps impossible, fairly to characterize all the nuances of the many vital exhibits involved, and the record was so bulky that even the most conscientious of judges would be disinclined to hunt for the originals. Indeed, in that particular brief, which extended to 159 pages, the first 153 pages were devoted exclusively to argument on the facts.

But, as I say, it is all a matter of judgment and proportion, depending on the nature and needs of the particular case.

Section 74. Quotations; Accuracy of quotations.—The caution that all citations must be checked is peculiarly applicable to quotations. Unless every quotation is carefully read, each against the original, significant words will become distorted, and, likely as not, whole lines will drop out. So—check against the original. You will kick yourself mentally around the courthouse square any time you neglect to do so—and it won't help your reputation for accuracy, either.

Section 75. Footnotes.—Perhaps no single implement of all the vast apparatus of scholarship is so thoroughly misused in the law as the footnote. There maybe some justification in the manifold areas of the academic world for that formidable display of learning and industry, the thin stream of text meandering in a vale of footnotes, but that sort of thing is quite self-defeating in the law: because it makes the writer's thoughts more difficult to follow—and hence far less likely to persuade the judicial reader.

The worst offenders on this score are undoubtedly the law reviews, whose student editors have at least the excuse of being still at the apprentice stage, and whose faculty editors may have had but insufficient opportunity to gain firsthand acquaintance with judicial psychology. Next in order are the attorneys at law who are not lawyers but who like to make a show of erudition.

It is entirely proper, and indeed helpful, to use footnotes in a brief (a) to indicate qualifications to statements in the text, where

---

[47] *United States v. Line Material Co.*, 333 U.S. 287.

such qualifications would interrupt the thought if they remained in the text, and (b) to include citations on points of secondary importance.

On occasion, some lawyers relegate to a footnote their reply to particular arguments made by the opposing party. This is a risky technique, which is proper only in very limited situations. In the usual instance, yielding to the temptation to minimize the other side's contentions by giving them footnote treatment will lead counsel into the error of dealing inadequately with important issues. In that situation, the usual result is that the footnote technique backfires.

It is only when a particular argument is totally lacking in factual record support that it is safe to dispose of it in a footnote. But unless the opposition argument is utterly devoid of support in the record, it deserves reply in the text of your brief, and it is only your case that will be hurt when you drop your own views down to a footnote.

It is similarly not proper, however, and can be of distinct disservice to your cause, to use footnotes as a means of setting out a parallel line of argument. Whenever you do that, you detract appreciably from the force of your contentions—and you may do serious damage to an important principle.

An unfortunate example of this double-stream-of-argument employment of footnotes appeared in the Government's brief in the *Schneiderman* denaturalization case.[48] The question was the meaning of the expression in the naturalization laws, "attached to the principles of the Constitution of the United States," which has been on the books since 1795. It was sought to show, by presentation of the legislative history, that the phrase meant more than mere law-abiding acceptance of American government by one who did not at heart believe in a republican form of government—and the legislative history in fact shows that very clearly.[49] But by dividing up the legislative history materials between text and footnote, the argument could not easily be followed, it was weakened, and in

---

[48] *Schneiderman v. United States*, 320 U.S. 118.

[49] James Madison had argued against the adoption of this requirement in 1795, saying (4 Annals of Congress 1023): "It was hard to make a man swear that he preferred the Constitution of the United States, or to give any general opinion, because he may, in his own private judgment, think Monarchy or Aristocracy better, and yet be honestly determined to support this Government as he finds it." But Congress adopted the requirement over Madison's objections (*id.*).

the end it failed to persuade the Court.[50] A few years later, in the *Knauer* case,[51] the same materials were set forth, without substantial additions of material but in one consecutive argumentative screed—and the Court chose to decide the case on other grounds.

Section 76. Record references.—At the risk of offensive repetition, I will emphasize again the matter discussed in Section 44, above: the imperative and absolute necessity for backing up every assertion of fact in your Statement of Facts with a record reference to show that what you say is established by the record and is not simply conjured up out of thin air, whole cloth, and similar material of spontaneous generation. It is well, too, to repeat the record references when you repeat the assertion in the Argument, certainly when the point is critical or even of substantial importance. At that latter juncture, when the judicial reader is bound to catch the significance of the asserted fact, his curiosity will be aroused. Don't make him thumb back to try to find the particular reference in a long Statement of Facts, and don't lead him on a species of treasure hunt with a tantalizing "(*supra*, p. 16)." Have the reference right there so that he can turn to it immediately: "(R. 298)." Remember also that a Statement of Facts or an Argument richly sprinkled with record references will always have a very reassuring effect on any legal reader.

And, here again, as in connection with citations and quotations, absolute and unswerving accuracy must be the goal; inaccuracies, particularly inaccuracies of substance, are generally unforgivable and always dangerous. A court particularly dislikes a citation to fact A when all that citation establishes is fact B, from which you proceed to draw an inference that fact A exists.[52]

---

[50] See the reference at 320 U.S. 118, 133, n. 12, to "the discursive debates on the 1795 Act."

[51] *Knauer v. United States*, 328 U.S. 654.

[52] "Even more inexcusable than defective documentation of the facts is the habit indulged in by some counsel of citing page and line for a statement of fact when a reading of the page and line cited does not sustain the point for which it is cited, but only some inference which counsel seeks to draw from the testimony. When counsel is referring to testimony to sustain facts testified to, all he needs to do is cite page and line. But when he is asking the court to make an inference from the testimony thus referred to, he should tell us, not only what the inference is, but from what the inference is drawn. There are plenty of words in the English language to express the fact of inference. Nothing is more annoying in studying a brief either as an advocate or a judge than to have citations given which do not directly support the facts for which they are cited." Vanderbilt [C. J., N.J. Sup. Ct.], *The New Rules of the Supreme Court on Appellate Procedure*, 2 Rutgers Univ. L. Rev. 1, 27–28.

So—have all record references checked, preferably by a person other than the one who has written the brief. Such others are invariably better proofreaders than the brief-writer—the latter is always unconsciously inclined to see the mental image of what the word or citation should be rather than the strictly visual image of what it actually is. Moreover, having a third party do the checking ensures independent scrutiny. It is much better to have your text questioned and doubted by an office associate in the first instance than by a court.

Section 77. Indicating emphasis.—Some courts have had rules that forbid the use of italics in briefs; most of them, however, have left such matters to the judgment and good taste of the brief-writer.

A sound general rule is to use italics sparingly. If they are used too freely in the text of a brief, they are apt to be regarded as (what indeed they frequently are in fact) insults to any reader's intelligence. It is perfectly possible to write a strong, forceful, even a fighting brief, without a single word italicized for emphasis.

The most appropriate use for italics, by and large, is to point up a particular passage in a quotation. At the very least, this will catch a reader's eye, because a good many lawyers and judges who read legal matter almost invariably tend to skip quotations at first reading.

In any event, never proceed beyond italics to capitals and worse, whether in quotations or elsewhere. I recall vividly a written comment on a brief, made by a most able lawyer in the U.S. Solicitor General's Office: "and for the love of God, no bold face!"

Section 78. Going outside the record.—It is permissible to go outside the record in these instances:

(i) As to anything in the realm of judicial notice—and in some courts that is a broad domain indeed.[53]

(ii) In the Supreme Court of the United States, as to administrative practice. That tribunal goes further than most other courts in receiving outside-the-record proof of administrative practice, and will give due and careful weight to official letters.[54]

(iii) In the federal courts, as to anything showing or tending to show that the controversy has become moot.[55]

---

[53] See e.g., 9 Wigmore, *Evidence* (3d ed. 1940), secs. 2565–2583; Morgan, *Judicial Notice* (1944) 57 Harv. L. Rev. 269; compare Davis, *Official Notice* (1949) 62 Harv. L. Rev. 537.

[54] See, e.g., *Vermilya-Brown Co. v. Connell*, 335 U.S. 377; *Foley Bros. v. Filardo*, 336 U.S. 281.

[55] The Supreme Court allows the greatest latitude in bringing such facts to the attention of the Court. For a discussion of available methods, with full citations to cases, see Robertson and Kirkham, *Jurisdiction of the Supreme Court of the United States*, sec. 252.

(iv) In some courts, as to almost anything resting in official files.[56]

(v) In all courts, as to anything in the particular court's own files.[57]

(vi) Possibly, but sparingly, in other situations. Thus, in the *Trailmobile* case,[58] where a returned veteran was the unfortunate victim of a bitter dispute between rival unions, the Government (representing the veteran) set out in its brief—and at the argument—relevant matters that had occurred since the ruling below.[59] But that is probably the verge of the law; even there the foregoing departures from the record encountered hard going.

Subject to the foregoing, you depart from the record at your peril; the courts will not listen to details resting only in the knowledge of the brief-writer, and generally resent any such efforts to supplement the record.

Section 79. "Things you cannot afford to do."—The four outstanding don'ts for brief-writers, in my judgment, are (a) inexcusable inaccuracy; (b) unsupported hyperbole; (c) unwarranted screaming; and (d) personalities and scandalous matter.

They are don'ts, not only from the point of view of one's own professional standards and self-respect, but also from the narrow aspect of intelligent self-interest: every one of these faults is bound to backfire—and most unpleasantly.

Below are listed some examples of these faults that I have encountered. In each of the instances I have indicated what the other side was able to do by way of reply; in none of these instances did success rest with the offending party.

---

[56] Thus, in *Red Canyon Sheep Co. v. Ickes*, 69 App. D.C. 27, 98 F.2d 308, the court judicially noticed certain proceedings in the Interior Department, including an unpublished Solicitor's opinion. In that case, counsel for the Secretary asked the court to go that far in order still to be able to move to dismiss, and to avoid trial. At the present time, the same result can be obtained simply by moving for summary judgment, and by bringing the relevant papers to the attention of the court in a covering affidavit, under Rule 56 or amended Rule 12 (b), F.R. Civ. P.

[57] E.g., *National F. Ins. Co. v. Thompson*, 281 U.S. 331; *United States v. Pink*, 315 U.S. 203, 216, and cases there cited.

[58] *Trailmobile Co. v. Whirls*, 331 U.S. 40.

[59] E.g., that, after the entry of the decree of the [Court of Appeals] adverse to the Union, the Union suspended Whirls from membership and requested the Company to suspend him from work; and that the Company, while telling Whirls not to report for work, had nonetheless kept him on the payroll, on leave of absence with full pay.

(a) *Inexcusable inaccuracy.* In one case of conspiracy, which for a number of reasons need not be more particularly identified, the charge was that two of the defendants, who will be called the Smiths, conspired to defraud the Government of the faithful services of an officer, who shall be called Captain Jones.

At an appellate stage, the Smiths, whose defense was that certain payments by them to Captain Jones had been extorted by him, complained that the trial judge had failed to charge the jury that, if they found that the payments had been extorted, there would be no basis for any finding of conspiracy.

The Smiths' handling of this contention is perhaps best shown reflexly, by setting out the answering excerpt from the prosecution's reply brief:

> The Smiths complain at some length that the trial court's charge as to the basic issues concerning them was inadequate (Br. 18-24).
>
> They say (Br. 20)—
>
>> As regards the Smiths, the basic issue in the case was whether or not the payments had been extorted by Captain Jones by threats to violate his duty, or had been made pursuant to conspiracy to seduce Jones from fulfilling his duty.
>
> They then go on to quote three sentences from the court's charge (Br. 21, 22, 23), and conclude (Br. 21)—
>
>> It will be observed that there was no statement by the Trial Court anywhere in the charge that the jury could find that there would in law be no conspiracy or agreement on the part of the Smiths as charged in the indictment if the jury believed the contention of the defense, namely, that the Smiths were the victims of a shrewd and ruthless plan of extortion.
>
> The difficulty with considering particular isolated sentences of a charge instead of the charge as a whole, or even a portion of the charge, is that important aspects are apt to be overlooked. The Smiths' sampling technique in this instance has produced the very consequences which might have been anticipated; they failed to note that the trial judge did in fact charge on the precise point with which they were concerned. He added, following the sentence quoted by the Smiths at Br. 22, and preceding the sentence quoted by the Smiths at Br. 23, the following (R. 1134)
>
>> However, as to the payments of money, if you believe that they were coerced by the defendant Jones, that is, that they would not have been made at all in whole or in part except for Jones' threats, then such payments would not be the result of agreement nor any evidence of a crime. And if you so believe, and also are not satisfied beyond a reasonable doubt by other evidence in the case that the conspiracy existed as

charged in the indictment, you should find all the defendants not guilty, as Jones is not here charged with extortion.

The foregoing intervening excerpt is nowhere quoted in the Smiths' brief.

Well, the Smiths went to jail. And, apart from any question of professional standards, it was a fact that, had the trial judge's charge been set out in full, without omissions, the omitted sentence would not have appeared to do nearly so full justice to the Smiths' theory as isolating it in the reply brief did.

(b) *Unsupported hyperbole*. Whenever a lawyer exaggerates any substantial distance beyond the record, he is simply asking for trouble—and the greater the exaggeration, the more devastating the impact of the inevitable reply.

I have in mind a criminal case involving tax evasion, where the essential defense was that the petitioners had made a disclosure of their tax discrepancies, so that, they contended, they had obtained immunity from prosecution. In their brief they stated that the court below

wholly failed to consider the important and undisputed facts pertinent to the question whether the Petitioners' confession, unique for frankness and completeness, was induced by the Treasury Department's promise of immunity.

This assertion, that the petitioners' confession was "unique for frankness and completeness," really left the lads wide open. Here are the answering paragraphs from the prosecution's brief

1. The District Court found as a fact that "at no time between February 28, 1945, and April 25, 1945, was any act of the defendants or of the corporate taxpayers prompted or brought about by any inducement held out to them by any person in authority or any person connected with the government" (Fdg. 19, R. 2176), and that "at no time" during those dates "were the defendants or the corporate taxpayers coerced or compelled or induced, either with or without process, to make incriminatory disclosures" (Fdg. 20, R. 2177).

The District Court likewise found as a fact that the March currency redeposits "were prompted by the belief that currency in bills of large denominations might in effect become contraband and not by any desire or intention voluntarily to disclose frauds on the revenue" (Fdg. 19, R. 2176), and that the filing of two additional fraudulent tax returns after substantial redeposits of currency had been made "conclusively establishes that the redeposit of currency was no evidence of any intention on the part of the defendants or the corporate taxpayers to make voluntary disclosure of the frauds theretofore practiced," and "that said redeposits had no connection with or bearing upon crimes against the revenue" (Fdg. 24, R. 2178). The Circuit Court of Appeals characterized the contention that the making of these deposits amounted to a voluntary disclosure in response to a promise of immunity as "fantastic" (R. 2196).

The District Court further found that "Neither the defendants nor the corporate taxpayers at any time prior to April 25, 1945, disclosed the fraudulent practices of the corporate taxpayers to any government official" (Fdg. 18, R. 2176), and also specifically found that statements submitted in affidavits to the effect that "voluntary disclosure" was discussed between E. Allan X_____ and Collector P_____ on March 26, April 10, 20, and 24, were false. (*Ibid.*). The Circuit Court of Appeals thought it "clear" that "the investigation began at the latest on March 24, 1945" (R. 2197–2198)." The first disclosure was that contained in the letters of April 25, 1945 (R. 2123–2124; see also R. 2134), which contained an invitation to examine the corporate taxpayers' books. Those letters, the District Court found, "were not frank and full disclosures, were not voluntarily made, and were delivered at a time when the defendants well knew that an investigation of their affairs and those of the corporate taxpayers had actually been initiated" (Fdg. 22, R. 2177–2178). "On April 25, 1945, the extent of the frauds practiced by the corporate taxpayers was not disclosed" (Fdg. 14, R. 2175). These "belated and partial revelations" (Fdg. 23, R. 2178) were "prompted solely by the fact that the defendants and the corporate taxpayers knew that an investigation of their affairs had begun and that an Internal Revenue Agent had made an appointment, deferred at the request of the defendants and of the corporate taxpayers, to commence an examination of the books of the defendant Henry X_____ on April 23, 1945." (Fdg. 19, R. 2176–2177). The subsequent investigation of the books of the corporate taxpayers, between May and August 1945 "was invited by the defendants and by the corporate taxpayers with full knowledge that an investigation had been commenced which would lead to the discovery of fraudulent entries in the books of the corporate taxpayers, and with full knowledge of the fact that said investigation could be commenced and continued with or without the consent of the defendants or the corporate taxpayers" (Fdg. 21, R. 2177).

The Circuit Court of Appeals likewise noted "that the corporate records were in no sense the result of any promise of immunity. They were furnished long after the government investigation had begun" (R. 2198).

These concurrent findings, accurately reflecting the record (see Statement, *supra*, pp. 13–23), need not be independently reviewed here. *Goldman v. United States*, 316 U.S. 129, 135, cf. *United States v. Johnson*, *319 U.S.* 503, 518; *Delaney v. United States*, 263 U.S. 586, 589-590. They make it abundantly clear that the questions suggested by the petition are academic, without actual relationship to the present record. Those questions happen to be without any substantive merit, though that is now beside the point. But it may be noted in leaving this aspect of the case that, considering all the circumstances, petitioners' reference to their April 25 letters as "confessions, unique for frankness and completeness" (Pet. 27), involves not so much hyperbole as irony.

Review was, of course, denied; and if the lawyers who penned the quotation in question had any sensibilities at all, they must (at least figuratively) have been eating off the mantelpiece for days and days.

So—don't exaggerate or overstate; the farther your departure from the record, the more painful the return trip will be. Consequently, whenever you are tempted to go all out for hyperbole, it is appropriate to remember the classic admonition to "take a pillow along, so that when you get thrown out of court you'll land soft."

(c) *Unwarranted screaming.* Exaggeration comes in both plain and fancy types. The latter model, which can be recognized by its emotional content, is now and doubtless always will be popular with crusaders.

There comes to mind a petition that raised certain questions involved in an expulsion from the West Coast by the military. It raised some difficult questions, too; but petitioner's counsel chose to slop over, as follows:

> It is a fair inference that in regard to the forcible expulsion, as in regard to the denial of a right to hearing (*supra*, pp. 16–20), respondent was chiefly interested in an assertion of the breadth of military power, rather than in a fear of harm to the country by petitioner.

Not only was that passage unnecessary, it was extremely unwise, because on the question of good faith and good motives, respondent was on impregnable ground—as his brief was at pains to point out:

> 3. * * * Respondent's removal of petitioner through the use of military personnel was specifically and expressly authorized by Secretary of War Stimson, by Assistant Secretary of War McCloy, and by General Marshall (R. 265-266). Moreover, he had been advised both by the Attorney General of the United States and by the Judge Advocate General of the Army that he could lawfully exercise such power (R. 248, 254). Respondent did not remove petitioner from California to Nevada until petitioner had prosecuted his injunction proceeding in the district court, seeking to enjoin respondent from "directly or indirectly by any means, method or device whatsoever from executing or causing to be executed" the exclusion order here in question (R. 247). The right to use military personnel in carrying out the order had been asserted before the court in the injunction proceeding (R. 256–257). Not until the district court had denied petitioner's suit for an injunction and had given judgment for respondent did the latter proceed to enforcement. Furthermore, as the district court in the present case concluded, respondent "acted in good faith and with the highest motives, and with an honest belief that Executive Order 9066 and Law 503 empowered him to lawfully do and direct" the acts and things for which it is here attempted to hold him liable (R. 299–300).

> Similar findings of good faith and reasonableness were made by the district court in the injunction case (R. 278–279, 281–282) and by the circuit court of appeals here (R. 337–338).

The temptation to indulge in a bit of counterscreaming was strong, but counsel refrained, adding only the following footnote at the end of the second paragraph just quoted:

In view of those findings, and in the face of other findings that the action here was taken pursuant to legal advice and after express approval by General DeWitt's military and civil superiors (*supra*, pp. 7, 11–12), the statement in the petition (Pet. 31) that "respondent was chiefly interested in an assertion of the breadth of military power, rather than in a fear of harm to the country by petitioner" is of course wholly unwarranted.

Review was denied; petitioner's screaming undoubtedly backfired, since it was shown to be without warrant in the record. Indeed, it approached and all but entered the realm of angry personalities.

(d) *Personalities and scandalous matter.* The argument *ad hominem* in a brief is always unpardonable, not simply because it is something no decently constituted brief-writer would include, but because, like all the other faults, it fails of its purpose: appellate courts have a hard enough time deciding the merits of the cases presented to them without embarking on collateral inquiries as to the personality or conduct of the lawyers involved. They recoil from any attempt even to ask them to consider such matters, and are always embarrassed by the request. So—granted that your opponent's disbarment is long overdue, granted in any event that his conduct in the particular case was shameful and thoroughly unprofessional, take those matters up with the grievance committee, and don't inject them into either the written or the oral argument of an appeal.

In much the same category, at least in my judgment, is the constant use of the adjective "learned" when referring to the judge or to the court below. A little reflection will show that it is always used, or very nearly so, as biting sarcasm. It adds nothing; it had better be omitted.

At the other extreme is the use of "honorable"—"we therefore submit that this Honorable Court should reverse the judgment below." Better leave that to the bailiff, who starts with "Oyez, oyez, oyez"—the last vestigial remnant of Anglo-Norman and Law French in American law—and who concludes, "God save the United States and this Honorable Court." Make it a rule to omit that particular adjective from briefs; judges don't like being fawned upon by members of the bar.

Finally, there are the two ultimate horribles. One is the brief which violates the rule of conduct that written arguments, "though often in sharp controversy, shall be gracious and respectful to both the court and opposing counsel, and be in such words as may be properly addressed by one gentleman to another."[60] The other is the brief that contains scandalous matter, i.e., that imputes improper motives to counsel or to a court. On occasion, such documents have resulted in disciplinary action, although usually they are simply stricken, frequently on the court's own motion.[61] Here again, the fault will be demonstrated reflexly, by printing in full the motion to strike that was filed by the Government promptly after the brief was filed:

Now comes the Solicitor General on behalf of the petitioner herein, and prays that the respondent's Brief in Opposition to the Petition for a Writ of Certiorari be stricken because it contains scandalous matter. *Green v. Elbert,* 137 U.S. 615, 624; *Royal Arcanum v. Green,* 237 U.S. 531, 546–547. Compare Cox v. Wood, 247 U.S. 3, 6–7, where, however, the language seems to have been more restrained.

The principal objectionable passages in respondent's Brief in Opposition in the present case are the following:

Petitioner sought to abuse and insult the intelligence of the Court of Appeals by this same type of unsupportable claim which he must of necessity know to be completely false. Yet he persists with this same technique of urging unsupportable arguments which he must know to be completely false in this Court again. It is outrageous that an officer of the U.S. under oath to uphold the laws of the United States and supposedly advised of the rudiments of ethical conduct should advance frivolous argument merely for the purpose of delay and should dare to use so contemptible and obviously dilatory a device which outrages common decency. (P. 13)

*   *   *   *   *   *   *

---

[60] *National Surety Co. v. Jarvis,* 278 U.S. 610, 611, *per* Taft, C. J. Compare *United States v. Miller,* 233 F.2d 171, 172, note 1 (C.A. 2): "A brief of a * * * purported 'friend of the court,' being a curious compound of scurrility and irrelevance, the filing of which is not objected to by the United States Attorney, may remain lodged in the files of the court as an example of how lawyers should not act."

[61] See J. Sup. Ct., Oct. T. 1934, pp. 105, 149–150, 79 L. ed. 1714 (six months' suspension and payment of a $250 fine); J. Sup. Ct., Oct. T. 1935, pp. 77, 159, 80 L. ed. 1411–12, 1414 (rule to show cause why counsel should not be disbarred; on counsel's apology, brief stricken, and rule discharged); *Missouri-K.-T. R.R. Co. v. Texas,* 275 U.S. 494 (brief stricken); *Knight v. Bar Association,* 321 U.S. 803 (brief stricken on Court's own motion); *Matter of Fletcher,* 344 U.S. 862 (same).

This problem seems to be a timelessly recurring one, as witness the following from a case decided by the Third Circuit (citation advisedly omitted):

"The petition for rehearing filed by the attorneys for the petitioners contains intemperate and gross language. The use of such language by members of the bar in a petition to

(continued)

Petitioner then assaults (at p. 20, brief for petitioner) the importance of title, a fundamental legal conception having vital necessity and meaning to all free peoples, and countless consequences in the law of sales. He forgets that *United States v. Lee* turned specifically on what he casually terms "technical doctrines of passage of title." He asks this Court to brush aside ownership of property as merely "technical." Many of his predecessors in this immoral doctrine, who have regarded the ownership of another as "technical," are filling our jails. (P. 18)

*   *   *   *   *   *   *

Toward the bottom of page 16, petitioner goes on in an attempt to place himself above the law by insinuating that he has some celestial status that removes him personally from the reach of the law to which "a recalcitrant private vendor" would be subjected. This is indicative of petitioner's concept of all law—namely, that he is above it, that he is the law himself, and that he is immune from the enforcement of the law upon him by this or any other Court.

*   *   *   *   *   *   *

* * * When the day comes that anyone in respondent's position cannot resort to the Courts for protection of his property under law merely because some bureaucrat seeks to hide his incompetence and injustice behind a protecting shield of sovereign immunity, both liberty and reason shall have perished from the land. (P. 15.)

*   *   *   *   *   *   *

The depths of petitioner's willful ignorance of these boundaries of sovereign immunity under a free constitution like ours is revealed by his misuse of *Goldberg v. Daniels*, 231 U.S. 218. (P. 16.)

The sequel: an apology tendered in person, and a "Motion for Leave to Withdraw" the offending document—which was promptly granted.

The moral of all the foregoing is simply this, that unprofessional conduct in appellate work just does not pay. I could put the matter on a higher plane, of course, but this section is written for those whose minds may still be open on the question.

Section 80. Signatures.—Who shall sign a brief and how is largely a matter of court rules and local practice. In some jurisdictions it is customary to add the firm name; in others only the names of individuals should be signed to briefs. Some courts

---

the court verges upon contemptuous conduct. A repetition of such conduct on the part of counsel will bring disciplinary action. The Clerk will be ordered to strike from the petition the language in question."

require the signature of counsel to be followed by his office address; in other courts the address is generally omitted.

Similarly, in some jurisdictions the name over at the left, which is designated "Of Counsel," is merely that of the forwarding lawyer or the lads who go on the brief just for the ride; whereas in New York the people who sign "Of Counsel" are those who are actually handling the case.

In the New York courts, both state and federal, it is customary to print at the top of the cover, "To be argued by," giving his name. I have never encountered this practice elsewhere.

In the Supreme Court of the United States it is the better practice to sign only individual names; the firm names are not carried into the reports, and so might better be omitted.[62] It is not necessary to add the addresses of counsel. And the printed signature suffices, except that the first of the forty briefs or petitions required to be filed should be marked "Original" on the cover, and then should have the pen-and-ink signature of the first lawyer named added over his printed signature at the end of the brief proper.

To generalize: Read your court rules, and, when there is no specific rule, be guided by the practice followed by the leaders of the particular local bar.

Section 81. Reply briefs.—This is probably as convenient a juncture as any to discuss the problem of reply briefs.

The basic problem here is—whether to file. My own view is that, in general, reply briefs should be sparingly used.

    (a) Normally, when the issues are clearly drawn, don't file a reply brief; you only discourage the court by burdening it with more matter to read.

    (b) When the other side fuzzes up the issues, and you can reclarify the discussion by filing a short reply brief, it may well be helpful to do so.

    (c) When the other side raises an entirely new point, you are well advised to meet that new point in a reply brief.

    (d) When the court (or any member thereof) asks at the argument whether you intend to file a supplemental memorandum on a particular question, you must do so. Regardless of its tenor or form, such an inquiry is the equivalent of a command.

If you decide not to file, that solves the problem. If, on the other hand, you feel that a last word is imperative, be sure that your reply

---

[62] The emphasis is on "the name of a member of the bar of this court." See, e.g., Rule 27(9).

brief is short, that it is not a rehash simply going over the same ground, and, preferably, that it hits hard. For instance:

The company's brief on reargument, filed October 8, 19— (hereinafter cited as A.B. 2d Br.), fails almost completely to meet the contentions made in the Government's main brief on reargument (cited as U.S. 2d Br.). In addition, the company's brief at a number of places misstates the record.

We shall endeavor to deal, as summarily as possible, with the basic errors contained in that brief, and thereafter with the specific matters in it which seem in most urgent need of correction.

I. THE COMPANY'S BASIC MISCONCEPTIONS

The company's position rests upon three basic errors which reach to the heart of the case.

First.—The Company's brief throughout proceeds on the assumption that the Act of June 25, 19—, declares a common-law forfeiture. Yet, as we have shown at some considerable length (Point I, U.S. 2d Br. 60–79), that assumption is wholly without foundation. Our argument on that point is not met, and the legislative material adduced in support of our construction of the statute is entirely ignored. Indeed, the company in effect ignores everything in the Act except the word "forfeited," and proceeds to impress upon that word its own interpretation of a common-law forfeiture. This basic fallacy underlies the whole of the company's brief, and necessarily removes its arguments a considerable distance from the issues in the case.

*   *   *   *   *   *   *

The Company asserts (A.B. 2d Br. 43) that the United States took no exception to the finding that the sales were made to the highest and best bidders where the lands were situated. To the contrary, that finding was very specifically objected to before it was made (R. 593, Objection 2).

*   *   *   *   *   *   *

The Company urges (A.B. 2d Br. 51) that "The United States, with full knowledge, has waived all rights, if any, it ever had." No record references are cited in support of this assertion, and we think that none are available.

*   *   *   *   *   *   *

An equally bold assertion appears at A.B. 2d Br. 62, where it is said that the statement that second indemnity limits were laid down only at the request of the company is incorrect. Again no record reference is cited; and again the record (R. 805) proves the correctness of the Government's statement.

Section 82. After the reply brief.—Some lawyers are uneasy unless they have the last word; and, after brooding over the argument, decide to file still one more written document.

Some courts do not permit the filing of anything after the reply brief without special leave, and others similarly limit the filing of any document whatever after the argument. What, then, is the lawyer with the last-word-itch to do?

The best advice for this sort of impulse is: don't! Far better to write out what you have in mind, read it aloud to as sympathetic an audience as you can muster—and then relegate it to your file, circular or otherwise.

Post-argument filings are justified in only a rigidly limited class of instances—and their form depends on the rules and practice of the court in question. In the Supreme Court, a letter to the Clerk is acceptable— which is to say, it will not be bounced back for being in letter form. In many Courts of Appeals, on the other hand, a motion for leave to file must be affixed to anything at all submitted after oral argument. Checking with the clerk in advance in this connection may save much embarrassment.

In my view, there are only two instances in which the filing of additional material after the argument is justified:

(a) First, when the court at the argument has asked counsel for additional data of any kind. If a memorandum has been requested orally, then that document should so state. E.g., "Pursuant to the Court's request, etc.," or "Pursuant to permission granted at the argument of this cause, etc." In courts where letters to the clerk are in order, be sure to provide sufficient legible copies for every member of the court, and do not fail to send a copy to opposing counsel.

(b) Second, in the unusual situation where, in a supplemental memorandum filed by your opposition in the situation just mentioned, you find a whopping misstatement. Since there is no other way to reply, a motion for leave to file—or a letter to the clerk—is then in order. Flyspecks or minor errors had better be passed over as one of the unavoidable incidents of litigation; further reply is justified only when the misstatement is both material and significant.

An example of such a communication in the latter situation is set forth in the note below, exactly as it was written to the Clerk of the Supreme Court.[63] The Clerk later advised that copies were distributed to the Court; there was no reply from the other side.

---

[63] 8 March 1957

John T. Fey, Esq.,

Clerk,

Supreme Court of the United States,

Washington 13, D.C.

Re: *Reid v. Covert*, No. 701, O.T. 1955.

Kinsella v. Krueger, No. 713, O.T. 1955.

(continued)

But, in the more usual situation—desist. Normally this kind of final final-word won't be given much attention, and although it may make *you* feel better, it really won't advance your case.

Section 83. Petitions for rehearing.—Petitions for rehearing can be more poetically—and more accurately— labeled as "Love's Labor Lost." The normal petition for rehearing has about the same chance of success as the proverbial snowball on the far side of the River Styx; the stronger courts grant only a very few each Term— never more.

Dear Mr. Fey:

A particularly glaring misstatement of fact in the Government's "Supplemental Memorandum * * * Following Reargument" impels this communication.

At page 14 of that document it is stated that I misunderstood the Government's position as to the power of Congress to subject dependents of military personnel to trial by court-martial, and I am correctly quoted from page 70 of the Ward & Paul transcript of the oral argument as having said:

"Then I must confess I was amazed when the Solicitor General said that it is only a question of legislative judgment that any time Congress wants to subject the good ladies at Fort Myer to trial by courts martial, they can do so."

The Government fails to quote, from the same transcript, what the Solicitor Generally actually said which evoked the foregoing reply. Here are those passages (Ward & Paul transcript, page 14):

"The Chief Justice: How about the wives and other dependents of military personnel who live on a cantonment in this country; are they camp followers too in the sense that that book describes it?

"Mr. Rankin: I would think they would be under the sense of this book. I think that that is provided for otherwise by the question of whether they are in the field, and the fact that Congress has expressly provided that if they are not in the field, they are subject to the jurisdiction of the courts.

"The Chief Justice: Then does Congress say that dependents of military personnel in this country who live on a cantonment are in the military service and would be subject to court martial as these women are?

"Mr. Rankin: I think so far as power is concerned.

"The Chief Justice: Yes, I am talking about power.

"Mr. Rankin: The power is there."

I would not for a moment question the Solicitor General's right to correct what on more mature reflection appears to have been an improvident oral statement. It is doubtless his duty to recede from untenable positions. But I submit that this duty can be fully discharged without the present post-argument attempt to attribute error to opposing counsel by less than full disclosure in a printed brief of what the transcript of argument shows to have been actually said in open court.

Respectfully,

/s/ Frederick Bernays Wiener

Counsel for Appellee in No. 701

And the Respondent in No. 713

cc: Hon. J. Lee Rankin

In general, of course, a petition for rehearing is an utter waste of time, labor, and good white paper, particularly when the points you are contending for are fully set forth in a dissent, i.e., have already been considered by the court. The only real chance a petition for rehearing normally has is when there has been an intervening statute or decision,[64] or when it raises an issue of public importance not theretofore presented,[65] or, rarely, when, after the original argument, there had been an affirmance by an equally divided court.[66] (To illuminate these practical hurdles, an example of a rare, successful petition for rehearing is examined in Chapter 10.)

At the intermediate appellate stage, there is sometimes this virtue in a petition for rehearing: the time for certiorari is counted, not from the date of the original opinion, but from the date of the denial of rehearing.[67] Filing the petition, therefore, extends the time for your client to raise additional funds for the next appellate step, or increases the possibility that some other circuit may rule the other way and so produce a conflict. But—these apparent advantages frequently collide with the usual requirement that a petition for rehearing must have appended thereto a certificate of counsel to the effect that it is filed in good faith and not for purposes of delay.

Section 84. Use of models.—I have earlier suggested (Section 20, above) the utility of studying briefs written by leaders of the bar, so that you may learn how the masters of the business turn it off.

To the extent that the several forms you examine differ, to the extent that several lawyers of equal eminence and learning employ varying styles, use your own judgment, make up your own mind, and, in the words of a now hackneyed but essentially tragic phrase of the twenties, combine the best features of each.

Be careful, however, not to follow any forms blindly; therein lies the pitfall of the form book, of what one of my associates used to

---

[64] E.g., *Zap v. United States*, second petition for rehearing granted, 330 U.S. 800, after the intervening decision in *Ballard v. United States*, 329 U.S. 187. For an intervening statute, see Sioux *Tribe of Indians v. United States*, rehearing granted, 329 U.S. 684; *Alaska Juneau Gold Mining Co. v. Robertson*, rehearing granted, 331 U.S. 793.

[65] E.g., *Elgin, J. & E. R. Co. v. Burley*, 325 U.S. 711, 327 U.S. 661.

[66] When the original argument was heard before less than a full bench, reargument is not infrequently granted, as for example after Mr. Justice Jackson returned from the Nuremberg trial. But when there has been a disqualification, a petition for rehearing after affirmance by a divided court is rarely granted. A recent exception was *Marzani v. United States*, 335 U.S. 895, 336 U.S. 910, 336 U.S. 922—and there the judgment was, after reargument, reaffirmed by an equally divided court.

[67] See *Citizens Bank v. Opperman*, 249 U.S. 448, 450; *Craig v. United States*, 298 U.S. 637.

call the Sears Roebuck catalogue. Use the form of other folks' briefs intelligently and eclectically.

Section 85. Significance and importance of accuracy.—I will end the discussion of briefs by recurring to that tiresome obsession of mine, the importance of accuracy.

Nothing quite so destroys a court's confidence in a lawyer or in his brief as its finding that he has made inaccurate statements, either through carelessness or through design. That statement is true of the entire document. *Per contra,* a court will have complete faith in the briefs of any lawyer who has established his reputation for accuracy. The finest tribute paid Government lawyers by the Supreme Court is the circumstance that, when the judges want to know what the case is about, they turn first to the Statement of Facts in the Government's brief. Those briefs have acquired, over the years, a reputation for accuracy, and that reputation is as jealously guarded as personal honor—which in a very real sense it involves.

A brief should be written to persuade; it should pull no punches; but it must be honest, and it must be accurate.

Part III

ARGUING THE APPEAL

CHAPTER 6

Essentials of an Effective
Oral Argument

Section 86. Should you argue at all?—At this point it will be assumed that your brief has been filed, that it is in satisfactory shape, and that it contains a minimum of misprints and typographical errors. You are then faced with the problem whether to argue the case or to submit it on briefs.

Appellate judges, virtually without exception, say that a case should never be submitted without oral argument. A good many are on record in print to the same effect, and add that they feel a sense of genuine regret whenever the clerk announces that a case is being submitted on briefs alone.[1] These expressions are thoroughly genuine, and reflect the fact that the task of judgment is infinitely harder when counsel is not present to be questioned regarding his exact position, or to be asked how far he deems that the principle he contends for should extend. Just as the trial lawyer objects to an offer in evidence of an affidavit by saying, "I can't cross-examine that document," so an appellate judge knows that he cannot obtain from a printed brief the clarification of issues and positions that questioning of counsel will afford. More than that, as Mr. Justice Frankfurter once wrote after he had been on the Court upwards of fifteen years, "Oral argument frequently has a force beyond what the written word conveys."[2]

Consequently it will also be assumed that you are prepared to argue.

It may be, of course, that the appellant's case is so completely devoid of merit that you, representing the appellee, will never be called upon, or that you will be told by the presiding judge, as you

---

[1] See Loughran [Ch. J., N.Y. Ct. App.], *The Argument of an Appeal in the Court of Appeals*, 12 Ford. L. Rev. 1, 6; Wilkins [J., Mass., Sup. Jud. Ct.], *The Argument of an Appeal*, 33 Corn. L.Q. 40, 48; Hiscock [formerly Ch. J., N.Y. Ct. App.], *The Court of Appeals of New York: Some Features of Its Organization and Work*, 14 Corn. L. Q. 131, 139.

[2] *Rosenberg v. Denno*, 346 U.S. 371, 372.

move toward the lectern, "The Court does not desire to hear further argument." In that event it is better to accept victory gracefully than to attempt to inflict your eloquence on the tribunal notwithstanding. And there may be instances where it will be desirable, on behalf of the appellee, to say little or nothing.

For example, in one case petitioner's lawyer took such a battering from the court that it was obvious to everyone that the judgment below would be affirmed. Counsel for the respondent arose, bowed, and said, "If the Court please, I must apologize for an error in my brief. At page 39, second line from the bottom, the citation should be to 143 Federal Second and not to 143 Federal." He paused until the members of the court noted the correction, paused again when they looked up, toyed with his watch chain, and proceeded: "Unless there are any questions, I will submit the respondent's case on the brief"—and sat down. I have it on excellent authority that it was one of the most effective arguments ever heard by that Court.

But of course, that is the exceptional instance—and a risky technique. Normally it is well to assume that the court desires to hear argument unless it affirmatively indicates the contrary, and normally, also, too cavalier belittling of an opposing argument is apt to backfire. Certainly where the appeal is a discretionary one, by permission of the court, it is unwise to suggest that after all there is nothing in the case to argue about; by allowing the appeal, the court in effect has held otherwise. At any rate, so far as I am personally concerned, I prefer to get up and talk. (For me, that's half the fun, besides which it is probably safer from the point of view of the case.)

Section 87. List of the essentials.—The really essential features are:

(a) Appreciation of the purpose of advocacy.
(b) Not reading the argument.
(c) Application of the fundamentals of good public speaking.
(d) An effective opening.
(e) Clear statement of facts.
(f) Complete knowledge of the record.
(g) Thorough preparation.
(h) Attitude of respectful intellectual equality.
(i) Flexibility.

These essentials are discussed in order below. The finer points, i.e., those that make the difference between a really good argument and one that is merely adequate, are considered in Chapter 8.

Section 88. Appreciation of the purpose of advocacy.—What is it that a lawyer seeks to do when he argues a case on appeal? Is he there to make a flamboyant speech? Is he there to put on a show for a client? Or is he there to win the case? The last named, obviously, if only for the mundane reason that higher fees are paid—and, usually, additional retainers become available—to the successful advocate. (Not that the public practice of the law is essentially different; Government or State or County lawyers also all want to win; losing a case is fully as painful to public counsel's psyche as it is to private counsel's pocket.)

Perhaps one of the most penetrating discussions of what a lawyer should strive to do when arguing an appeal appeared in an obituary address written by Mr. Justice Frankfurter some years back on the occasion of the untimely death of one of his former law clerks.

> From the first he showed that the stuff of the advocate was in him, and by the time he left the Government, when the Supreme Court adjourned in June, 1952, he had fashioned himself into an accomplished practitioner of the art of persuasion. When he appeared at the lectern, erect and handsome, with an agreeable voice, serene rather than self-confident, tactful but firm, and always master of his case, the Court increasingly was assured of an argument that gave pleasure as well as enlightenment. He respected the traditions of the Supreme Court as a tribunal not designed as a dozing audience for the reading of soliloquies, but as a questioning body, utilizing oral arguments as a means for exposing the difficulties of the case with a view to meeting them. He held up his share of the probing process, and members of the Court were kept alert to observe the responsibilities of the questioner. It is fair to say that in a few short years Stanley Silverberg had attained a stature as an advocate matched by few lawyers coming before the Court, including the most eminent and experienced members of the Bar.[3]

Putting to one side for the moment the quality of the tribute, the significant point in the present connection is the Justice's definition of an advocate: "a practitioner of the art of persuasion." I emphasize that definition because of its importance, and because one would never dream from hearing some appellate arguments that they were being made to persuade a court to agree with the speaker.

The frequency with which counsel will fight a court, either generally or on specific unessential propositions, serves only to underscore the extent to which some lawyers overlook the obvious. One never persuades by antagonizing. You may take a dim view of a particular judge or of a particular decision, or of a whole series of decisions, or

---

[3] Frankfurter, *Of Law and Men* (1956), 321–322.

indeed of the prevailing trend of the particular court—but when you appear before that tribunal on behalf of a client—private, corporate, or public—your job is to win your client's case, not to tell off the court, or particular members of the court, or to go all out on any tack not necessary to the case.

I place first among the essentials, therefore, the truism that advocacy is the process of persuasion.

Section 89. Not reading the argument.—Never read your argument. *Never read your argument.* NEVER READ YOUR ARGUMENT.

Once a lawyer begins to read to the court, whether it is his formal written brief, or the set piece he has written out to constitute his text for the argument, he raises up a curtain between himself and the court. Talk to the court, don't read to them! It is really amazing how many lawyers of ability and reputation will write out an "oral" argument and then get up and read it to the court—and equally amazing how many courts will tolerate the practice.

There are not many phases of oral advocacy on which one is warranted in being quite dogmatic, but this is one of them: Don't read. It is wrong, all wrong. Occasional addresses, i.e., *Remarks on the Dedication of a Memorial to the Former Members of the Society*—something prepared for a particular occasion, where the form of every sentence counts and where there are no interruptions—those can and should be read. (Make sure, however, that even in that instance you read from the paper, and not *at* it.)

But in court, when you are engaging in argument, subject to instant, insistent (and frequently fairly constant) interruption, reading just doesn't go over. It raises a veil between the speaker and his auditors. No advocate worthy of the name will ever read his argument to the court—and if the unequivocal character of these statements leaves you unconvinced, just go to court some day and listen to the readers.

Not only that, but an oral argument loses much of its spontaneity if it is written out in advance. It is more natural—and hence more effective—if it is delivered from notes. Chapter 7 discusses the problem of how extensive those notes should be, and whether and to what extent they may safely be discarded altogether. The point made here is that the advocate should use his notes as a guide, not as a text.

Section 90. Application of the fundamentals of good public speaking. An effective appellate advocate must have an appreciation of and an ability to apply the fundamentals of good public speaking—and that does not mean oratory, because oratory is not necessary. An appellate court is not a jury. It may react like a jury, as witness the timelessness of the observation that hard cases make bad law, but it dislikes to be harangued as though it were in the box instead of on the bench. The play on an appellate court's emotions must be subtle and restrained if it is to be effective.

Nonetheless, an argument differs from a dinner table conversation; and although of course the present chapter does not and cannot purport to be a text on public speaking (any more than Chapter 3 is a manual on how to write good English), there are certain fundamentals that can be briefly stated.

(a) *You must be heard.* Once you are up on your feet, talk is the only medium by which you can communicate your thought to the court, and unless you can make yourself heard you are wasting your time and the court's time and are endangering your client's cause. If you are arguing to a bench of five, seven, or nine judges, the end men must be able to hear what you are saying.

It is all very noble to assert (as I have heard some earnest and upright young men say) that honesty precludes resort to any artificialities. The fact of the matter is that a certain degree of artificiality is necessary in order to convey a realistic likeness. Consider, for instance, actors in a play: In order to present to the audience the picture of persons sitting around a table talking quietly, the actors must themselves talk in a considerably louder tone of voice so that the people in the back of the theater may hear them; and in order that they may be seen, the actors, however manly, must put on grease paint and theatrical lipstick. Artificial? Yes, but without that kind of artifice the audience cannot obtain an impression of realism.

It is the same with a lawyer in an appellate courtroom—most of which have wretched acoustics. He must speak loudly enough so that he can be heard and understood.

(b) *You must use proper emphasis.* Here again, emphasis is a species of artifice; but the spoken word without emphasis would be as ineffective—and often as unintelligible—as the written word without punctuation or capitalization. A lawyer worthy of the name cannot afford to use the same tone for "This case comes here on appeal from a decree of the District Court for the Eastern District" as for "This is the gross and shocking fraud that was perpetrated by these respondents."

The matter of proper emphasis can be broken down into not more than four basic admonitions:

(i) *Avoid a monotone.* Perhaps the best way to attempt to reproduce a monotone in print is to set out a paragraph without punctuation: "At this point the shipper called on the railroad to deliver livestock directly to its siding but the railroad refused to do so contending that by reason of its contract with the stockyards it was bound not to deliver such competitive traffic over the track in question without the payment of yardage charges which yardage charges it was no longer willing to absorb and thereupon the shipper instituted its complaint against the railroad before the Commission." That sort of thing is just as difficult to follow by ear as by eye.

(ii) *Avoid the ministerial cadence.* Here the voice goes up and down but without emphasis on particular words, like this

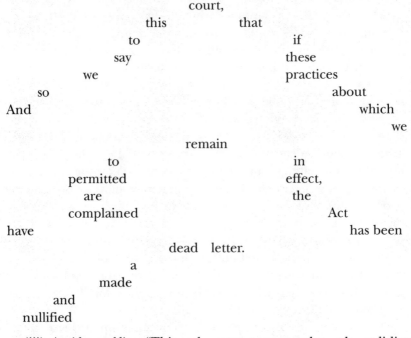

(iii) *Avoid mumbling.* "This—ah—case, turns on the—ah—validity of the—ah—Gadget Restriction Act of—ah—1958. We—that is, the petitioners—ah—contend—ah—that—the—measure—ah—clearly transcends—ah—the powers vested in the—ah—Congress." And so on, and so on.

(iv) *Use the pause.* The only way that an oral statement can be punctuated is by a pause—a short one for the commas (which, after all, are simply signals for a breath), a longer one at the end of sentences, and a still longer one when you reach the end of a paragraph. If you want more emphasis, as for instance to mark your taking up an entirely new point, underscore the pause and make it longer by taking a sip of water.

The pause is also helpful as a device to regain the court's attention. Sometimes the learned justices just aren't interested. Sometimes that is the fault of the case, more often it is the fault of the lawyer, and sometimes they just aren't paying attention anyway. They are whispering, and passing notes, and reading at the record. Your main proposition is coming up. How to make certain that it will have their full attention? Very simple; just use the public speaker's oldest trick: Pause. The sudden silence makes everyone look up, every member of the court eyes the speaker expectantly—and then you give them your big point. It's an ancient dodge, but still one of the most effective.

Section 91. An effective opening.—High on the list of essentials is the admonition to lodge effectively in the court's mind in the opening two minutes what the case involves, so that interest and understanding will be seized and held. This generally involves the use of a good opening sentence or paragraph. The important point to remember is that the first two minutes are critical, that counsel must catch and hold the court's interest and attention in that time. If he is for the appellant, he must give a thumbnail epitome of "what this case is all about." If he is for the appellee, he must in his opening sentence seize upon the central feature of the case, and, by driving it home, dispel the impression left by his adversary.

The opening should, after the technique of the newspaper account, tell the whole story in the first paragraph, after which it is time to go back and fill in the details. And, like the competent newspaper reporter, the advocate must never keep his audience in suspense; on the contrary, he must give his secret completely away right at the outset.

The process of formulating an effective opening is probably easier when the lawyer is topside, i.e., when he appears for the appellant or petitioner, because then he can work out and polish his opening well in advance. More flexibility is necessary when the advocate is bottomside; then, very frequently, he must improvise in order to be able to tie on to something said by the preceding speaker. In either event, counsel must avoid trivia—and, when he is the second man up, he must, however great the temptation and/or provocation, avoid personalities.

On the whole, I think a good opening is probably more important when the advocate is bottomside, for the appellee or respondent, because then the court is extremely anxious to get, in a nutshell, the gist of the reply to the argument it has been hearing for twenty, thirty, or forty-five minutes. The appellee's case sags perceptibly if counsel, facing this expectant bench, commences with a recital of minor corrections. The court is perhaps not equally alert when appellant rises, because at that point there is generally a certain amount of intellectual clearing of the throat, so to speak.

(a) Here are some examples of openings, drawn from my own practice and observation, that have held a court's attention:

(i) [For petitioner.]

Respondents were convicted by a jury of conspiring to defraud the United States of the disinterested services of one of its officers. Their judgments of conviction were reversed by the Second Circuit on four separate grounds, and the case is now here on certiorari.

Two of the questions, involving alleged errors on the part of the trial court, concern only the Bayers. Two concern only Radovich—whether a confession of his was admissible, and whether his plea of double jeopardy was a valid one. I shall deal with each of those questions separately in the course of the argument.

The basic facts can be briefly stated. Etc., etc., etc.[4]

Analytically, this opening does two things. First, "convicted by a jury" is pure semantics, resorted to in order to sway sympathy away from the respondents by appealing to that palladium of liberty, the twelve good men and true in the box. Second, it states the issues in a nutshell, so that the court has the bare outline of the case in mind, and will not ask impatient, interrupting questions while the basic facts are being developed.

(ii) [For petitioner.]

This case, which is here on certiorari to the Ninth Circuit, involves the protection to be accorded the Government–soldier relationship.[5]

That states the question concisely—and phrases it in such a way as to present the petitioner's contention, i.e., that there is something to be protected, as sympathetically as possible. (If the flag is to be waved effectively in an appellate court, the motion should be languid—as though the flagstaff were a fan.)

(iii) [For respondent.]

Two days after this Court's decision in the *Schwimmer* case, a bill was introduced in Congress to change the rule of naturalization there announced. Hearings were held on the bill, it was discussed on the floor—but it never got out of committee.

And on the first day that Congress was in session following this Court's decision in the *Macintosh* case, a similar bill was introduced in Congress to reverse

---

[4] *United States v. Bayer*, 331 U.S. 532.

[5] *United States v. Standard Oil Co.*, 332 U.S. 301.

the result in that case. Hearings were held on that bill, that bill was also discussed on the floor—and that bill never emerged from committee either. Indeed for eleven successive years, through six successive Congresses, the same bill was introduced and reintroduced—and Congress never saw fit to pass it.[6]

That opening focused attention on the strongest point in the Government's case, i.e., not that the *Schwimmer* and *Macintosh* decisions were right, but that they had subsequently been approved by Congress. That argument, as has been noted (Sections 49 and 68), did not prevail, but the substance of the opening found its way into a strong dissent written by the late Chief Justice.[7]

(iv) [For respondent.]

The question in this case is whether a good Nazi can be a good American.[8]

This was a denaturalization case, the first to reach the Supreme Court since the process of denaturalization had run afoul of the decisions in *Schneiderman v. United States*,[9] and *Baumgartner v. United States*.[10] It was far stronger for the Government than either of the other two, but I felt that I needed an opening that would really rock the Court on its heels, and make them sit up and take notice. This opening did just that, and the *Knauer* denaturalization was sustained.

(b) It may also be helpful to set down an example or two of how not to do it.

(i) [For petitioner.]

This case comes here on certiorari to review a judgment of the Circuit Court of Appeals for the Eleventh Circuit which reversed an order of the District Court for the Western Caroline Islands that dismissed a bill of complaint for lack of federal jurisdiction.

The facts involve an action for damages brought by a native chieftain of those islands against a medical officer in the Navy etc., etc., etc.

The first paragraph is unintelligible orally (and not too easy to understand in writing). The second launches directly into the facts. It will be some time before the court learns what questions are involved. They will either lose interest—or else interrupt. Sometimes judges are reduced to prying the facts out of counsel by a species of cross-examination, which means that counsel isn't doing his job—and isn't helping his case.

---

[6] *Girouard v. United States*, 328 U.S. 61.

[7] See 328 U.S. at 73–74.

[8] *Knauer v. United States*, 328 U.S. 654.

[9] 320 U.S. 118.

[10] 322 U.S. 665.

In this particular situation, the whole matter could have been very simply and clearly presented as follows:

This case is here on certiorari to the Eleventh Circuit, and involves the question whether an action for damages arising out of an alleged false imprisonment, said to be in violation of the constitutional guaranty of due process of law, states a cause of action within federal jurisdiction in the absence of diversity of citizenship. Otherwise stated, the single issue is whether an action seeking damages for a tort involves a federal question whenever the tort is alleged to have been committed in violation of a constitutional provision.

The facts alleged in the complaint and in the affidavits submitted on the motion for summary judgment are as follows: etc., etc., etc.

When the opening is thus presented, the court knows at the outset just what the question is, and will listen to the facts with some appreciation of their relevance.

(ii) Here is an example of how counsel for a respondent can make or break his case at the outset:

Action by the United States to recover public money paid out through mistake of law and in reliance on the defendant appellant's fraudulent representations. Appellant's counsel is questioned by the court just before he sits down.

Judge X: "Are there any facts reflected in the present record which were not before the officers of the government in 1923 and 1924 when the payments were made?"

Appellant's counsel: "No." [He sits down.]

Respondent's counsel: "May it please the Court: This case involves an interesting question regarding the scope of judicial review of the acts of administrative officers. Etc., etc., etc."

And the case sags. What respondent's counsel could have said with the record he had was this:

May it please the Court: I will undertake to answer from the record the question just put to Mr. Y.

There are many facts reflected in this record that were not before the departments concerned when the payments were made.

To begin with, appellant said in 1923 and 1924 that he always believed he had been an American citizen. But this record shows that he swore under oath in 1912 and again in 1914 that he was a subject of Germany, and the record shows that the government officers who passed on his claim were not aware of his earlier inconsistent statements.

And appellant said in 1923 and 1924 that he was an American who was detained in Germany by a sick wife. But appellant swore in 1912 that he was a resident of Germany, and in 1914 that he was a nonresident of America—and here again the officers passing on his claim did not know of his earlier representations to the contrary. Etc., etc., etc.

Such a beginning would electrify the court. First, it effectively undermines appellant's presentation, because it points up the inaccuracy of that presentation. Second, it shows that appellant was a wicked man. (Fraud always sways a court, whether the opinion turns on fraud or not.) So long as it is relevant and not simply dragged in by the ears as an abusive personality, it always makes an impression; and a case that analytically may be one of dry-as-dust administrative law very often turns, in fact, on the circumstance that a decision one way would favor the fraudulent party, whereas a decision the other way would strip him of his ill-gotten gains.

Respondent's counsel in fact got three votes out of six—enough for his purposes, since the judgment below was in his favor. But with a proper opening he would have been arguing in an entirely different atmosphere, and might well have got all six.

Section 92. Clear statement of facts.—"The great power at the bar is the power of clear statement!" If that expression standing alone seems unduly sententious, just listen some day to a really able lawyer outlining a complicated fact situation to a court or jury, and compare his exposition with the efforts of some garrulous dowager at the bridge table to explain just what happened to the girls at the last big country club dance. The lawyer states the essentials first, then develops and unfolds the details; the dowager runs on endlessly and repetitiously, expounding whole masses of trivia.

But it is not a matter of circumstance, or even of lack of training. Everyone knows that there are innumerable lawyers who always start with the dreary details, or who attempt to state a case by carefully embroidering the periphery at the outset.

No matter how complicated a set of facts may be, it can always be presented in its simple essentials. Mr. Justice Brandeis used to say, "There isn't anything in the world that can't be explained to a jury"—a comment that really stands as a challenge to every lawyer.

Now, how to go about this business of explaining a set of facts? First, ask yourself: How would you try to learn it? What would you want to know first? What would you want to know next? After that it is simply a matter of explaining the same things in the same order to the court.

Bear in mind always the basic psychological fact that knowledge is cumulative, and work from your essentials outward toward the details. Start with the trunk, take up the branches next, and end with the leaves. Or, in more concrete terms, always headnote your arguments. It is much easier for the court to follow you if you give them an oral outline, not only for the facts, but for the law as well.

Suppose you were retained as counsel by another lawyer: How would you want him to explain his case to you? If you know that, all you need to do is to restate the matter to the court in the same way.

Below, in Sections 110 and 111, are discussed certain of the fine points connected with the process, as, for instance, the elimination of unnecessary details and the necessity for sketching the picture in clear, broad strokes after it has been outlined. Here is considered only the immediate essential, namely, will the court—or any listener—know what the case is about when you have finished stating the facts? If the answer is a resounding "Yes!," you are ready to pass to preparing the legal portion of your argument. If the answer is anything less than that, you had better work over the facts some more.

Bear in mind also that you cannot cross-reference in an oral argument. Specifically, suppose you have a case involving two unrelated points. In the brief, you will set out, under your Statement of Facts, the facts bearing on point A and follow them with the facts relating to point B. The brief then continues with the law on point A, followed by the law on point B, and if any reader wonders about the facts as to B at that juncture, all he need do is turn back a few pages. In other words, your order in writing is *FA, FB, LA, LB,* where *F* = facts and *L* = law.

But if you argue the case orally in the same way, the court will find such a presentation confusing in the extreme, and this is particularly so if there have been questions regarding *LA.* It is impossible to cross-reference by ear, even for the most acute, and if you are facing even a single judge whose mental uptake is on the slow side, his questions born of honest confusion will completely disrupt your presentation. In the case put, the only sound way to present the case is to state the facts as to A, mention that you are deferring the other facts until you reach B, and then argue *LA* where it logically belongs, i.e., after the facts out of which it arises. Next you take up *FB,* followed by *LB,* and, once again, everyone is able to follow you.

The same is true in a case involving numerous unrelated points. For instance, in *United States v. Bayer,*[11] four questions were involved, two of which concerned the Bayers and two Radovich. The first had to do with the admissibility of a confession made by Radovich, and the second with the availability of Radovich's plea of

---

[11] 331 U.S. 532.

double jeopardy. Point Three was whether the trial judge properly exercised his discretion in refusing to permit the Bayers to introduce additional evidence four hours after the jury had retired, and Point Four involved the question whether the trial judge's concededly accurate charge was so cryptic as to require reversal. Even in the brief, we preceded each point under the argument with a summary of the facts bearing upon it. At the oral argument, the Government's case, after being set out in general outline, was divided up so that the facts bearing on each point immediately preceded the legal argument on that point. Or, using the symbols already employed: General statement, *FA, LA, FB, LB, FC, LC, FD, LD.*

Section 93. Complete knowledge of the record.—If I were asked to name the advocate's secret weapon—a weapon, indeed, that remains a secret to many—I should say that it is complete knowledge of the record. In this field, preeminently, knowledge is power, and in this field, also, forensic reputations painstakingly established can be thrown away by a single lazy lapse. No lawyer, no matter how able he may be, can afford to argue any case in ignorance of the record. It is done, of course, but it is risky; it never results in a really good argument; and whenever any lawyer gets to the point of believing that he no longer needs to know his record, then hardening of the forensic arteries has set in.

Of course, experience begets a familiarity with the learning process, and an old hand can pick up—and pick out—the essentials of a record far more easily than a tyro. But the lad who really knows his facts is a far more dangerous opponent even on his first time up than the polished veteran of hundreds of appellate arguments who has given the record a glib once-over-lightly. I have seen lawyers of reputation utterly demolished in a courtroom when they went free-wheeling away from a record they obviously had not read, and were then caught up short by opposing counsel who knew it inside out. The otherwise gentle visages of appellate judges harden perceptibly when such misstatements are exposed. A lawyer simply has no business getting up to talk about a case he does not thoroughly know.

There are a number of aids to learning a record. First of all, read it. Don't rely on abstracts. Read it yourself. If the case is going to turn on facts, if the other side is going to attack findings in your favor, if the litigation has any complexity at all, there is just no escape from that harsh solution. The admonition to read the record may be a counsel of perfection, but no painless substitute for it has yet been invented.

Second, reread the critical portions. Here again, there is no softly padded, anesthetized road to learning.

Third, tab the record with index tabs, so that you can readily find any material portion without thumbing through it or looking in the index. The details of this process are discussed below in Section 100. Tabbing in order to learn the record is principally valuable in assisting you to envisage its scope and in viewing the case in outline.

Fourth, the record will stick in your mind more firmly when you write the brief yourself. When you do that, the case becomes a part of you more than when you simply soak up a brief that someone else has written. But very frequently, whether in governmental or private practice, the brief (or at least a finished first draft) will have been written by another hand, so this may be another counsel of perfection.

Fifth, a good memory helps. Some people are born with what a friend of mine used to call a flypaper mind—everything sticks. It's a distinct advantage to a lawyer to have one, just as it is a distinct advantage to a woman to be born beautiful or a man to be hand-some. But memory can be trained—just as, unless the advertisers are wholly wrong, people can be beautified.

At any rate, when you get up to argue your case, you must know your record better than the court does, because the court relies on counsel to present the facts. You must do the exploratory work; no court is going to plow through thousands of printed pages to find the critical bit of testimony that will win your case. And no court is going to think much of your argument or be impressed by your knowledge of the case if, when a judge asks you a simple question—"Where is the order of the Commission in the record?" "Where is the final contract as agreed upon by the parties?"—you stand there fumbling, unable to put your finger on the vital documents. The judges become impatient, you will feel embarrass-ment, the client sitting in the courtroom isn't going to think well of you at all—and if opposing counsel stage-whispers to you, "Page 28," that isn't just kindness of heart on his part. Rather, it is a signal to the court that, if they want to learn about this case, he is the one they had better ask, not you.

Section 94. Thorough preparation.—No lawyer would dream of filing with the clerk the first rough draft of his brief. Why then pres-ent to the court the first draft of your oral argument? Many lawyers, too many of them, do just that—which is why such a lot of sorry oral arguments are heard in courts of appeal throughout the land.

There are, of course, some virtuosos, some people who have a flair for the extemporaneous. If you are one of those fortunate few, the paragraphs that follow are not for you. But if you are a simple, run-of-the-mill fellow, like the rest of us, a carefully rehearsed and prepared and revised presentation will always be better than one that is just rolled off the cuff.

Preparation and rehearsal will save you from going off on unprofitable or even untenable side issues, will spare you the waste of precious minutes on nonessentials, and will substantially assist you in eliminating unhappy turns of phrase.

I myself feel that I must go over what I am to say if only for one reason: to time my remarks. There is something inexorable about the ticking of that courtroom clock, particularly when a firm judge is presiding. When your time is up, when the Chief Justice leans over and says, "Your time has expired"—well, you sit down. The stories told of Chief Justice Hughes—that "on one occasion he called time on a leader of the New York Bar in the middle of the word 'if,'" and that "once on being asked by the same gentleman how much time remained, he replied, with beard bristling, "'14 seconds,'"[12]—may be apocryphal, but they contain more than a germ of truth. Consequently, you had better know before you start just how much or how little time your direct presentation will take. If you have three points, and can only cover two in your 45 or 60 minutes, revision is imperative— and you had better make that discovery before you address the court.

But, apart from timing, I feel that repeating what I want to say is helpful in many other respects. In going over the case orally, I generally think of other points to make. Questions arise in my mind that must be checked, questions of fact and of law alike. I progress gradually to a smoother presentation, and can sense what to stress, what to eliminate, where to expand, and where to compress.

More than that, by practicing the oral argument several times, it becomes fixed in my mind so that when I appear in court I no longer need detailed notes, but can rely with assurance on headings and subheadings. I thus avoid the need for elaborate notes that tempt one into reading, or nearly reading, the argument.

If possible, I plan to go over the argument two or three times. That is often enough to get the context of the contentions in mind, to smooth out the more obvious infelicities, and to learn precisely just how many precious minutes I am using; yet I have not so

[12] McElwain, *The Business of the Supreme Court As Conducted by Chief Justice Hughes*, 63 Harv. L. Rev. 5, 17 (1949).

over-rehearsed as to sound in court as if I had committed my argument to memory.

The result is, by the time I get up in the courtroom with my striped pants neatly pressed, the court hears, not my first draft, but my fourth. Frequently that draft still leaves a good deal to be desired—but at least it is a much more finished performance than the first.

Section 95. Planning the argument.—Not only must you prepare your argument so that it will fit into the allotted time, you must plan its absence as well. This breaks down into four major aspects.

(a) *Selection of Points.* What points are you going to make? Are you going to repeat what was said by other counsel in the related case just ahead of you? Are you going to stress the points that the other side virtually concedes? Or are you going to argue at length some unimportant issues that are very much in dispute? A lot of lawyers choose some or all of these alternatives—which is another reason for the paucity of good arguments.

Planning in this area involves elimination, but a different kind of elimination than the process of cutting weak points out of your brief. When you plan your oral argument, the weak points have already been taken out of your case, and you now must decide which of the points that remain you had better relegate to the briefs, and which you will discuss orally. Never be afraid to say, "The remaining points are not abandoned, but in view of the limited time, we rest those on our brief."

(b) *Avoiding Unnecessary Complexity.* Any argument planned to cover too many points will leave a fuzzy impression. An argument in its essential outline must be kept relatively simple, else it will fail to leave with the court a feeling that the case should be decided in a particular way.

It is far better to cover the really important points orally so as to make a firm impression and then to yield back some of your time, than to use up all of your time to treat all of your points and then leave the court up in the air. As Mr. Justice Jackson wrote, "The impact of oral presentation will be strengthened if it is concentrated on a few points that can be simply and convincingly stated and easily grasped and retained."[13]

(c) *Avoiding Improper Emphasis.* Most cases present a mixture of questions; some are easy, some are difficult—often very difficult.

---

[13] Jackson, *Advocacy Before the Supreme Court: Suggestions for Effective Case Presentations,* 37 A.B.A.J. 801, 803.

Suppose you have two issues, one in each category. Why stress the hard one when you can win your case on the one that avoids a great many difficulties? Of course, even after arguing some difficult, not to say untenable propositions, you may win in the end. But why go at it the hard way? At any rate, one of the subjects for planning is to select the easier points for the argument, the ones that will generate less opposition from the court.

(d) *Arguing Principles.* Finally, when you are on your feet, argue principles, and argue them broadly. Leave the details of the decisions to your brief, where they can be more helpfully discussed. Effecting that differentiation will be an important feature of your planning.

None of this, of course, means that you can be sure of following your plan. Again to quote Mr. Justice Jackson,

> I used to say that, as Solicitor General, I made three arguments of every case. First came the one that I planned—as I thought, logical, coherent, complete. Second was the one actually presented—interrupted, incoherent, disjointed, disappointing. The third was the utterly devastating argument that I thought of after going to bed that night.[14]

This from the man of whom Mr. Justice Brandeis said that he should be Solicitor General for life![15] But—and here is a question for the rest of us—what chance would an advocate have who had never planned his argument in the first place?

Section 96. Attitude of respectful intellectual equality.—Another essential of an effective argument is a proper mental attitude on the part of the advocate.

(a) It will not do to say of a court, as one may perhaps say of one's spiritual advisers, "They will show us our errors." Because if a judge asks, "Where does this power end?" and counsel answers, "That is for this court to say," then, inevitably, the judge will reply, "I am asking for guidance." (I once heard just precisely this colloquy in the Supreme Court of the United States.) Moreover, if the lawyer approaches a court with an appreciation that amounts to awe, perhaps verging into fear, he will not be able effectively to stand up to the court's questioning. Counsel simply cannot afford to have a litter of intellectual kittens in the courtroom while he is arguing his case—certainly not if he expects to win it for his client. I have myself witnessed case after case being lost, cases that could have been won, basically because counsel was so terrified of the

---

[14] *Ibid.*
[15] Frankfurter, *Of Life and Men* (1956), 192.

tribunal and so in awe of its individual members that their questions threw him completely off balance, and, through the mere fact of being asked, quite disabled him from answering. If you set out to argue an appeal, you must be able to engage in give-and-take with the court. They can point out errors only as errors are pointed out to them.

(b) By the same token, it will not do to talk down to a court, however much the individual advocate may have been more generously endowed with quick perception than some of the judges whom he addresses. Sometimes the lawyer's attitude of superiority rests simply on his own keen sense of self-appreciation. On other occasions its basis may be a view widely prevalent at the bar that old Judge Overshoe just isn't very bright. And on other occasions the lawyer may feel that he is such an outstanding expert in the particular field of law involved in his case that he is the professor and the judges simply students—not particularly bright students at that—who are listening to an expository lecture. But, whatever the explanation in any given situation, such an attitude is wrong. It is wrong as a matter of protocol, because the theory is that the judiciary is superior to the bar. And it is particularly wrong as a matter of advocacy, because advocacy is the art of persuasion, and you do not, by talking down to him, ever persuade a man who has the power to decide against you.

(c) The only proper attitude is that of a respectful intellectual equality. The respectful part of it is the same quantum and manner of respect that a younger man should show when speaking to an older one, or a junior officer in the military service when engaged in official discussion with a superior much senior to him, or a parishioner talking to a priest, or the law clerk taking up a point of law with the senior partner. Beyond that, however, the argument of an appeal must be undertaken by the advocate on the basis that it is a discussion among equals, whether the argument is made directly or in response to questions from the bench. Counsel must stand up to the judges quite as he would stand up to the senior members of his own firm. If he permits himself to be overawed by comments or questions simply because they emanate from judges, if he proceeds on the footing that a chance, offhand remark from the bench is sacrosanct because of its origin and without regard to its intrinsic merits, if he becomes completely unnerved by a judge saying, "Well now, I don't know about that," then he—and his case—are well on their way to being lost.

Section 97. Flexibility.—An appellate argument is not a set piece. For one thing, it is in most courts far from being a monologue, and for another it must be adjusted and trimmed according to the reaction it evokes.

Naturally, counsel must make allowance for questions (and, if topside, for rebuttal) when he plans his argument. If the rules of court permit only 45 minutes on a side, and judges are prone to ask questions, then, unless the direct presentation is kept to 30 minutes, counsel will simply not, in the ordinary course, be able to cover all his points.

In the Supreme Court of the United States, unless the case is on the summary docket or comes up on certificate or additional time has been allowed, the limit is 60 minutes on a side. There, the Justices ask many, many questions. Consequently, any lawyer who appears for a petitioner or an appellant must plan a direct presentation of not over 40 minutes. Beyond that, he has no assurance that he will ever be able to reach everything he needs to say. Moreover, if the questioning takes up a great deal of his time—more than he has made allowance for, he must telescope and thus eliminate subsidiary points. He may, of course, conceivably get an additional allowance of time by reason of the Court's having used up a great deal of his assigned time. That has varied in the past, largely with the individual reaction of Chief Justices; some have sympathized with counsel, others have had more sympathy with the clock. The governing principle has been that counsel is not entitled, as of right, to compensation for time taken by judicial eminent domain.

Therefore, the lawyer must have the essentials of his case so firmly in mind that, whenever his time is in fact cut down, he will know where and what to cut, so that, by the time he must sit down, he will have covered all the vital points. It is not an easy process, particularly when the argument as finally prepared is already a drastically pruned production; and, absent such preliminary trimming and cutting, it is, of course, well-nigh hopeless.

Sometimes, in the case of a split argument, counsel can reframe his remarks overnight, or during the recess. But he must be prepared to make his revisions on a substantially extemporaneous basis.

Counsel must also be sufficiently flexible to vary his argument on the basis of the reception it receives. If he has planned to spend, say, ten minutes on Proposition A, and finds that his initial statement thereof gets nods of approval from the bench, he need not—indeed, he should not—proceed to elaborate that proposition further. He should move on to Proposition B. If his statement of that second principle evokes a similar attitude of assent, he should once more move on. If the court does not react, he should proceed to elaborate upon the bare statement. And if he encounters doubts or active opposition, he may have to expand and detail his argument on Proposition B far beyond what he had originally planned.

Sometimes these alternative contingencies can be planned far in advance by setting up one's notes on each point in three parts: the basic proposition, its elaboration, and its further elaboration. Then, depending on the reaction from the court, the lawyer can use one, two, or all three portions.

It is perhaps easier, though quite as important, to be similarly flexible when appearing bottomside. If counsel for the appellant has had stormy going on Proposition A, counsel for the appellee is wasting not only his time but the court's as well if he belabors the argument that Proposition A is simply not so. The mere statement should suffice, since the court obviously is on appellee's side. And more time will be available to argue down Proposition B, as to which the court's reaction appeared favorable to appellant.

It is not easy to attain the necessary flexibility. (If it were, anyone could do it.) But it is, I am convinced, essential to effective argument.

CHAPTER 7

Suggestions for Preparation
for Oral Argument

Section 98. In general.—How should you go about preparing for the oral argument of a case on appeal? Preparation is essential, as anyone will soon find out if he ventures to argue a case without preparation. This chapter will discuss the several aspects of the process, and will set out some approaches and methods that I have found helpful in my own practice. Here, preeminently, the question of which is the best method depends upon the personality and personal characteristics of the advocate; methods one lawyer finds helpful may not be so for any other lawyer. The best method is the one that best enables the particular advocate to attain his maximum effectiveness. But the problem can be expressed and discussed in terms applicable to all lawyers and to all cases. For the rest, my justification for treating particular methods is that the discussion will at least be suggestive, and that, here also, the methods which have helped one lawyer may similarly be of assistance to others.

Section 99. Analysis of the problem of preparation.—The task of preparation involves essentially three phases. First is attaining mastery of the case, becoming thoroughly familiar with the facts, the applicable law, and the implications of both. Next is the process of compressing that mastery within the confines of the medium, i.e., within the allotted time, so that the essentials can be orally conveyed to the court. Finally, there is the matter of preparing the necessary notes, as an aid to memory while actually up on one's feet. These three aspects of the basic task will be discussed in order.

Section 100. Mastery of the case through tabbing of record and briefs.—One very helpful aid to learning a record, already suggested above in Section 93, is to tab the record with index tabs, so that any material portion can be found without thumbing through the pages or looking in the index.

Nothing is more awkward or embarrassing in open court than that long and painful pause that takes place when a lawyer is trying to find a critical document in a record. He thumbs through it, and gets flustered and nervous; co-counsel do the same; and the court gets annoyed and impatient. Their time is being wasted by the delay—by this so thoroughly unnecessary delay. With a tabbed record, counsel need not waste a minute of his time or of the judges'; he can turn instantly to whatever matter is in question.

At the preparatory stage, tabbing is even more valuable, because it places the elements of the case in their proper perspective; it enables the lawyer who first comes into the case on appeal to get the feel and the relative position of the pleadings and of the testimony. This is particularly so in a case of any length or complexity.

I generally tab all the more important pleadings, all the witnesses (except possibly some of the purely formal ones who can be lumped together under a single heading), and all the more important appellate stages.

Thus, in the *Haupt* treason case,[1] an intricate criminal appeal with a record running to 958 printed pages, the following items were tabbed; they are given here in the order in which they appeared in the record:

Indictment; charge; motion for new trial; sentence; defendant's exceptions; assignment of errors; opening arguments; testimony of two witnesses; colloquy involving a charge of perjury on the part of a witness; testimony of each of some 28 witnesses, some of whom (e.g., several F.B.I. agents testifying to the same point) were lumped together; motion for directed verdict; testimony of each of four defense witnesses; colloquy re overt acts; colloquy re instructions to jury; court's draft of instructions; prosecution's requests for instructions; defendant's requests for instructions; closing arguments; jury's return; rereading of testimony; charge re rereading; verdict; bill of exceptions; evidence on insanity issue; C.C.A. opinion; C.C.A. dissent; petition for rehearing; reply to petition for rehearing; dissenting opinion on denial of rehearing.

All told, including recalled witnesses, this ran to some 64 separate tabs.

In the *Line Material* case,[2] a long and complicated antitrust suit with a record of 2,340 printed pages, the following items were tabbed:

Complaint; answers of each of 11 defendants; interrogatories; three stipulations; testimony of each of 11 witnesses; opinion of the district court; findings;

---

[1] *Haupt v. United States*, 330 U.S. 631.

[2] *United States v. Line Material Co.*, 333 U.S. 287.

final decree; motion to amend findings; order denying motion; assignment of errors.

There were several hundred exhibits, handled as follows: separate tabs for each of 25 Government exhibits, i.e., G X 1, G X 26, G X 51, through G X 476; one tab for the last one (G X 498) and one for G X 400, a large tabulation out of order; a separate tab for each group of defendants' exhibits, marking the larger groups in intervals of 25 exhibits each. In addition, each cross-license agreement involved in the proceeding was separately tabbed. In all, there were some 89 separate tabs for the entire record of the case.

Naturally no such elaborate apparatus is required in order to absorb and learn a short record, but even in the very thinnest of records tabbing is helpful at the argument in facilitating reference to significant portions or particular pages without fumbling. And see Section 116, below, for the tabbing of quotations that are to be read to the court.

Section 101. Mastery of the case through reading and rereading of pertinent materials.—I have already discussed above, see Section 93, the indispensable if harsh method of learning a record: reading it, and then rereading its critical portions. The problem at the present juncture, however, is the more immediate one of preparation for oral argument. Assuming that you have a fair knowledge of the case already, how can you bring that knowledge into sharper focus for the supreme test of oral argument—the final examination, the time when you must know it, the final event to which all else has been building up?

It will generally be most helpful if you start your final preparation by sitting down and reading all the briefs, consecutively and slowly. In that way you acquire a working grasp of the arguments on both sides, soaking up the elements of the case until you become as familiar with them as you were when you wrote your brief. If someone else wrote the brief, and you contributed little more than your signature, then necessarily this part of your preparation will take longer.

Next, reread the leading decisions on which both of the parties rely. Here again, if this is your first glance at the briefs, your preparation will take longer. But even if you wrote every word of your side's brief by yourself, and looked up all the law single-handedly, you will still find it helpful to go over the controlling authorities. Frequently a last rereading will be productive of values and emphases that just never occurred to you earlier. And of course, if you are dealing with a brief that someone else wrote, you may be able to get from your reading of the decisions thoughts that never suggested themselves even to the able colleagues or juniors who did the research and writing. In either event, however, rereading of the cases as the day of the argument approaches is a must if you are to be properly prepared.

It is not necessary to read every case cited in the brief, at least not after you attain a certain familiarity with the process of advocacy. One's first argument—that is different. The eager beaver lawyer on his first time up will have read and reread every citation, even the statutory provision under which the appeal was taken, and will probably carry into the courtroom an abstract of every case cited. I am not ashamed to admit that I did just that the first time I had a case to argue in the Supreme Court of the United States. And I knew many Assistant Attorneys General who invariably prepared for argument by setting one or more juniors in their division to preparing such abstracts for their use.

I don't feel that this is really necessary for an advocate of any experience. First of all, with experience one gets the feel of a case, and can judge which are the critical authorities, i.e., those on which the case will turn, and those concerning which the court will ask questions. Those are really the only ones that need to be thoroughly studied—and if you don't know those when you are on your feet, the abstracts so laboriously prepared by your juniors won't help you. As for the others—well, in the unlikely event that some judge should ask, "What were the facts in *Jones v. Schmaltz?*," you can always take refuge in, "Well, your Honor, I don't recall them now, but I do know that that case supports the proposition for which we have cited it, namely, that post-mortem declarations are inadmissible." It is far more profitable to employ your time in rereading and learning the controlling decisions than in reading and learning the collateral ones.

The critical portions of the record should similarly be reread. You must know the opinion below, or the decree, or the findings, or the commission's order—the points on which your case turns. You must have mastered those. Similarly, you must be familiar with the crucial portions of the testimony. The rest of it is not so important. And, of course, with experience you will learn which portions are, and which are not, vital in the particular case.

Section 102. Rehearsal; Compressing the case into workable compass.—One judge of my acquaintance once told me that in his judgment the art of the advocate lay in a lawyer's mastering the case without letting the case master the lawyer. You must compress your case into workable compass, so that you can present it within the allotted time and still leave a positive impression when you sit down. That process involves compression, emphasis, and elimination— and to be certain that you have succeeded in your endeavor you must go over your presentation. In short, you must rehearse your argument, so that the court will hear a finished draft of oral argument and not simply a first rough.

I have already indicated (see Section 94, above) the principal reasons why rehearsal is necessary: to time one's remarks, to smooth out infelicities, to ascertain where to expand and what to eliminate. In the following sections will be discussed some of the methods of rehearsing.

Section 103. Rehearsal; Informal methods.—I always find it extremely helpful to engage in informal rehearsal. Even while the briefs are still in a very formative state, I find it helpful to discuss the case with all comers. (Since the record is settled by this time, there is no question of revealing professional confidences.) I discuss the case with anyone who will listen (and probably with some who would prefer not to), at lunch, or in the course of conversation, or while bending the elbow over the beer or better—and, by all means, with people who reflect all sorts and shades of opinion, in order to obtain as wide a variety of reactions and to evoke as many objections as possible. If my case involves an antitrust question, I want the big business point of view as well as that of the trust-busting crusaders. If it turns on an interpretation of the Bill of Rights, I want the reactions not only of the libertarian Children of the Dawn, but also of those who subscribe to the more rugged give-'em-a-fair-trial-and-hang-'em school of thought. Those of your listeners who come up with objections as you expound your views will force you to devise new arguments that you may have overlooked until then. The more shades of opinion you can sample, the slimmer the possibility that you will be caught flat-footed or taken by surprise when you actually argue.

This method of informal discussion is also helpful in assisting you to evolve an intelligible and effective statement of facts. Whenever someone asks, "What's this next case of yours really about?," you have an opportunity to rehearse a brief thumbnail exposition. And when you have explained your case to people at lunch in such simple terms that they can follow you between gulps of that day's Blue Plate Special, you are well on your way toward being able to explain it to a court. By the time *they* understand you, any court will.

Section 104. Rehearsal; Formal methods.—The foregoing helps you to work out arguments, to formulate effective phrasing, and to block out the essentials of your statement of facts. But the time will come when more formal methods are necessary, if only to ascertain how much time you are using.

There are three or four methods most generally used, and of course no single one works well with every person. Some lawyers prefer to try out their preliminary efforts on their spouses. Others inflict it on a moot court of generous friends. Still others undertake the task in decent seclusion, preferably at night, when one is neither disturbed nor disturbing. And a fourth method is to use a sound tape or similar recording device, and then play back one's golden words. As I say, no particular method will work well for every person.

The moot court method is considered very helpful by many lawyers, and so it is—provided that the members of the moot court ask questions to develop the critical points in the case, and not simply to inject witticisms. The real difficulty with this method is that the moot court just never thinks of the questions that the real court will ask the next day; it is difficult, if not impossible, to prophesy just what questions will be asked from the bench, even by judges whose general outlook is fairly predictable.

A variant on the moot court method is to find an audience of one, preferably a lawyer with appellate experience, who will listen as you go through your argument. His comments and criticisms will be helpful to you in polishing up the next draft.

Still another method is to talk into a recording device and to play it back. This method has many obvious advantages—although its use may be somewhat disconcerting, for it is probably correct to say that the most unsettling experiences a person can have are the first glimpse of one's own profile and the first time one really hears one's own voice.

For myself, I prefer to go over my notes in decent privacy, all the way from "May it please the Court" down through "We therefore submit that the judgment below should be reversed." I note the moment of beginning, to time the argument, and speak right up. Then I revise my notes, expanding, eliminating, altering, and changing emphasis wherever necessary.

Section 105. Notes for argument.—When your case is called for argument and you get up, what sort of notes should you place on the lectern before you? Should you have your argument written out, neatly arranged in a loose-leaf binder? Is it better to have informal notes instead, which may be either extensive or fragmentary? Or should you venture to argue without any notes at all?

This is another field where, preeminently, individual aptitudes and habitudes govern. Nonetheless, there are some general observations that can usefully be ventured.

(a) *Argument fully written out?* I have no hesitation at all in saying "No," emphatically "No," to the suggestion that an argument be written out in full. If your argument is fully written out, you will read it, and reading one's argument is high on the list of Things Not to Be Done. See Section 89, above. Again, if what is there written fails to convince you, go to court and listen to the readers. After all, if the task of the advocate were the simple one of reading what he (or someone else) has written out in advance, it would save time and anxiety all around if the recording of his sound effects were simply played to the court.

(b) *No notes at all?* I would recommend against arguing without any notes at all, for two reasons.

First, any lawyer before an appellate court is under distinct mental pressure: he must be alert, he must have complete control of his materials, he must be able to make immediate response to questions. Why then add a second form of mental pressure, the need to keep in mind the precise order of presentation and every detail of the argument? Notes prevent this second kind of pressure, and free one's mind accordingly. For it is a distinct pressure, even when the advocate is blessed with the famous flypaper memory, where everything sticks. Even advocates who are phenomenal mnemonic athletes, whose feats of memory are still talked about years after the event, will say that they prefer to argue with notes before them.

Second, arguing a long case without notes is so very obviously a stunt that it detracts from the effect the argument should make. It is as though counsel were simultaneously juggling five balls while talking—a wonderful and amazing feat, without question, and one that few individuals can accomplish. But performing it takes the court's mind off the argument, and so the effort fails of its purpose. The object of an argument, after all, is not to show the court what a wonderful fellow the lawyer is; it is to show the court what a wonderful case the client has. Anything that detracts the court's attention from the merits of the client's case is poor advocacy. Of course, no lawyer should ever strive to appear at less than his best, and there are many instances when a flash of genuine memory pays off, but the obvious and planned effort to show off one's own prodigious powers of memory not only does not contribute anything to a case, it generally detracts therefrom.

(c) *Extensive or fragmentary notes?* The question whether one's notes should be extensive or fragmentary is, of course, the place where the personal equation looms largest. Once my preference was for rather extensive notes, so that all my material was available, but not so extensive as to tie me down to a prepared text. I have come to prefer very fragmentary notes, essentially of headings and catch-words, designed to prevent me from overlooking any points or taking them up in the wrong order. These notes are annotated when necessary, following the practice described in subsection (d), below.

The reason for using fragmentary notes rather than fairly extensive ones is a simple one: I found that, whenever I let myself slip into writing out notes that were too detailed, I became so dependent on them that it was difficult to talk without referring to them, and so was virtually in the rigid and unprofitable position of a speaker with a prepared manuscript before him, unable to meet the judges eye to eye, and hence hampered in establishing rapport with them. So—now I use headings and catch notes.

And, as has already been indicated, by rehearsing the oral argument several times before actually making it in court, its substance has become sufficiently fixed in my mind that the fragmentary notes, which relieve the pressure of having to remember the number and the order of points, are entirely sufficient.

(d) *Use of references.* Regardless of how detailed or compressed your notes are, they should contain references to the record and to pertinent cases and statutes, *not for the purpose of citing them during the argument,* but so that you have them ready to meet questions and to avoid the necessity of fumbling through your papers.

Thus, it is well, whenever a case turns on conflicting evidence, to have your notes contain a record reference to every statement of fact you make. Don't, don't, don't read those references to the court as you go along; make your assertions without more; but when a judge leans over and asks, "Where do you find that in the record?," you are instantly prepared with the page in question, because you have it right there before you.

In a sharply contested case, this kind of preparation, involving as it does some fairly extensive documentation, will take a good deal of time. It is, however, well worth while, because it means that whenever the court makes inquiry of the lawyer who has just made a challenging or apparently questionable statement, counsel is prepared to support what he has just said with the record itself. After a while, the questions will reflect interest and curiosity rather than doubt, and a little later, after the lawyer has several arguments under his belt, his statements will have been so regularly backed up by the record that he will have acquired a reputation for accuracy and reliability. The goal to aim for is the stage at which the judges will think—or even say—of you, "When Mr. X tells us that the record shows so-and-so, we know that it does." So—annotating your notes pays.

Similarly, include references to the decree, or to the findings, or to any critical portion of the record about which the court will ask, i.e., which it will want to examine for itself. Do the same with controlling statutes or decisions, and similarly mark any portions of brief or record that are important enough to be quoted verbatim to the court.

Needless to say, the habit of marking record references on one's notes is excellent insurance against inadvertent inaccuracy. By checking your proposed statement against the record you will avoid any distortion into which zeal or wishful thinking might, but for such check, unfortunately lead you.

Contrariwise, the lack of record references may cause serious embarrassment. I once heard an eminent practitioner get up in the U.S. Supreme Court, for a fee that must certainly have run well into five figures, and begin by saying, "Pursuant to the division of the case which the various petitioners have made among themselves, I am going to discuss paragraph X of the decree." Question from the bench: "Where is that in the record, Mr. Y?" And there ensued an anguished and frantic fumbling that lasted for some time.

How much confidence, do you suppose, did a start of this kind generate in the judicial mind for what was to follow?

Section 106. The actual process of preparation.—This will be largely a summary of the foregoing, set out in the order in which I have personally found it helpful to proceed.

After having discussed the case with everyone who would listen, and when the day of argument begins to approach, you have reached the time to prepare in earnest.

I sit down and read the briefs, slowly and consecutively (i.e., appellant's first, regardless of who wrote it). See Section 93, *supra.* If there is then any doubt in my mind as to the precise holding or language of the controlling decisions, I read those too, not neglecting those relied on by the other side. Next, I try to formulate the argument with a view to making the most effective presentation; this may or may not be the order set forth in the brief.

After that, I outline the argument and thereafter make my first draft notes. I have found it most helpful to use a legal size scratch-pad, and to scribble notes large enough so that I can read them easily in court. Then I fill in the necessary record references, and fill in the indications for matters to be read to the court. When I am through, I am ready to go over and time the argument for the first time. See Section 102, above.

Next, I revise wherever revision is necessary, changing emphasis, adding, or eliminating, as the case may be. It will frequently be necessary to check against the record, or to reread a leading case or so, or to embark on an entirely new bit of research. Then, I go over the whole argument again, once more timing it, until finally I feel that I am ready to face the court.

If pressure of other work permits, I find it helpful at this point to reread portions of the record, or even the entire record if it is a short one. Frequently this last rereading will turn up something I had earlier overlooked, or something that assumes a different significance in the light of the additional research since the first reading. And, in any event, this final rereading of the record always serves to fix it more firmly in mind.

I never put my notes for argument in a binder, because I feel that this interferes with flexibility. If, for example, the court asks a question about a topic I had originally planned to cover later on, so that I must now turn to it earlier, it is much easier to have unbound notes; that enables me to discuss the topic inquired about by pulling out the appropriate pages, and then to resume where I left off when diverted. Ideally, the notes on each topic can be clipped together. At any rate, unbound notes will, I believe, be found easier to handle.

Section 107. Peripheral preparation and last-minute revisions.— One of the most important finer points of preparation is what may be called peripheral analysis, i.e., a study of the points on the fringes of your central questions that are apt to interest an active and well-informed judicial mind. The only safe rule is to familiarize yourself fully on all related details and on the background of the law of your case before you get up to argue. Much of this kind of work turns out to be love's labor lost, because the questions to which you have so painfully worked out answers may not be asked after all. But if the lightning really strikes, then the extra effort has been well worth while, and that which you know down deep to have been just a stroke of luck may to the court and to the listening bar appear to be a touch of genius.

It is well to bear in mind, also, that neither your notes nor your preparation, however complete and thorough each may be, should ever be regarded as final. I know that when I used to cram for college and law school examinations, I had the feeling on the morning of the day when the misery was going to take place, "Well, if I don't know it now, I never will." But with arguments it has been brought increasingly home to me that it is a mistake to consider even one's most carefully prepared efforts as set pieces and that it is always possible, even at the last minute, to effect useful additions and revisions that will add to the persuasiveness and clarity of the ultimate performance. I can think of a good many arguments I have made that were measurably improved by some change I wrote into my notes in the morning before going to court. Indeed, in one or two instances I effected the changes or additions while actually in court, waiting to go on. And of course rebuttal arguments (see Section 125, below) must be worked out substantially on an extemporaneous basis.

One final caution: Get plenty of sleep the night before. Fatigue slows up the most acute mind, and the lawyer who is physically tired is therefore at a distinct disadvantage both in presenting his case and in replying to questions. And I can add, also with the heartfelt sincerity derived of experience, that the night before an appellate argument had better not be devoted to class reunions or get-togethers with the lads with whom you fought the war. A courtroom is a mighty uncomfortable place for working off a hangover.

Section 108. All alone.—Once you are up on your feet, you are on your own, and there just isn't anyone who can help you if you aren't prepared. Your colleagues and the young men can pass notes and all that, but those are desperate palliatives for anything but minor details. Unless you know your case at this point, it won't be known; the time for planning, for joint endeavor, for cooperative enterprise, has passed; the situation is one for individual initiative, and you are that individual.

Holmes once said

Only when you have worked alone—when you have felt around you a black gulf of solitude more isolating than that which surrounds the dying man, and in hope and in despair have trusted to your own unshaken will—then only will you have achieved.[3]

Well, once you are up on your feet in a more or less crowded courtroom, it isn't exactly a black gulf of solitude—but you will certainly have to rely on your own unshaken preparation, and unless at that point you are well prepared, you won't achieve.

---

[3] Holmes, *The Profession of the Law*, in *Collected Legal Papers*, 29, 32.

CHAPTER 8

The Finer Points of Oral Argument

Section 109. In general.—Having previously considered and discussed the essentials of an effective oral argument, and the process of preparing to get ready to make one, we are now in a position to take up some of the finer points, namely, wherein a good oral argument differs from one not so good. Here again, trifles make perfection, but perfection is no trifle.

An excellent way to pick up these points by oneself is to go up to court and just listen. If you are about to argue a case before an unfamiliar tribunal, it is a very good idea, time permitting, to get there a day or so ahead of time, and then simply to sit and listen to the cases ahead of your own in order to get, so to speak, the feel of the court—how the judges react to the particular propositions and approaches, to what extent they are willing to let counsel proceed in his own way, to what extent and when they will interrupt with questions, and the like.

Indeed, even in more familiar surroundings, the student of advocacy—and every really able advocate remains a student always, since there is always something to be learned, or relearned—the student of advocacy can invariably pick up useful pointers simply by listening to the arguments of other lawyers. In a sense, he is like the intern going on ward rounds. By listening to the really able members of the bar, he will learn what to do, and how the masters of the business turn it off. And, by listening to the not so able members of the bar, he will acquire the equally valuable knowledge of what not to do. Regardless of the quality of the forensic performance, time spent listening to arguments in court is never wasted.

Section 110. Appreciation of the limitations of the medium.—Perhaps the most illuminating insight into the refinements of oral advocacy is acquired through an appreciation of the limitations of the medium employed. You are speaking, not writing. Your words are received by ear, not by eye. Your impact is evanescent; your audience cannot go back and pick up something they may have missed. There is rarely a permanent record of what you have said—unless you hire a stenographer at your own expense to take down your deathless prose, and even then the result is something for your own files, which the court will seldom see.

This salient fact, that oral argument must depend on the fleeting impression it makes, conditions the entire process. Consequently, the basic caution is, don't let your argument get lost in details. Concentrate on the broad strokes. To use a visual metaphor, you are painting a billboard, not constructing a fine-screened halftone. That admonition carries through everything you say while on your feet, because any oral explanation or exposition that is too detailed simply gets lost. In the paragraphs that follow are set forth some applications of this governing principle.

Section 111. Avoid excessive detail as to dates, facts, and figures.—Never be more detailed on facts, dates, or figures in oral argument than your case requires you to be. Normally, counsel should eliminate months and days in stating dates, and should use good round figures—except only when the more detailed presentation is an essential part of the case.

For instance:

Petitioner was convicted by a jury in Nineteen Hundred and Thirty-Eight. He did not appeal. Thereafter he brought four successive petitions for habeas corpus, Nineteen Hundred and Forty, Nineteen Hundred and Forty-Two, Nineteen Hundred and Forty-Five, and Nineteen Hundred and Forty-Six. The last petition is the one now before the Court.[1]

Compare the foregoing with the more accurate statement that follows:

Petitioner was convicted by a jury on April twenty-nine, Nineteen Hundred and Thirty-Eight. Thereafter, he brought four successive petitions for habeas corpus. The first was filed on June four, Nineteen Hundred and Forty, the second on September twenty-four, Nineteen Hundred and Forty-Two, the third on August six, Nineteen Hundred and Forty-Five, and the fourth on January 2, Nineteen Hundred and Forty-Six. It is this fourth petition that is now before the Court.

The latter statement would not be out of place in a brief, but by cluttering up the years, which are the essential dates, with the unessential days and months, the lawyer who has framed his oral

---

[1] *Price v. Johnston*, 334 U.S. 166.

statement along the lines of the second example has made it very difficult for the court to follow him by ear. (Have someone read the second statement to you, if you doubt what is here said about it.)

On the other hand, there are cases where time is of the essence, as for example the case of the Station-Platform Warrior, the lad who reported for the draft on Armistice Day, 1918, and then sought a writ of mandamus in 1945–1946 to compel the Secretary of War to issue him an Honorable Discharge from the Army.[2] See Section 31. There it was vital to the argument for the Court to know that he reported for duty on November 11, 1918, that he was told to go home the same day, that on November 14 he was released from any further obligation to report, and that in January, 1919, he received a Discharge from Draft plus a check for four days' pay.

More generally, however, it is only the framework that is important; if you cover that with too much ornamentation and bric-a-brac, the essentials of your structure tend to get lost.

It is the same with figures; use good, thumping round numbers in the usual case, and don't go into the odd dollars and the pennies unless the case turns on the little discrepancies—or unless the very coincidence of the odd figures reflects very close action in concert!

Normally, avoid confusing details; use years for dates and round numbers for figures. Paint in broad strokes, because the court gets it only by ear.

Section 112. Don't attempt to dissect individual cases in open court.—Mr. Justice Cardozo once wrote: "There is, of course, no formula that will fit all situations in appellate courts or elsewhere. If, however, I had to prepare a list of 'Don'ts' for the guidance of the novice, I think I would say that only in the rarest instances is it wise to take up one decision after another for the purpose of dissection. Such autopsies have their value at times, but they are wearisome and gruesome scenes."[3]

You will be well advised, therefore, to state your cases simply as establishing broad propositions, and to leave all the details of the particular decision to your briefs. Unless you do just that, the main thread of your argument will become lost.

---

[2] *Patterson v. Lamb*, 329 U.S. 539.

[3] Cardozo, *Law and Literature* (Harcourt, Brace and Co.), p. 37.

Here are two examples of how a case can be stated in court;
the problem is whether postmortem declarations are admissible in
evidence:

(A)

Post-mortem declarations have been held to be utterly inadmissible for any
purpose, ever since Chief Justice Marshall's justly celebrated opinion in
Schmaltz against the *Chosen Freeholders* in the 13th of Wheaton.[4] Their inadmis-
sibility has never been questioned since the time of that decision, which has
stood as a landmark of the law of evidence, and which has been followed and
affirmed and reaffirmed in a whole stack of cases, all of which are collected
and discussed in our brief. Indeed, but for the decision below, we should have
thought that the proposition was not subject to successful question.

(B)

The question of the admissibility of post-mortem declarations was first
passed upon in the case of *Schmaltz* against the *Chosen Freeholders of East
Overshoe,* reported at 13 Wheaton 743. That is a leading case, hence it may be
helpful to state the facts out of which it arose:

One Oscar Schmaltz claimed a tract of 120 acres in the Township of East
Overshoe, as devisee under the will of his uncle, Joseph Schmaltz. New Jersey
had a statute at that time—this was in the year 1799—to the effect that the
estates of Revolutionary War veterans should be exempt from taxation. If the
elder Schmaltz were such a veteran, then the land in question passed to his
nephew Oscar, the plaintiff-in-error. But if Joseph Schmaltz were not a veteran,
then his estate escheated for nonpayment of taxes to the township, represented by the Chosen Freeholders. Now, Joseph Schmaltz's status as veteran or
nonveteran turned on a declaration made, etc., etc., etc.

Question: Which statement more effectively lodges in the court's
mind the proposition for which you are contending? Question
Two: Didn't Mr. Justice Cardozo hit the nail on the head? So—state
your proposition, and don't dissect individual cases in open court.
Relegate their details to their proper resting place, viz., your brief.

---

[4] (a) Of course there are only 12 volumes of Wheaton.

(b) The older lawyers always used to cite reports orally as "the 4th of Wallace," "the
114th Massachusetts," "the 229th United States," and so on. When I first began
to listen to arguments in the United States Supreme Court, the brighter young
lawyers (who had picked up the practice from their seniors) used to do so too.
It may be a little bit old-fashioned these days, but it adds a little flourish, and so
might well be encouraged and preserved.

(c) Please note that the page reference is not given orally. It is omitted for the same
reason that dates and figures should be simplified (Section 111, above; Section
113, below), viz., to leave a clearer impression of the essentials.

There is one exception to the foregoing: When the court asks you about a particular case, it is perfectly proper to dissect and distinguish—because then you are talking about details that are familiar to your questioner, rather than cluttering up and confusing a broad proposition you are attempting to establish to a court that is temporarily unaware of it.

Section 113. Don't cite too many individual cases in open court.—In a brief, every proposition of law must be supported by authorities, but this is really not necessary in open court. Indeed, it may be more effective not to attempt to rest every proposition on a particular case. This is a matter partly of individual emphasis and partly of the habits of the particular court.

In the main, however, the following standards for oral presentation may safely be followed:

Generally, do not cite any cases by name in support of undisputed or hornbook propositions.

Again, do not bother to cite cases by name in support of every subsidiary proposition of your presentation.

Where, however, the immediate subject matter of a principal heading has not come up recently or involves a somewhat obscure point, it is well to cite a few of the leading, landmark cases as you go along, by way of reassuring the court that you are not just reciting law by ear but have solid authority to support you. Remember—just a few, not the sort of collection you may properly set out and discuss in your brief.

If the field you are discussing is one in which there have been a number of recent decisions, it is generally safe to assume, certainly at the outset, that the judges are acquainted with their own precedents. It should not therefore be necessary to cite many supporting cases orally. Exception One: When it becomes apparent from the reaction you are evoking that the judges are in fact not familiar with the decided cases supporting your proposition, you must of course refresh their recollections. Exception Two: When a court sits in divisions or in panels of varying composition, it may more frequently be necessary to acquaint the sitting judges with what their brethren have decided.

In any event, do not cite the little cases that simply apply a principle established by a well-known or fairly well-known leading case, except—for these matters cannot be disposed of by rigid rules—except when the satellite or subsidiary case is right on all fours, and except when you are asked about a particular decision.

As a matter of fact, there is really nothing like a pat citation for silencing a persistent judicial questioner.[5]

Finally, regardless of the occasion, when you do cite cases orally, content yourself with a simplified citation. For instance: "And that was held by the *Smith* case in the 303rd United States, and again by the *Johnson* case decided earlier this Term." "That proposition is fully supported by the *Quercia* case, which is discussed at length in both briefs." "There hasn't been any question about that rule of law since *Brown* against the *State*, with which your Honors are of course familiar."

Don't, for the reasons set forth in Section 112, above, go into further detail. When you say orally, "There hasn't been any question about that rule of law since *Brown v. State*, 69 R.I. 894, with which your Honors are of course familiar," you don't add anything helpful to the presentation, and you only make your thought more difficult to follow by ear.

Section 114. Other matters that cannot be conveyed by ear.—By the same token, it is generally not very profitable to attempt to state legislative history orally, unless the whole case hinges on it, in which event more detailed treatment is justified. An example of the latter was *Girouard v. United States*,[6] discussed above in this connection in Section 91. Even for that case, however, it was necessary to state the legislative history in broad and simple terms.

In general, it is well to rely exclusively on the brief for anything that is so detailed that it sounds fuzzy when you attempt to present it orally. The only test is to try it, i.e., rehearse it, orally. Regardless of what it is, whether law, or facts, or whatnot, if it doesn't leave a distinct impression by ear, relegate it to the brief where it can be

---

[5] When I argued my first case in the Supreme Court, *United States v. Summerlin*, 310 U.S. 414, Mr. Justice McReynolds was in his last year of active service. He was the last survivor of the Old Guard, and no doubt his only remaining amusement was the heckling of new Government counsel as they appeared. He began to question me rather intently about "Wasn't there a case a few years back that held—" something to the effect that the United States in commercial transactions is bound by commercial rules. Through dumb good fortune, I had tried in the U.S. District Court for Northern Alabama, the previous fall, a check case that turned on the decision in *United States v. National Exchange Bank*, 270 U.S. 527. It came to mind, luckily enough, and I asked, "Does your Honor mean the case of United States against the *National Exchange Bank*, somewhere around the 270th United States?" "That's the case!" exclaimed McReynolds, J. It was easy enough to distinguish, and the old gentleman didn't bother me further during the remainder of the proceedings.

[6] 328 U.S. 61.

more leisurely—and more effectively—absorbed by the eye. And never be afraid or ashamed to say, when you are up on your feet, "We have discussed these cases [or that evidence, or the legislative history] fully in our brief, so that I won't take the court's time by discussing the details here."

Section 115. The handling of questions from the bench.—Replying to the questions asked by the judges is without doubt the most difficult aspect of oral argument; certainly it is the most stimulating aspect, and it is unquestionably one of the most important. Yet the basic principles of this particular problem can be broken down into about three admonitions.

(a) *Learn to think on your feet.* As to this, familiarity with the case helps, and so does thorough preparation, because the more questions you anticipate, the more answers you will have available to put out when the test comes. Undoubtedly a ready wit is of substantial aid; practice helps, and experience helps too, although in large measure quick-wittedness is congenital: you either have it or you haven't.

I have known some lawyers, able and intelligent citizens, too, who were simply struck dumb by questions from the bench, questions which they had anticipated beforehand and on which they were prepared. The ensuing silences caused those associated with the case to burn their eyes onto the floor, hoping against hope that some trap door would open up through which they could disappear from the horrible scene they were witnessing. If you are one of those forensically weak, silent men—well, the only known cure is to stick to brief-writing and office conferences. It's much easier on all concerned.

At the same time, no advocate, however able, will ever be completely satisfied with any answer he has given. A better one will always come to mind in the taxicab back to the office. I once hoped to be able to invent a gadget that would make the taxicab answer jump up and hit me while still on my feet in court, but up to now I have still to report utter lack of success. Perhaps the quest for the perfect answer comes under the heading of vain regrets, on a par with that dream brief discussed in Section 20, above. But, like the other, it is probably one of the inescapable pangs of advocacy.[7]

---

[7] That Grand Old Man of American law, Professor Samuel Williston, had this to say of his only argument in the Supreme Court, *Boston & Maine Rd. v. Hooker*, 233 U.S. 97: "A defeated counsel often regrets his failure to give the best possible answer to questions
(continued)

(b) *Never refuse to answer a question.* The precept that counsel
should never refuse to answer a question holds good even if the
question is not in his case, for the normal reaction of the judge
who asked the particular question will be, "Well, I realize that, but I
should like to know your position on the point just the same." The
judge will insist, so you had better be prepared in advance on the
more obvious questions that lie around the edges of your case. If
you are not prepared, or if the question comes out of the blue in a
case in which you are otherwise prepared up to the hilt, it is better
to say, "I should like to consider that question further before ven-
turing an answer," or even to offer to submit a supplemental memorandum, than to refuse point-blank to answer or, what is just as
bad, obviously to try to evade an answer.

Unreasonable on the part of Judge X to insist? Certainly. But you
are endeavoring to persuade him, so you had better cater to his
unreasonableness.

Here again, there is an exception: Don't answer in any detail if
to do so will take you far away from the thread of the argument, off
on an unprofitable tangent, or when there is a possibility that you
may be led to discuss an issue that is not, and from your point of
view should not be, in the case. In such a situation you must be
firm, and you must indicate very respectfully that you will not be
drawn into any such peripheral dissertation.

How can you tell whether you should or should not answer in
full? Here again—it all depends. On the other hand—

(c) *Never postpone your answer.* Almost as bad as refusal, outright
or barely concealed, is the all too familiar, "I am coming to that
later." Few replies are quite so annoying to a person whom you are
endeavoring to persuade; he asks you now because he is interested
now, and you dampen his interest in your case if you fail to answer
now. Apart from that consideration, which should be fairly obvious
to anyone who has thought about the matter, the fact is that promises that "I will take that up later" are left unperformed in appellate
courts quite as frequently as promises that "I will connect that up
later" are broken in trial courts.

Moreover, and this is another point frequently overlooked, the
circumstance that the particular matter inquired about comes at a

---

put to him from the bench, and I have always regretted a failure to answer to my own
satisfaction, at least, an inquiry put to me by Mr. Justice Hughes." But he added, "A man
convinced against his will is of the same opinion still, and the decision of the Supreme
Court carries no mandate to the logical faculty." Williston, *Life and Law*, p. 283.

different place in your own prepared outline is really not an adequate reason for declining to make an immediate reply to a judge who reaches the point somewhat sooner in his own analysis of the case.

Some judges simply refuse to accept a postponement. It is said that once when a question asked by Mr. Justice McReynolds was answered with the too usual "I am coming to that," the Justice snapped back, "You're there now!"

Actually, there is only one solution: Namely, to supply a stopgap answer and move on. That is the best solution, if not the only one. When Mr. Justice Y asks, "Is it your position that the statute is invalid?," answer, "Yes, that is our position"—and state that you will develop it more fully later, adding a good reason for postponing full discussion, as, for example, that the reason will appear more intelligibly after you have first sketched in your position on points B, C, and D, or after you have outlined the legislative development of the statue, and so forth.

But remember, you must have a better reason for postponement than the happenstance that the point inquired about appears in a different relative position in your own plan of argument.

Section 116. Quotations in open court.—The reason for the basic admonition, "Never read your argument" (Section 89, above), is that reading draws a veil between the advocate and the court. What is true of arguments as a whole is likewise true of lengthy quotations from documents or testimony or opinions. So—never read long quotations to a court. Here again, if you are not prepared to take this precept on faith, just go to court and listen to the lawyers who read to the judges copious quotations from decisions or records.

I will not urge, "Never read a quotation"; that would be dogmatic, and unsound. I do insist, however, that you should never undertake to read a quotation that is over four sentences or so long, because at about the fourth or fifth sentence the veil begins to form. Therefore, if you do read, the quotation should be short, and above all pat, else departure from the normal standard is not justified.

Moreover, if a particular quotation is so essential to your argument that you feel you must read it, tab it specially in the brief or record (as the case may be), so that it is ready for you without fumbling, and so that you can read it smoothly, with perfect transition and without any jerky, jumpy pause. (But remember that if your quotation is at, say, page 83 in the record, and you want to turn to that page when you lift up the tab, you must paste the tab on the leaf that carries pages 81 and 82. If your tab is pasted to page 83, you will turn up pages 84 and 85.) Two other cautions: First, read from the paper, not at it; look at the court while you are reading, don't bury your nose—and your voice—in your text. Second, read slowly, so that you convey the full effect of the passage. There is always a strong tendency, even among the best advocates, to rush the reading. If you want your quotation to be really effective, you must overcome that very natural urge.

If you keep your quotations and excerpts short, and tab them so that they can be reached without delay, and read slowly from the original—then there is no reason why any veil should come between you and your judicial audience.

Section 117. Use of a striking phrase.—In order to present your contentions in simplified form, it is frequently useful to employ a striking phrase—a dignified slogan, if you please, but a slogan nonetheless.

Perhaps this point will be somewhat more clear after a discussion of examples.

(a) The issue turned on the constitutionality of an involved regulatory statute. The entire case was effectively summed up by the statement, "Petitioner is not being denied due process; on the contrary, this statute affords him undue process."[8]

(b) One of the cases involving the military trials of civilian dependents, where it was proposed to retry the relator by court-martial at Bolling Air Force Base in the District of Columbia;

"The question in this case is whether a woman, who all of her life has been a civilian, may be tried by an Air Force court-martial in time of peace, here in the District of Columbia and literally within the shadow of the Capitol dome."[9]

(c) A denaturalization case: "The issue is whether a good Nazi can be a good American."[10]

(d) Habeas corpus to review a conviction by court-martial, the contention being that the preliminary investigation under old

---

[8] *Sunshine Coal Co. v. Adkins*, 310 U.S. 381. There are two schools of thought on the source of this particular gem; one attributes it to Mr. Justice Jackson, then Attorney General, who argued the case, the other to Chief Justice Hughes, who presided over the Court that heard it. Mr. Justice Jackson writes, "I would like to claim it but if my title is no better than my memory, it is cloudy."

[9] *Reid v. Covert*, 354 U.S. 1, at the original hearing in the District Court. The passage in the text was quoted in *In re Varney's Petition*, 141 F. Supp. 190, 204 (S.D. Calif.).

[10] *Knauer v. United States*, 328 U.S. 654.

Article of War 70 was inadequate. The issue, as phrased by Government counsel, was "Whether, after a fair trial and painstaking review of the record by the agencies provided by law for that purpose, the convicted person will be set free because of alleged errors occurring *in the hinterland of the proceedings* long prior to the actual commencement of the trial."[11]

If the slogan you have devised is good—really good—it will make an indelible impression, one that will persist in the minds of the judges long after the rest of the argument has evaporated and been forgotten.

There is another kind of slogan that will fit almost any kind of situation—but that can probably be used only once before any particular bench. One of these is the opening, "This is a most remarkable case." Now, assuredly, that will make any court sit up and take notice, even when it later occurs to the judges that the case is really not so remarkable after all. Another is the expression, to be delivered with all solemnity, "If ever there was a case that"—and then you add whatever may be appropriate, and pause—"*this* is that case."

Both are effective. But, pretty clearly, they can't be usefully repeated, day in and day out, before the same judges.

Section 118. Use of maps and charts.—The need for graphic presentation of matters difficult to describe otherwise—"one picture is worth a thousand words"—justifies inclusion in the brief of maps, charts, or patent drawings. You must have those visual aids in your brief so that the judges can study them at their leisure when the case is under consideration. But it is a great mistake to rely on the map in the brief when arguing the case in open court, and equally a mistake to hand up one set of the applicable exhibits for the use of each member of the court. What you should do is to have an enlarged copy of the map or drawing in the courtroom, on a stand or easel, and one sufficiently large that it can be seen by every member of the bench. (Try it out in the empty courtroom

---

[11] See *Humphrey v. Smith*, 336 U.S. 695. The point had been extensively litigated in several circuits. See *Waite v. Overlade*, 164 F.2d 722 (C.C.A. 7), certiorari denied, 334 U.S. 812; *DeWar v. Hunter*, 170 F.2d 993 (C.A. 10), certiorari denied, 337 U.S. 908; *Henry v. Hodges*, 76 F. Supp. 968 (S.D.N.Y.), reversed, 171 F.2d 401 (C.A. 2), certiorari denied, 336 U.S. 968; *Becker v. Webster*, 171 F.2d 762 (C.A. 2), certiorari denied, 336 U.S. 968; *Hicks v. Hiatt*, 64 F. Supp. 238 (M.D. Pa.); *Anthony v. Hunter*, 71 F. Supp. 823 (D. Kan.).

I had used the phrase italicized in the text in some of my own briefs, but its author was my learned friend Colonel William J. Hughes, Jr., of the District of Columbia bar.

beforehand to make sure it is really large enough for all essential details to be seen by all the judges.) And, when you argue, use a pointer as you explain your exhibit.

Why all this trouble? Because if each judge simply has a map before him, he will study it and let his mind wander. All sorts of memories will come to mind. "Wallula—oh, yes, there it is. Gosh, I haven't been there since the summer after graduation. Hmmmm, I wonder whatever happened to Suzy." Or "Peckham. Yes, there was a fellow in my class named Peckham who came from Portland and whose father owned a store. I wonder whether that's the same family." While these reveries go on, while each judge is demonstrating what a wonderful distraction a map can be, the court is listening to counsel with only half an ear. But if there is only a single map up there before the bench, counsel is the center of attraction, particularly when he is using his pointer; all the judges are listening to him, and none is making personal excursions to irrelevant portions of the drawing.

Here again, if you doubt any of the foregoing, just watch what happens in court whenever a lawyer relies on a map he has handed up—and then you will certainly agree that it a great mistake to rest on the map that is in the record or in the briefs if you want the court really to understand the case.[12]

There may, of course, be cases that are helped by a lack of understanding on the part of the bench. I once argued a motion to dismiss in a mandamus case in the former Supreme Court of the District of Columbia on behalf of the Secretary of the Interior. The case turned on whether a certain tract of land had been appropriated and set apart for public use. That question depended on an interpretation of maps and reports contained in Congressional documents. Well, I ran back and forth between counsel table and bench, pointing first to one map and then to another—"Now point A on this map, your Honor, is identical with point G on this second map"—and so on, until the judge became thoroughly confused and finally said, "Well, this is a very complicated matter, so complicated that I cannot interfere with the discretion of the Secretary, who obviously was not acting arbitrarily. I will grant the motion to

---

[12] I have used large maps in the courtroom on three occasions—and won the case each time. (a) *United States v. Northern Pac. Ry. Co.*, 311 U.S. 317. (b) *United States v. Baltimore & O. R. Co.*, 333 U.S. 169. (c) *Hunter v. Wade*, 169 F.2d 973 (C.A. 10). The latter case was affirmed on certiorari, 336 U.S. 684—and prevailing counsel used the same map in the Supreme Court.

dismiss." But, as I say, this technique is not to be recommended when you are setting out to clarify rather than to confuse.

Section 119. An appropriate peroration.—An appellate advocate's closing words are important, and they should leave an impression of combined strength and dignity. They must be more than simply a shouted conclusion while the judges are folding up their briefs and turning to the papers in the next case. And, although an appellate court can be moved, it is not a jury; the scope for emotional impact is distinctly limited when the case is on appeal.

Fashioning a proper peroration presents a difficult problem in any circumstances, and a particularly difficult one when counsel's time has been so taken up with questioning that his planned ending no longer serves. All that can usefully be ventured are the following considerations:

First, you must have some sort of an ending in order not to leave your argument up in the air, and to avoid tacking on the purely formal "We therefore submit that the judgment below should be reversed." Come up with a conclusion in a nutshell, at the very least. For instance:

> The result is that, without pausing to repeat or even to sum up, the totality of errors in this record, particularly those discussed orally, is such that the conviction now under review simply cannot be permitted to stand.

Next, you should, as a general and all but invariable rule, remain calm and dignified, making your closing as impressive as possible, carefully avoiding anything that is even faintly irrelevant.

Thus, if the question for decision is whether the practices in a particular industry violate the Sherman Antitrust Act, it is a waste of breath and worse for counsel to wind up on a note of how much the industry concerned contributed to the war effort. And if the case turns on the sufficiency of the allegations in a petition for habeas corpus, a peroration built around a letter from the prisoner, which has obviously been censored through the use of shears and which is waved under the eyes of the judges, is simply cheap.

On the other hand, genuine, relevant emotion may be very effective, as witness the closing by Senator George Wharton Pepper in the AAA case:[13]

> My time is fleeting and I must not pause to sum up the argument I have made. I have come to the point at which a consideration of delegation is the

---

[13] *United States v. Butler*, 297 U.S. 1, 44.

next logical step, and that is to be dealt with effectively by my colleague, Mr. Hale. But I do want to say just one final and somewhat personal word.

I have tried very hard to argue this case calmly and dispassionately, and without vehement attack upon things which I cannot approve, and I have done it thus because it seems to me that this is the best way in which an advocate can discharge his duty to this Court.

But I do not want your Honors to think that my feelings are not involved, and that my emotions are not deeply stirred. Indeed, may it please your Honors, I believe I am standing here today to plead the cause of the America I have loved; and I pray Almighty God that not in my time may "the land of the regimented" be accepted as a worthy substitute for "the land of the free."

All who were present agree that this was most effective—"too effective" was the way one lawyer on the losing side put it—and even today, in the cold print of the reports, it still moves the reader. One reservation, however, may not be inappropriate: The foregoing passage from the lips of a man of less stature than Senator Pepper might well have failed to accomplish its purpose.

For those who are still a considerable distance from the top of the profession, something more impersonal is necessary for a close. Perhaps I may be pardoned for including two of my own perorations—the combined batting average of which was .500.

In the *Girouard* case,[14] which turned on legislative ratification *vel non*:

Thus it is clear that the decisions of this Court in the *Schwimmer* and *Macintosh* cases have been legislatively ratified by the Congress. Accordingly, unless this Court is now to sit as a Council of Revision, it must affirm the judgment below.

Well, the judgment was reversed, which prompted Chief Justice Stone to say, concluding his dissent:[15]

It is not the function of this Court to disregard the will of Congress in the exercise of its constitutional power.

And, announcing that dissent, on the very day he was stricken, with the last coherent words he ever uttered, he had said, "There has been too much of this judicial tinkering with statutes."[16]

---

[14] *Girouard v. United States*, 328 U.S. 61.

[15] 328 U.S. at 79.

[16] The reader may perhaps wonder at my preoccupation with the *Girouard* case. I can only say, by way of at least partial extenuation, that it worried a good many other people besides losing counsel. See Horack, *Congressional Silence: A Tool of Judicial Supremacy*, 25 Tex. L. Rev. 247; *American Citizenship: Can Applicants Qualify Their Allegiance?*, 33 A.B.A.J. 95; and the several sequels to the article last cited, 33 A.B.A.J. at 323, 540, and 663.

Another example, from the *Line Material*[17] arguments:

* * * So we say, overrule the *General Electric* case. But whether you overrule it or simply distinguish and limit it, we submit that it is impossible to justify the sort of thing that was done here, because this sort of thing is a constant menace to the public interest in free competition—and it is nothing new.

It is nothing that has just recently been dreamed up. It goes back many years—not, perhaps, to Adam—but certainly to Adam Smith.

I would like to bring this argument to a close with a single sentence from Adam Smith's *Wealth of Nations*, which is just as timely—and just as timeless—as when it was first written over a century and a half ago.

"People of the same trade seldom meet together, even for merriment and diversion, but the conversation ends in a conspiracy against the public, or in some contrivance to raise prices."

We submit that the judgment below should be reversed.

That one got five votes.

Section 120. Courtroom manners and mannerisms.—It might seem unnecessary to include pointers on how not to behave, but the list of don'ts that follows has been collected because observation has indicated that violations occur with distressing regularity.

(a) *Never interrupt opposing counsel.* It is an unpardonable breach of manners to interrupt opposing counsel. I add this remark here because I have heard such interruptions even in the United States Supreme Court.

(b) *Don't wander from the lectern.* Judges find most annoying the practice some lawyers have of wandering from the lectern.

(c) *Don't see-saw with glasses.* One of the unhappiest mannerisms, and one of the least pleasant to watch, is the habit some lawyers have of putting their glasses on and then taking them off again, waving them back and forth as though see-sawing. If you need glasses for close reading, but can't see the judges' faces through them, or if you need glasses for distance vision, but can't read with them, then there is only one solution for your next appellate argument: get a pair of bifocals, and wear them while on your feet. Relax and enjoy your maturity; don't annoy your judicial listeners by refusing to admit to membership in the bifocal bracket.

(d) *Avoid unpleasant gestures.* Don't, for instance, point an admonitory finger at the bench, or indulge in similar unpleasant gestures.[18]

---

[17] *United States v. Line Material Co.*, 333 U.S. 287.

[18] Compare the remarks of the Hon. William D. Mitchell, Solicitor General 1925–1929 and Attorney General 1929–1933, at the *Proceedings in Memory of Mr. Justice*
(continued)

(e) *Never grimace.* Don't assume a derisive smile while opposing counsel is addressing the court; this is very bad manners. The only safe rule, for counsel's weak points as well as for his good ones, is to keep as set a poker face as you can muster: Don't sneer at his poor arguments—and don't look worried at his good ones. There is one exception: When the court laughs, don't hesitate to laugh right along with them—quite regardless of the quality of the humor.

(f) *Desist when your time has expired.* When your time is used up, and the other side has had the last word, don't say anything more—except possibly to ask for permission to file a reply brief. Don't attempt to say anything more, because the court will not permit it, and above all, don't argue for the opportunity to be heard. Some of the most painful courtroom scenes in living memory have been the result of lawyers' insisting on talking when they had no right to do so and when the court had already indicated that it did not desire to hear them.

Section 121. Courtroom attire.—When in Rome, do as the top-drawer Romans do. This precept is particularly applicable as a guide to what the properly dressed lawyer will wear while arguing a case in an appellate court.

In most appellate courts, it is customary to wear simply a business suit. Where that custom obtains, it would be a mistake to appear in more formal attire. But a decent respect for the bench requires that the lawyer's suit be dark and reasonably conservative, and that his tie be not too strikingly chromatic.

At the same time, the latitude of colors permitted one's garments may well vary with the geographical latitude involved. A white linen suit in a New England court would be regarded as an affront to the bench, but in the Supreme Court of Hawaii it would not be out of order.[19] (In the Supreme Court of Puerto Rico,

---

Van Devanter, 316 U.S. v, xvi, xviii–xix: "* * * In the same spirit, he was very kind and helpful to me. During my early experiences as Solicitor General he found the opportunity, very tactfully, and privately, to suggest ways of improving my court manners. I learned through him how important it is that the Solicitor General, whom the Court must listen to week in and week out for years, should be free from annoying mannerisms. The Court can stand them on occasions, but as a steady diet they become quite unbearable."

[19] My learned friend Garner Anthony, Esq., of the Honolulu bar, advises that "there is no written or unwritten rule in the Supreme Court of Hawaii as to what counsel should wear. It depends upon the individual." He adds, however, that his former senior partner, the late judge A. G. M. Robertson, "was always meticulous in appearing in the Supreme Court of Hawaii with a stiff batwing collar, a dark suit, and a white waistcoat."

however, the advocate, in accordance with the old Spanish tradition, was once required to wear a toga.)[20]

In the Supreme Court of the United States, some years back, counsel would not even be listened to if attired in anything less than a long coat. Consequently, the Clerk used to keep on hand, for the benefit of practitioners hailing from the forks of the creek (up East Overshoe way), three long coats: large, medium, and small. Gradually, however, a relaxation crept in, and the Court began to deign to listen to counsel arguing in business suits.[21]

I assume, however, that the argument will do the costume justice. There is extant a lovely story concerning one Government lawyer (not now in public life) who on the occasion of his first argument in the Supreme Court appeared in a new—and obviously wholly owned—cutaway that was a masterpiece of the tailor's art. He had rough going from the outset, and indeed had not proceeded very far before Mr. Justice X, an acidulous and caustic man, leaned over to Mr. Justice Y, sitting next to him, and stage-whispered all too audibly, "Better dressed than equipped!"[22]

Section 122. The saving grace.—The saving grace is best used sparingly; intentional, deliberate humor in an appellate court is a dangerous ingredient in untrained hands, and an attempted joke that falls flat chills the atmosphere into a deep freeze. In this field much depends upon the court—some are deadpan, sitting like a collection of wooden Indians, others have a more ebullient temperament. Moreover, much depends on the advocate concerned; it is only the real leaders of the bar who can afford to say things that in other mouths would be inappropriate liberties.

---

[20] I am indebted for this information to my distinguished and learned friend, Mr. Justice Snyder of the Supreme Court of Puerto Rico, who cites Rule 14 (b) of that tribunal, and writes:

"The toga has a satin collar extending to the waist, satin reveres to the floor in front, and 16 box pleats across the back. These togas are exactly like those worn by the Justices, with the distinguishing feature that our togas have lace cuffs. The only lawyer permitted to wear the lace cuffs is the Fiscal of the Supreme Court, roughly translated as Solicitor General. This is because under the Spanish tradition he was considered as attached to the Court rather than to the Executive Department.

"Under the Spanish regime a six-sided satin *birrete* was also worn, but this was abandoned under American sovereignty."

However, the learned justice adds, the law graduates of the University of Puerto Rico still wear a *birrete* at their graduation ceremony.

[21] See Palmer, *What Lawyers Wear—Reverie on a Pink-Shirted Lawyer*, 33 A.B.A.J. 529.

[22] A word for the ladies: In any court, on any occasion, wear your best basic black dress or suit with a touch of white at the throat.

It may be noted, however, that the danger zone for younger practitioners lies in the realm of deliberate, purposeful humor, carefully (and often all too obviously) planned in advance. Spontaneous wit, so long as it is not lacking in the necessary quantum of deference, is hardly ever resented; to the contrary.

In the view that it may be of interest to examine some examples of permissible light touches, I include a few that have passed muster, or, at least, that have not backfired.

(a) Proceeding by the United States to file a claim in a probate proceeding; the State Supreme Court held the claim invalid because it was not filed in time. Government counsel urged that the United States was not bound by state statutes of limitations; counsel for the estate urged that the state enactment was not a statute of limitations, but a statute of nonclaim. On rebuttal:

> The contention seems to be that a rose by some other name—might prove less thorny.[23]

(b) The *Girouard* naturalization case,[24] already mentioned at some length. The basic issue was whether Congress, by refusing to amend the naturalization laws after the *Schwimmer*[25] and *Macintosh*[26] decisions, and by thereafter reenacting the provisions construed in those cases, had legislatively ratified those decisions. Former Attorney General Cummings, for the petitioner, had argued that the Congressional refusal to amend was inconclusive, because the issue was, as he put it, a "hot potato."

Counsel for the Government urged the significance of the reenactment of the earlier provisions in the Nationality Act of 1940:

> Now this reenactment, as the legislative history shows, had its origin in the report of a cabinet committee, of which Mr. Cummings, then Attorney General, was a member. And whatever may be the attitude of individual members of Congress, certainly no one could ever fairly accuse my former chief of lack of courage where legislative proposals were concerned, simply because they involved *burning* issues.

The reference was, obviously, to the Court Plan of 1937, and every member of the Court laughed loud and lustily—joined, let it be noted, by the former Attorney General.

(c) The case of the Postprandial Patriot, the man who had lunch with his draft board on Armistice Day, 1918, and then years later

---

[23] *United States v. Summerlin*, 310 U.S. 414.

[24] *Girouard v. United States*, 328 U.S. 61.

[25] *United States v. Schwimmer*, 279 U.S. 644.

[26] *United States v. Macintosh*, 283 U.S. 605.

attempted to mandamus the Secretary of War to issue him an Honorable Discharge from the Army.[27] (Earlier—in Section 111—I referred to this individual as the Station-Platform Warrior, but that may well have been an exaggeration, because the record fails to show that he ever even got to the railway station.) His counsel had been asked to say in what branch of the service he had been, and counsel had not really satisfied the Court on that point. Government counsel on rebuttal:

> I will endeavor to answer that question. Now, he wasn't an infantryman, because he had never been assigned there; nor was he an artilleryman or a cavalryman, because, as we have shown, he wasn't really in the Army. But he did have lunch with his draft board, so I suppose he could be called a trencherman.

Well, that will give some idea of what can be done, within permissible limits and along wholly relevant lines, to brighten up the proceedings.

Section 123. Avoid personalities.—Never confuse or detract from your argument by dragging in personalities. They are bad enough in briefs, but they are infinitely worse in oral argument.

It may well be, of course, that your opponent's disbarment is long overdue, or that the court below is widely referred to as "Old Man Necessity" because (of course) Necessity knows no law. Don't introduce such considerations into argument. The question for decision on appeal is not whether opposing counsel is a Servant of Brotherhood, it is whether his client was. And if you are trying to get Judge Schmaltz reversed, the question isn't whether he is wise or ignorant, it is whether his decision in this particular case was right or wrong. (Besides, if he is really as obtuse as you think he is, the appellate court will be aware of that, too; they are likely to have seen more of his rulings than you have.)

Moreover, counsel on appeal is still a lawyer, and so must maintain the bar's traditional respect for the judiciary, even when the district judge in question is known to every member of the appellate court to be wrong more frequently than he is right. He is still a judge; if the appellate judges think ill of him, they are free to say so privately; you, however, cannot even intimate his shortcomings publicly. As a perceptive friend of mine once put it, "Never forget that there is, after all, a judges' union." Not only do trial and appellate judges frequently lunch together, in most circuits District Judges in

---

[27] *Patterson v. Lamb*, 329 U.S. 539.

varying degrees of frequency sit as members of the Court of Appeals. Like Lord Nelson's captains, they are, certainly with reference to the bar, a band of brothers. Counsel will be well advised, therefore, to keep his disagreements with their rulings on a purely intellectual basis.

And don't row with counsel, either. Remain calm, dignified, and professional. If the opposition is in fact a disgrace to the profession, you should be at pains not to descend to his level.

Section 124. Sarcasm and bitterness.—Anything in the nature of sarcasm or bitterness is in the nature of a personality, because it injects an emotional element into what should be essentially an intellectual difference of opinion. Hence these also are improper and should be avoided.

On occasion the temptation to indulge in either or both is a strong one. In my own experience, I probably yielded to both emotions in the original argument of the first court-martial cases;[28] some examples—fairly horrible examples, too—are noted in the margin.[29] I will not say that these cases could or would have been won on the first hearing had a more objective and dispassionate argument then been made, but the items referred to did not help my cause, and in the cold, clear, and infinitely painful light of the morning after the original decisions, I became more and more aware of the probable harm that these expressions of personal resentment had done.

---

[28] *Kinsella v. Krueger*, 351 U.S. 470; *Reid v. Covert*, 351 U.S. 487.

[29] "So that the tradition which the Government invoked in its brief is of only 15 years' standing. And I cannot help being reminded of the freshwater college that was trying to inch into the Ivy League, announcing that 'It is traditional here that freshmen will uncover as they cross the Memorial Quadrangle. This tradition began last Monday.' The tradition of trying civilians by court-martial in the American service is only 15 years old." Ward & Paul transcript, p. 44.

"So I say, I suggest, that it would be much better for the Air Force to devote its very considerable talents to the material and terrific problem of maintaining our air supremacy, in a word, sticking to the wild blue yonder, instead of trying civilian women by court-martial." *Id.*, p. 52.

"But if we can assume that these agreements purported to enlarge the jurisdiction of American courts-martial, then we have this situation—that as applied to the *Covert* case, a woman in the District of Columbia, who normally could claim her double guarantee of jury trial, is, by reason of the act of a foreign parliament, following an executive agreement which does not mention women, deprived of that right to a jury trial here in the District of Columbia. And of that I say, in the language of Mr. Justice Grier, on the last page of the 24th of Howard, *Haud equidem invideo, mirror magis*—it is not so much that I am angry, but rather that I marvel at it." *Id.*, p. 55.

Once more to stress the obvious, in an appellate court emotion must have an intellectual foundation on which to rest, and it is far better for the tribunal to be moved to a sense of outrage on its own than for the advocate to expound his personal feelings of chagrin.

If it is permissible to descend to the jargon of Madison Avenue in this connection, the situation is one where the "soft sell" is indicated, where understatement is the most telling weapon. And, lest any reader think this an admonition too quixotic for a realist world, let him ponder the sheer power of restrained statement exemplified by the opinion written by Mr. Justice Brandeis in *Wan v. United States*.[30] To quote Professor Felix Frankfurter (as he then was), "in the terrible case of Ziang Sung Wan, his restraint attains austerity."[31] Read that opinion, and ask yourself whether any degree of emotionalism could possibly have been as effective.

Section 125. Rebuttal.—The first and undoubtedly the most troublesome problem in connection with rebuttal is whether, when you represent the party complaining of the decision below, you should get up at all for a second time. This is a problem—indeed it is frequently a dilemma—that cannot be solved by rote; in the end one's answer boils down to a matter of judgment—tempered by the advocate's own temperament.

Advocates of great distinction and ability have suggested that the privilege of the appellant or petitioner to argue in rebuttal should be sparingly exercised. Mr. Justice Jackson wrote:

I would not say that rebuttal is never to be indulged. At times it supplies important and definite corrections. But the most experienced advocates make least use of the privilege. Many inexperienced ones get into trouble by attempting to renew the principal argument. One who returns to his feet exposes himself to an accumulation of questions. Cases have been lost that, before counsel undertook a long rebuttal, appeared to be won.[32]

"Now, how to deal with them. I have suggested the traditional method for punishing extra-territorially committed crime, namely, by trial in the first district to which the person is brought or is found. That was not deemed too difficult in the post-war treason cases. It is true that there is no power to subpoena witnesses, but the Government had no difficulty last month in flying eighteen Italian subjects, whom it could not subpoena, here for the Icardi case. Of course, when that case was thrown out [*United States v. Icardi*, 140 F. Supp. 383 (D.D.C.)], it was rather too bad, because those were witnesses that could not have been used over again in other cases." *Id.*, p. 58.

[30] 266 U.S. 1.

[31] Frankfurter, *Mr. Justice Brandeis and the Constitution*, 45 Harv. L. Rev. 33, 105, reprinted in Frankfurter, ed., *Mr. Justice Brandeis* (1931), 49, 124.

[32] *Id.*, at 804.

And the late Mr. William D. Mitchell, who was a distinguished Solicitor General and Attorney General, said in his review of the earlier version of the present work:

Discussing whether reply briefs or reply arguments are desirable, the author is inclined to resolve doubts by favoring their use. The conclusion might well have been the other way. It should be a rare case where either a reply brief or reply argument is justified. In his brief and oral argument an appellant should be able to cover adequately his case and anticipate his adversary's. Able judges of appellate courts do not wobble back and forth to be captured by the litigant who insists on having the last word.[33]

The considerations governing the filing of reply briefs have been discussed in the light of the foregoing, in Section 81, *supra*. The present section, covering reply arguments, has been rethought with the comments of Justice Jackson and Mr. Mitchell in mind, and has been thoroughly rewritten.

First. If your opponent has been obviously demolished by the court, it is well not to trample on him further by way of a gloating "me too." Not only is it considered poor taste and worse sportsmanship to kick too hard a man who is down, but, more important—because a lawsuit is not a game, it involves serious consequences for the client—more important, such tactics are apt to kindle a feeling of sympathy for your opponent on the part of the court. Rebuttal in such a situation has precisely the opposite effect from what a good closing argument should be designed to accomplish.

Second. Rebuttal is, however, essential, whenever there is a real argument to answer, or whenever the court is obviously in doubt, or whenever there is a palpable misstatement to be corrected or even a residuum of honest confusion to be cleared up. On that score there can be but little disagreement. While I can look back on quite a few rebuttals that added little beyond the satisfaction of having had the last word, I can recall one or two that really advanced the case. It may be helpful to mention them briefly as examples.

(a) In *United States v. Summerlin*,[34] the question was whether a claim of the United States, tardily presented in a probate proceeding, could be barred by a state statute of limitations that was sugarcoated by being called a statute of nonclaim. In rebuttal, I read from the record that portion of the decree of the state court which

---

[33] Book Review, 64 Harv. L. Rev. 350, 351.
[34] 310 U.S. 414.

in terms held the claim "void."[35] Chief Justice Hughes really raised his eyebrows at the sound of that word—and wrote the unanimous opinion reversing the State supreme court.[36]

(b) In another case that will not be otherwise identified, I appeared for the Government, which was seeking to overturn the reversal of a criminal conviction. There were a number of difficult and fuzzy issues in the case, which, quite frankly, could have gone either way. My opponent, a lawyer of reputation, had apparently reached the stage of neglecting preparation; in any event, his argument was rested on a factual foundation that was demonstrably inaccurate. In ten minutes of rebuttal time, I exposed the inaccuracy, the judges' faces hardened noticeably, and the respondents went to jail. In that particular instance, I have no doubt whatever that the outcome of a case that was far from open-and-shut, not only inherently but also throughout most of the argument, ultimately turned on the circumstance that a vital misstatement of fact was exposed by the rebuttal.

Third. Don't get up a second time simply to rehash what has already been fully covered. The court's questions will normally indicate whether any tag ends imperatively require buttoning up. Rebuttal is justified only when it concentrates on the areas of genuine doubt.

In that connection, it is extremely undesirable to come up, ostensibly by way of rebuttal, with newly generated ideas on essentially tangential points that could not possibly have been thought through. Don't risk fuzzing up the final impression your argument left by injecting untested new departures.

Fourth. When you do get up for purposes of contradiction, be sure to go for the essentials. One of the most outstandingly poor rebuttals I have ever heard anywhere began with the announcement that "Petitioner's counsel has been guilty of a misstatement." The courtroom waited expectantly—and then the mountain

---

[35] "The Court is of the opinion that the United States with respect to filing its claim is in the same position as any other creditor of the estate * * * and that therefore the claim of the United States is void for the reason that it was not filed * * * within * * * months from the time of the first publication of the notice to creditors * * *." R.12, No. 715, Oct. T. 1939.

[36] "So far as the judgment goes beyond the jurisdiction of the probate court and purports to adjudge that the claim of the United States is void as a claim against the estate of the decedent because of failure to comply with the statute, the judgment is reversed." 310 U.S. at 418.

brought forth this mouse: "He said petitioner was president of the corporation when the record plainly shows that he was simply its vice-president."

Section 126. Preparation of the rebuttal.—Once past the painful question *whether*, the next problem is *how* to prepare an oral rebuttal.

If you are bottomside, representing the appellee or respondent, you can work your reply arguments into your own notes as you listen to opposing counsel, inserting them at the appropriate places. It is generally a good idea to use a red pencil for the purpose, so that you won't overlook the new matter as you come to it.

If you are topside, the process is much more difficult. Indeed, the preparation of an effective rebuttal is really one of the hardest points in the business. And yet it should not be neglected, because, as has already been indicated, it is often preferable to reply when there are unanswered or confused questions still floating around to which decisive answers are available.

Rebuttal argument should hit the jugular and concentrate on the big issues; it should avoid a long list of little things, or a whole lot of minor discrepancies that do not bear on the essentials of the case. Years ago, our debating coaches at college used to distinguish between rebuttals on the hunk system and rebuttals on the bird-shot system. I am glad to echo their advice here: eschew birdshot rebuttals.

The process of composing a rebuttal is, necessarily, a continuous one. First, during your opponent's argument you take notes of matters that he is misstating or as to which he is wrong, and that you can usefully reply to and correct. After a while, you can proceed to make tentative formulations of your outline for reply. That tentative outline will generally need to be revised as the argument proceeds, because if you have answer *X* to your opponent's contention *A*, and the court picks up *X* on its own and pretty well tramples *A* beyond all recognition, then, for reasons already set forth, you can cross out that item—and move to another.

By the time your opponent's argument is drawing to a close, you should have a pretty good idea of the points that are significant enough to warrant mentioning in a reply—and any doubts should be resolved in favor of elimination.

As to the items that you decide to mention, two principles are applicable. First, the opening of your rebuttal should, whenever possible, tie closely on to your opponent's conclusion. Whenever you can do that, you add immeasurably to the effectiveness of your reply. Second, unless you have a great deal of time left over so that you are not pressed by the clock, it is not safe to leave your choicest bit for the very end—because the court's questions may eat up your time and thus prevent your ever reaching that final forensic morsel.

The process of preparing an effective rebuttal, while not easy, is less difficult than the process of deciding where to reply, and on what issues. In this particular corner of the field, preeminently, one can only learn the hard way, viz., by doing—and by reflecting on the rebuttal (or the lack of one) in the light of the result attained. One's hindsight is of course always 20/20, but continuous retrospective introspection on rebuttals is bound to sharpen the advocate's vision for arguments still to come.

CHAPTER 9

The Task—and the Goal—
of the Advocate

Section 127. The task of presentation.—The basic responsibility of the advocate, after all, is the task of presentation—to present the law and facts of his particular case so that the court will know what the controversy is about, and will want to decide it in his favor.

That task is conditioned by three factors: the length of the record—the facts; the complexity of the questions involved—the law; and the interval allowed for argument—the time.

Each of these three factors varies from case to case. The record may consist of not over ten printed pages, as for example when the appeal involves review of the dismissal of an indictment or of a complaint. The record may run to several hundred or a thousand or even several thousand pages, when the case represents an appeal in a long criminal trial, or in a rate-fixing proceeding, or in the usual antitrust case. Indeed, on occasion, the advocate must deal with what are literally monster records; examples are the 12,719 printed pages in the North-South rate case,[1] 16,532 printed pages in the *Hartford-Empire* antitrust case,[2] and 16,832 printed pages in the *Cement Institute* basing-point case.[3]

The law factor is similarly a variable. The advocate may have a very narrow legal question to present, one that can be fully and comprehensively briefed in not over 20 pages. He may have a number of very substantial points that will have to be carefully condensed to fit within the limits that courts impose on the lengths of briefs. Or, perhaps, he may be dealing with a very complex series of legal problems or with a novel and highly significant question of

---

[1] *New York v. United States*, 331 U.S. 284.

[2] *Hartford-Empire Co. v. United States*, 323 U.S. 386, 324 U.S. 570.

[3] *Federal Trade Commission v. Cement Institute*, 333 U.S. 683.

constitutional law that cannot be adequately treated except in a brief extending to several hundred printed pages.

The factor of time is perhaps the least variable of the three; you get just so much time—30, 45, or 60 minutes—and it takes a very considerable showing to get more from any court, what with the pressure of overcrowded dockets everywhere. In the cases that have monster records, generous allowances will be made, but even so the advocate's problem remains, because the enlargement of time is never in direct ratio to the enlargement of the record.[4]

Moreover, if the advocate is to succeed, he must make a favorable impression: his task is to compress the law and the facts of his case into his allotted time—less interruptions—so that the court will obtain not only a clear conception of the case by the time he is through, but a favorable impression of his side as well. This is perhaps the most compelling reason, though assuredly not the only one, why so many experienced lawyers insist that advocacy is essentially an art, which can be mastered only through practice in the application of its governing principles.

Section 128. The task of presentation; A concrete example.—In the first version of this work, there is set out the complete stenographic transcript of the arguments in a closely contested antitrust case decided by the Supreme Court—*United States v. Line Material Co.*[5] It was twice argued, and, when finally decided, resulted in three opinions—majority, concurring, and dissent—that alone aggregate 76 printed pages in the reports.

The record in the case extended to 2,340 printed pages, of which all after the first 560 were exhibits—some 500 Government exhibits, and nearly 200 more introduced by the several defendants. By antitrust standards it was perhaps not a very long record, but it was fairly sizeable none the less.

The principal legal question was the scope of the *General Electric*[6] doctrine, i.e., the extent to which price-fixing under patent cross-license agreements was legal notwithstanding the prohibitions of the Sherman Antitrust Act. There were numerous subsidiary

---

[4] In the cases just cited, eight hours were allowed for argument in *New York v. United States*; thirteen hours were allowed for the original argument in the *Hartford-Empire* case, and eight more for the reargument; and eight hours were allowed in the *Cement Institute* case. These figures include the time for argument on both sides.

[5] 333 U.S. 287.

[6] *United States v. General Electric Co.*, 272 U.S. 476.

questions, some involving the Sherman Act,[7] some turning on the Federal Rules of Civil Procedure,[8] and some concerning the patent law.

That case had to be compressed into a single hour of argument on each side, since requests by both sides for extra time, made for both argument and reargument, had been denied.

Essentially, the task of the lawyers who argued the *Line Material* case was the same as that of lawyers who present any kind of a case in any appellate court: to condense the mass of their materials into an understandable and palatable verbal capsule—to make the case clear to the court, and to persuade the court to decide it in their favor.

How would you have tackled that assignment?

Section 129. Keying the oral argument to the brief; Selection and arrangement of points for oral argument.—Obviously, all the manifold details of a case, particularly of a complicated case, cannot be presented in the limited time allotted to oral argument, even when that time has been enlarged. Some portions, frequently many portions, must be left to the brief. As has already been pointed out, the basic principle is that the essentials should be conveyed orally, whereas the filling in of the details is best left to the brief. Similarly, because the principal propositions should be covered on oral argument, the subsidiary points must be relegated to the written argument. There may well be cases where it is desirable to discuss only the facts orally, leaving all discussion of law to the brief. No single rule of thumb, here or elsewhere, will fit every case. But it is essential to understand fully the advantages and the limitations of each medium, and to apportion your points between speech and writing in order to achieve the maximum effectiveness in the combined presentation.

A little thought and plenty of preparation will generally suffice to separate those matters that can best be presented orally from those that are better left to the written argument. The more difficult task of selection is to take the points that can be effectively set forth in the oral argument and to eliminate those that your allotted time will not permit you to cover orally. Suppose you have three major

---

[7] E.g., whether the facts brought the case within the rule of *United States v. Masonite Corp.*, 316 U.S. 265; *Interstate Circuit, Inc. v. United States*, 306 U.S. 208; and *Standard Sanitary Mfg. Co. v. United States*, 226 U.S. 20.

[8] Whether the District Court's findings were "clearly erroneous" within Rule 52(a), F.R. Civ. P., and whether in any event they were entitled to particular weight, being based primarily on documents.

points; each of them is important, but your time will allow you to develop only two of them convincingly. Which two will you pick?

That sort of problem is the elimination test that will separate the cream of the lawyers from the skimmed milk of the mere attorneys at law; because, after all, in the famous last analysis, given brains and learning and a competent grasp of legal techniques, the quality that distinguishes the outstanding lawyer from the lawyer who is simply very good is a highly developed sense of relevance.[9]

And advocacy in open court requires even more: If, as will frequently be the case, the three propositions in the situation just put are equally relevant, to what other test for survival or elimination should they be subjected?

Some advocates will select the two propositions that are most dramatic or arresting, others the two they consider most sympathetic or appealing, still others those propositions they conceive to be the strongest as a matter of logic and hence most satisfying intellectually.

On occasion, the same advocate who would select one set of propositions for presentation to one tribunal would argue the case quite differently if he appeared before another court or before the same court differently constituted. Indeed, there may be instances where the division in a particular court has been so marked that one or two judges will be the swing men on a particular type of case—and in that event the argument is most effective if addressed essentially to them.

All these techniques, obviously, require more than even the most highly developed sense of relevance: They call for a keen appreciation of the principles of psychology. It may well be, of course, that psychology in its present flowering is neither an exact science nor indeed a science at all. Even so, that circumstance only serves to underscore the view, rather widely held at the bar, that advocacy in its more expert applications is very much an art, because certainly in this instance there is no single answer or formula to solve the problem.

It should be repeated here, also, that the order of presentation of points in the brief is not necessarily the most effective order of presentation for the argument. Frequently it is; often it is not. The

---

[9] "Mr. Justice Frankfurter compared the lawyer and the scientist. The lawyer, he said, is distinguished as an 'expert in relevance.' Since the law touches life in a wider and perhaps deeper way than any other profession, this ability to ferret out the relevant considerations of any type of problem is a necessary qualification for the lawyer. The scientist, however, though highly trained in what is relevant within the limited area of his field, becomes lost among the maze of conflicting forces that operate outside his particular specialty." *Harvard Law School Record*, vol. 5, no. 9, December 2, 1947.

written brief can more easily develop the several propositions involved in their strictly logical order, whereas the oral argument may need to depart from that arrangement in order to take up at the outset the crucial issue, or, it may be, the one that appears to be the only one really in dispute.

Where, for example, an appeal involves a jurisdictional question or one of appealability, in addition to issues on the merits, the former issue is almost necessarily the one first reached in the brief. But it can frequently be deferred or omitted in oral argument, depending on the treatment given it by the other side in its brief, or on the court's reaction to it at the outset of the argument.

There is no set formula that will fit every case. The only standard is that of flexibility; the decision in the end must depend on the advocate's judgment of the way the argument is developing.

Section 130. An exercise in persuasion.—The presentation of a case to an appellate court, like any other instance of advocacy, is an exercise in persuasion: You seek to make the judges decide in your favor. Everything must be bent to that end—every sentence in the brief, indeed every footnote; every sentence in the oral argument; every mannerism, every gesture, even the advocate's attire. Every form of oral advocacy involves the impact of one personality on others. In an appellate court, it is the impact of the lawyer on three, five, seven, or nine judges. Though the number on the bench may vary, the advocate's aim remains the same: He must always, persistently, constantly, unflaggingly seek to persuade a majority of his listeners to agree with him.

That being so, he does not help his cause if he antagonizes his judicial audience or any of them. One never persuades by antagonizing. You may take a dim view of a particular judge, or of a particular decision, or of a whole series of decisions, or indeed of the prevailing trend of the particular tribunal—but when you appear before the judges on behalf of a client, your job is to win that client's case, not to tell them off, or any of them, or to go all out on any tack not necessary to your case. Flank the difficult forensic obstacles if hitting them head on repels your listeners. The frequency with which counsel will fight a court, either generally or on specific unessential propositions, serves to underscore the extent to which some lawyers overlook the obvious, viz., that advocacy is an exercise in persuasion.

Section 131. The dangers of crusading.—A crusader, in this connection, is any lawyer who identifies himself too closely or too emotionally with his cause. Once a lawyer starts crusading, he loses the objectivity he needs, he begins to slop over, he rapidly diminishes his effectiveness, and he becomes that stock, hackneyed, and yet constantly reappearing character, the lawyer who represents himself and who in consequence has a fool for a client.

My favorite story on the difference in function between lawyers and crusaders may be apocryphal, though I heard it many years ago from one of high authority who could qualify as "a source believed to be reliable." Here it is:

After the landslide election of 1928, President-elect Hoover was experiencing some indecision regarding the appointment of an Attorney General, in consequence of which he called upon Chief Justice Taft and besought that eminent statesman's counsel.

The Chief Justice warmly urged the merits of Solicitor General Mitchell, praising that gentleman's learning and competence, and stressing the respect and esteem and confidence with which the Supreme Court regarded him.

Mr. Hoover did not at first warm to the suggestion. Yes, Mr. Mitchell was a fine lawyer, "but he hasn't got an aggressive enough personality. I want someone who will take this issue of Law Enforcement"—this was still in the era of the Experiment Noble in Purpose [Prohibition]—"who will take this issue of Law Enforcement to the people, and really go crusading on it."

"Why, Mr. President!" said the Chief Justice, who had himself been Chief Executive, "you don't want a crusader. You've got to do the crusading yourself. What you need is a lawyer!"

I wish it were possible for me to document, with chapter and verse and collection of horrible examples, the timeless truth and the enduring wisdom of Chief Justice Taft's remark. I wish I could cite the numberless instances, since 1933, in court and out, of the ineffectiveness, not to say incompetence, of the attorneys at law who took to crusading, when by remaining detached they could have done an infinitely better, an infinitely more professional, and an infinitely more effective job.

At this juncture I shall have to content myself with a single example, exact identification of which will necessarily be fuzzy.

Some years back a man was convicted under extremely unfair circumstances. A crusading organization became interested in the case, and it retained a well-known, well-advertised, and (financially) completely successful lawyer to perfect the appeal. That appeal was heard by an appellate court of which the less said the better; some of its members later resigned, some were indicted, and its judgments in quite a number of cases were later set aside after extensive litigation because of the corruption with which they had been tainted. This was the court that affirmed the judgment of conviction.

The well-known lawyer thereupon loudly announced that he would petition for a writ of certiorari. Without question, he had a good cert. case, and even the old Court—this was before 1937—would have reversed. But, even as counsel was talking pretty big about what he would do in the Supreme Court, he failed to move for a stay of mandate, the mandate went down, sentence could not be stayed further, and the great case became moot. "You don't want a crusader, Mr. President; what you need is a lawyer!"

One further caution may not be out of order. When you are opposed by a crusader, avoid the temptation to go counter crusading against him. His emotional instability, his muddy thinking, will all strongly tempt you to have at him in kind. Resist the temptation. Remain detached, lawyerlike, and professional. If you have to operate on him, do so with the calm, impersonal deftness of a surgeon with a scalpel. It may not be so much fun, but it will be more effective—and your crusading opponent will find your technique, if not so immediately painful, certainly more deadly in the end.

Section 132. Inner conviction.—Assuming that the advocate has the technical equipment, assuming that he has mastered not only the principles of advocacy but also the art of applying them, what extra, added feature is there that distinguishes the really outstanding advocate from the run of just able advocates?

In my view, it is an inner conviction of the soundness and correctness of his case. That is not just fervor, and most assuredly it is not crusading, what with its screaming and its inevitable concomitant inaccuracies. It is, rather, an abiding conviction that law and justice are both on your side, certainly as to the points you are making. This inner conviction is often self-induced, frequently by an involved process of rationalization, but it is none the worse for that. The important thing is that you have it, so that you believe what you are saying, or at least believe the reasonableness of what you are saying, and that you are not simply repeating a line of patter, tongue in cheek.

As I review the cases I have argued in appellate courts, it seems to me that, in the present connection, they fall into three groups. Some I believed in wholeheartedly from the start, even passionately, so much so that it took an effort to avoid slopping over. Others were essentially indifferent cases, as to which I had no particular conviction one way or the other at the start, but where the joy of battle, as it were, eventually induced a belief that I was right. (O.K., turn the psychologists loose on that one!) In a third group, I had grave doubts when I started, and I needed to explore the cases very thoroughly before I found an approach or a theory to which I could really subscribe. Not until then was I able to argue those cases with conviction.

Possibly a concrete example may serve to clarify the sort of mental turmoil that precedes the acquisition of the requisite inner conviction.

In the *Line Material* case,[10] the Government's original argument had hammered at the doctrine of the *General Electric* case,[11] which had held that price-fixing under a patent license did not violate the antitrust laws. That argument rested in part on economic grounds, in part on some strongly held views as to the social values implicit in a patent, and in part (by way of conclusion from the foregoing) on what was conceived to be the proper scope of the patent grant. That argument was nothing more or less than a statement of the credo of the Antitrust Division of the Department of Justice, the Gospel according to Thurman Arnold, and it had been ably presented by Assistant Attorney General Wendell Berge. It failed, however, to gain the concurrence of a majority of the Court, and, Mr. Berge having meanwhile resigned from the Department, the *Line Material* case was set down for reargument.[12]

It was then assigned to me, and I had the benefit, not only of the briefs originally filed, but of a stenographic transcript of all the original arguments. I studied record, briefs, and arguments, read a good many cases, and soaked myself in the atmosphere of the antitrust patent field. Of course I wanted to win, and, whatever the merits or demerits of the case, I viewed it as the leader of the defeated faction in a primary looked on the party's nominee: "Sure, he's a so-and-so—but he's *our* so-and-so now." But—I could not subscribe to the tenets of the Antitrust Religion. Perhaps salvation lies that way; no matter, I could not with conviction recite the patter of the anti-*General Electric* syllogism. As the old preacher said, "And if I do not march in step, it is because I hear a different drummer."

Thereafter, I got busy on the facts, and proceeded to analyze the *General Electric* case as a matter of logic. Eventually I convinced

---

[10] *United States v. Line Material Co.*, 333 U.S. 287.

[11] *United States v. General Electric Co.*, 272 U.S. 476.

[12] Journal, U.S. Sup. Ct., Oct. T. 1946, p. 275.

myself that, on the facts, the Government was entitled to a decree without any change in law, and I likewise convinced myself, at least to my own satisfaction, of a logical flaw in the *General Electric* case, viz., that the provision in the agreements in question for the maintenance of the patentee-licensor's own prices did not contribute to the protection of the patent, which was the sole announced justification for the *General Electric* doctrine.[13] After that I had no more inner qualms, and whatever else may be said of my efforts on reargument, they certainly cannot fairly be criticized for reflecting any want of conviction.

To resume: It is, I am convinced, essential to effective advocacy that the advocate have, before he gets up, an abiding inner conviction of the justice of his cause. How he acquires that feeling—whether he starts with it or generates it in the process of preparation—is not really important. But if he is going to carry conviction to his listeners, he must first carry conviction within himself.

Section 133. The ultimate tribute.—We have been going upward and onward in this chapter, from the task of presentation as such to the art which, over and above any technical equipment, that task requires; and we have discussed also the advocate's need for possessing a highly developed sense of relevance and an abiding inner conviction of the rightness of his cause.

He must have all those qualities if he is to reach real heights. What, then, is the ultimate to which he may aspire?

I venture to suggest a fitting goal for the advocate, one that may well be unattainable for all but a few, but that is worth striving for nonetheless. It is this: So to present a case that judges will say to themselves when they hear him, as Chief Judge Cardozo of the New York Court of Appeals used to say when he heard Mr. Charles Evans Hughes, "How can I possibly decide against this man?"

When your argument evokes such a reaction—that's Effective Appellate Advocacy!

---

[13] "If the patentee * * * licenses the selling of the articles, may he limit the selling by limiting the method of sale and the price? We think he may do so, provided the conditions of sale are normally and reasonably adapted to secure pecuniary reward for the patentee's monopoly." *United States v. General Electric Co.*, 272 U.S. 476, 490.

PART IV

OTHER ISSUES

CHAPTER 10

Rehearings

Section 134. Petitions for rehearing; In general.—Petitions for rehearing can be more poetically—and more accurately—labeled "Love's Labor Lost": The normal petition for rehearing has about the same chance of success as the proverbial snowball on the far side of the River Styx. This is particularly true when the points raised in such a petition have been fully set forth in a dissent, which is to say that they have already been considered by the court. In that event, to ask for a rehearing by the same judges is an utter waste of time, money, labor, and good white paper. After all, if the dissenting judge or judges were unable to persuade their brethren in the conference room and in chambers—i.e., in oral discussions face to face and without any limitations as to time—it is absurd, indeed it is fatuous, to suppose that losing counsel will meet with more success simply by presenting a necessarily abbreviated written document.

Section 135. Petitions for rehearing; Basic reasons for denial.— Charles Evans Hughes, in the interval between his two terms of service on the Supreme Court, wrote that "Petitions for rehearing are an improvement on the tavern[1] as counsel may enjoy the luxury of telling the Court to its face what is thought of its opinion * * * ."[2] Later on in the same passage, he quoted Mr. Justice Bradley on the subject, a quotation which goes to the heart of the matter:

It ought to be understood, or at least believed, whether it is true or not, that this Court, being a Court of last resort, gives great consideration to cases

---

[1] Compare Section 2, p. 3, *supra*. See also Jackson, *Tribute to Country Lawyers: A Review*, 30 A.B.A.J. 136, 139: "* * * this vanishing country lawyer * * * never quit. He could think of motions for every purpose under the sun, and he made them all. He moved for new trials, he appealed; and if he lost out in the end, he joined the client at the tavern in damning the judge—which is the last rite in closing an unsuccessful case, and I have officiated at many."

[2] Hughes, *The Supreme Court of the United States*, 71.

235

of importance and involving consequences like this, and there should be a finality somewhere. This custom of making motions for a rehearing is not a custom to be encouraged. It prevails in some States as a matter of ordinary practice to grant a rehearing on a mere application for it, but that practice we do not consider a legitimate one in this Court. It is possible that in the haste of examining cases before us, we sometimes overlook something, and then we are willing to have that pointed out, but to consider that this Court will reexamine the matter and change its judgment on a case, it seems to me, is not taking a proper view of the functions of this Court. Your application is a proper one to be made, but this matter of motions for rehearing has become—I won't say a nuisance, but very disagreeable to the Court.[3]

Except where something has been overlooked, the routine or indiscriminate granting of rehearings reflects inadequate consideration of the appeal on the original hearing. As Mr. Justice Frankfurter said in his concurring opinion in the *Western Pacific Railroad* case,[4]

Rehearings are not a healthy step in the judicial process; surely they ought not to be deemed a normal procedure. Yet one who has paged the Federal Reporter for nearly fifty years is struck with what appears to be a growth in the tendency to file petitions for rehearing in the courts of appeals. I have not made a quantitative study of the facts, but one gains the impression that in some circuits these petitions are filed almost as a matter of course. This is an abuse of judicial energy. It results in needless delay. It arouses false hopes in defeated litigants and wastes their money. If petitions for rehearing were justified, except in rare instances, it would bespeak serious defects in the work of the courts of appeals, an assumption which must be rejected.

The other side of the coin appears in an opinion of the same Justice dissenting from the denial of a petition for rehearing:

Because I deem a reargument to be required, I do not mean to imply that it would lead to a different result. The basis of an adjudication may be as important as the decision. The Court has rightly been parsimonious in ordering rehearings, but the occasions on which important and difficult cases have been reargued have, I believe, enhanced the deliberative process.[5]

Section 136. Petitions for rehearing; Additional reasons for denial.—In part, of course, the low batting average of petitions for rehearings illustrates a very human trait. Most persons do not like to change their minds once they have made them up—and most judges share that well-nigh universal reaction. There is extant a letter from Mr. Justice Holmes that says, "I guess * * * that the

---

[3] *Ibid.*, 71–72.
[4] 345 U.S. 247, 268, 270.
[5] *Detroit v. Murray Corp.*, 357 U.S. 913, 915.

defeated side will apply for a rehearing hinting that we don't understand the patents and that the application will be denied in the belief that we damned well do."[6] Rarely has a prediction been more fully—or more quickly—fulfilled.[7]

It is only on the rarest occasions that a judge can be induced to view the same case differently once he is publicly committed to a particular course of reasoning on the issues that case involves. Confessing error afterwards does not involve the same degree of painful anguish; witness the announcement of three justices that they had changed their views on the flag salute issue,[8] and the comment of another that he would vote differently than he once had on the scope of the Fourth Amendment.[9] Where the earlier view had been expressed in a different capacity, backtracking is of course easier; here the classic instance is the graceful admission by Mr. Justice Jackson that an opinion he had signed as Attorney General on the same issue was, on reflection, completely wrong.[10]

Where, following the first argument, no opinion has been delivered, no one is publicly on record, and many votes in such situations have gone the other way following reargument. The Income Tax case in the 1890s is the best known instance,[11] though there

---

[6] Letter from Holmes to Laski, Feb. 14, 1930, 2 *Holmes-Laski Letters* (Howe ed. 1953) 1224.

[7] The case was *Minerals Separation Corp. v. Magma Copper Co.*, 280 U.S. 400, decided Feb. 24, 1930 (No. 71, Oct. T. 1929). A petition for rehearing, filed March 21, 1930, urged *inter alia* at p. 15 "misunderstanding of the meaning and effect * * * of the direction in" the patent in suit. The files in the case—this was before the denial of petitions for rehearing was noted either in the journal or in the reports—disclose that the petition was denied on April 14, 1930.

[8] See *Jones v. Opelika*, 316 U.S. 584, 623.

[9] See *On Lee v. United States*, 343 U.S. 747, 762.

[10] *McGrath v. Kristensen*, 340 U.S. 162, 176. The Attorney General's opinion in question was 39 Op. Att. Gen. 504.

Another example is *Lewis v. Manufacturers Nat. Bank*, 364 S. 603, 610, where Mr. Justice Harlan disavowed an opinion in which he had joined while one of the Circuit Judges for the Second Circuit.

See also Frankfurter., J., dissenting, in *Henslee v. Union Planters Bank*, 335 U.S. 595, 600: "Wisdom too often never comes, and so one ought not to reject it merely because it comes late. Since I now realize that I should have joined the dissenters in the *Merchants Bank* case, 320 U.S. 256, I shall not compound error by pushing that decision still farther. I would affirm the judgment, substantially for the reasons given below. 166 F.2d 993."

[11] On the first argument, the question of the constitutional validity of the income tax was reversed, due to an equally divided court, Mr. Justice H. E. Jackson being ill. *Pollock v. Farmers' Loan & Trust Co.*, 157 U.S. 429, 586. On rehearing, even though Justice

(continued)

have been others.[12] But when an opinion has once been announced and subscribed, it requires a rare degree of open-mindedness and intellectual humility for any judge to admit error on the identical issue in the very same case. Mr. Justice Harlan's opinion on rehearing in *Reid v. Covert*[13] is an example of this most unusual kind of admission—the only one, to my knowledge, that is to be found in the Supreme Court reports.

Section 137. Rehearings granted in Courts of Appeals.—By way of preliminary, it should be noted that, in this section as well as in those following, "rehearing" is used in its narrow technical sense of a second consideration following a decision. Otherwise stated, "rehearing" does not include a mere "reargument," which follows a court's failure to arrive at or to announce a decision following its original consideration of the cause.[14]

Petitions for rehearing in Courts of Appeal that succeed not only in being granted but that induce the same three judges to arrive at a different result are, necessarily, infrequent.[15] Occasionally a petition for rehearing, while in form denied, nonetheless broadens the scope of the order remanding the case.[16] In most other instances, the grant of a rehearing reflects a later controlling decision[17] or a later controlling statute or regulation.[18] In any Federal court, the question of its own jurisdiction is always open,

---

Jackson voted in favor of the validity of the statute, it was invalidated. *Pollock v. Farmers' Loan Trust Co.*, 158 U.S. 601. One judge, very plainly, changed his mind; his identity has never been established.

[12] E.g., *United States v. Grimaud*, affirmed by equally divided court, 216 U.S. 614; on rehearing, unanimously reversed, 220 U.S. 506. See Frankfurter and Landis, *The Business of the Supreme Court* (1928) 15–16, note. 43.

[13] 354 U.S. 1, 65.

[14] See *In re Fidelity Tube Corporation*, 278 F.2d 777 (C.A. 3), which was argued three times before any opinion was handed down. The last reargument (and, in all likelihood, the first reargument) was in banc.

[15] E.g., *Anderson Co. v. Trico Products Corp.*, 267 F.2d 700 (C.A. 2); *Verbeeck v. Black Diamond Steamship Corp.*, 273 F.2d 61 (C.A. 2).

[16] E.g., *Smith v. Flinn*, 264 F.2d 523 (C.A. 8); *Cross v. Pasley*, 270 F.2d 88 (C.A. 8); cf. *Forman v. United States*, 259 F.2d 128, 261 F.2d 181, 264 F.2d 955 (C.A. 9), affirmed, 361 U.S. 416.

[17] E.g., *Great Northern Railway Co. v. Hyde*, 241 F.2d 707 (C.A. 8); *Needleman v. United States*, 261 F.2d 803 (C.A. 5); cf. *King v. Waterman Steamship Corp.*, 272 F.2d 823 (C.A. 3).

[18] E.g., *McGehee v. Commissioner*, 260 F.2d 818 (C.A. 5) (statute); *United States v. Gibson*, 225 F.2d 807 (C.A. 9) (regulation).

and one circuit frankly told counsel that he need not apologize for raising a jurisdictional question only on petition for rehearing.[19]

Normally, then, the only petition for rehearing that is likely to succeed is one that, in the language of the Eighth Circuit's Rule 15(a), is restricted to "directing the attention of the court to some controlling matter of law or fact which a party claims was overlooked in deciding a case." Unless your petition is thus limited, you are wasting your time and your client's money.[20]

Section 138. Rehearings granted in banc in Courts of Appeals.— In circuits that have five active circuit judges or more, losing a case by a divided vote is not the end. Losing counsel may petition for a rehearing in banc.[21]

This practice was first employed in the Third Circuit, and, being challenged, was sustained by the Supreme Court in the *Textile Mills* case,[22] decided in 1941. The 1948 revision of the Judicial Code formalized the practice, and provided specifically for hearings in banc, by all the active circuit judges of the circuit.[23] When the Ninth Circuit struck from its files as unauthorized an unsuccessful litigant's petition for a rehearing in banc, the Supreme Court in the *Western Pacific Railroad* case [24] reversed, pointing out, however, that whether a rehearing in banc should be granted could be determined either by the original panel or by the entire court. The practice accordingly differs from circuit to circuit, but parties are clearly free to request in banc rehearings.

Inasmuch as a rehearing in banc augments the tribunal hearing the cause, it has frequently happened that the court in banc reaches a result just the opposite of that reached by the

---

[19] *Cummings v. Redeeriaktieb Transatlantic*, 242 F.2d 275 (C.A. 3). See also *United States v. New York, New Haven & Hartford R. Co.*, 276 F.2d 525 (C.A. 2), where a suggestion of lack of jurisdiction was fully considered on a second petition for rehearing.

[20] For another excellent statement, see *United States v. Procter & Gamble Co.*, 19 F.R.D. 247, 248–49, note 1 (D.N.J.), quoting a District Court rule that similarly formulates the proper nature of reargument.

[21] I follow the statute, cited below, in rendering this as "in banc" without italics. Actually, since the expression is of great antiquity, from the days of Law French, the correct form is "en banc," and hence preferably italicized. Would that the only deficiency of the Revisers of Title 28 had been their ignorance of philology!

[22] *Textile Mills Corp. v. Commissioner*, 314 U.S. 326.

[23] 28 U.S.C. § 46(c). Note that hearings in banc in District Courts have long been authorized. *FCF Film Corp. v. Gourley*, 240 F.2d 711, 714 (C.A. 3); see *Kovrak v. Ginsburg*, 177 F. Supp. 614 (E.D. Pa.)

[24] 345 U.S. 247.

panel.[25] For, not only will a rehearing in banc add from two to six additional circuit judges to the original bench, depending on the number in the circuit, but, inasmuch as such a rehearing is limited by the statute to "all the active circuit judges of the circuit,"[26] it will frequently exclude two of the original panel,[27] and may of course exclude all three, in view of the great statutory flexibility for the composition of a Court of Appeals.

Section 139. Practical details in connection with petitions for rehearing in Courts of Appeals.—While, as has been indicated, the normal petition for rehearing in a Court of Appeals gets fairly short shrift, it does have one undeniable virtue, namely, that the time for certiorari runs, not from the date of the original opinion, but from the date of denial of rehearing.[28] (There are refinements in respect of motions for modification of the judgment and second petitions for rehearing,[29] but the general rule is unquestioned.) Consequently, the filing of a petition for rehearing extends the time for your client to raise additional funds for the next appellate step, and may increase the possibility that some other circuit will rule the other way and so produce a conflict. But these apparent advantages frequently collide with the requirement, imposed by the rules of most courts, that every petition for rehearing must have appended thereto a certificate of counsel that it is filed in good faith and not for purposes of delay.

It has already been noted that in the Eighth Circuit a petition for rehearing is restricted to "directing the attention of the court to some controlling matter of law or fact which a party claims was overlooked in deciding a case." The limitation in the Court of Customs and Patent appeals is to "points supposed to have been

---

[25] E.g., *Howard v. United States*, 232 F.2d 274 (C.A. 5); *G. H. Miller & Co. v. United States*, 260 F.2d 286 (C.A. 7); *Reardon v. California Tanker Co.*, 260 F.2d 369 (C.A. 2); *Noah v. Liberty Mutual Ins. Co.*, 267 F.2d 218 (C.A. 5); *Leary v. United States*, 268 F.2d 623 (C.A. 9). Compare *Sperry Rand Corp. v. Bell Telephone Laboratories*, 272 F.2d 29 (C.A. 2) (different result as a matter of law, same result in exercise of discretion).

[26] 28 U.S.C. § 46(c).

[27] E.g., *Reardon v. California Tankers Co.*, 260 F.2d 369 (A. 2) (two retired circuit judges on original panel); *Herzog v. United States*, 226 F.2d 561, 235 F.2d 664 (C.A. 9), certiorari denied, 352 U.S. 844 (district judge and retired circuit judge on original panel).

[28] See Robertson and Kirkham, *Jurisdiction of the Supreme Court of the United States* (Kurland & Wolfson ed. 1951) § 414 (which incorporates by reference § 384).

[29] See Stern and Gressman, Supreme Court Practice (2d ed. 1954) ch. V(A), pp. 163–66, and see particularly *Federal Trade Comm. v. Minneapolis-Honeywell Co.*, 344 U.S. 206.

overlooked or misapprehended by the court."[30] (Whether that formulation is really a limitation may well be doubted; every petition for rehearing urges, indeed screams, that the opinion just filed is full of misapprehensions.)

Since this is not a practice manual, there is no occasion in these pages to discuss stay of mandate, supersedeas, or bail pending appeal, nor to warn counsel that failure to make timely substitution of public officers will make the cause abate.

Suppose, however, that you are winning counsel, relaxing in your office while savoring the eternal verities and soothing nuances of the opinion in your favor: Is there anything you should or can do when the opposition, ignorantly refusing to stay licked, files a petition for rehearing? Four circuits do not permit the filing of a response to a petition for rehearing,[31] two plus the Court of Customs and Patent Appeals specifically allow a response,[32] and the rules of the others are silent. In practice, two circuits will ask for a response if they are troubled by the petition.[33]

The soundest advice in this situation is, Sit Tight. You will have ample opportunities to say your say if and when you are called on for a response, or if and when your opponent seeks certiorari. Until then, there is nothing to be gained, financially or spiritually, in rearguing a case you have already won.

Section 140. Rehearings in the Supreme Court of the United States.—How to discourage the unmeritorious petition for rehearing that is filed as a matter of course, and yet to leave the door slightly ajar for that rare instance in which a rehearing should be granted, may well be an insoluble problem. Certainly the Supreme Court's short-lived effort to stem the tide by reducing from 25 to 15 days the time within which to petition for rehearing was unsuccessful;[34] it was accordingly abandoned in the 1954 Rules.[35] There is really only one way to discourage unmeritorious applications for rehearing, and that is to deny them.

---

[30] Rule VII.

[31] Second Circuit, Rule 25(a); Fourth Circuit, Rule 12; Sixth Circuit; Rule 22(d); Eighth Circuit, Rule 15(c).

[32] Seventh Circuit, Rule 25(a); District of Columbia Circuit, Rule 26(b); Court of Customs and Patent Appeals, Rule VII.

[33] The Second and Tenth, to my knowledge; but my experience in the former on this point antedates the present version of its Rule 25.

[34] Amended Rule 33, 332 U.S. 857, 875; see 68 Harv. L. Rev. at 83–84.

[35] Rule 58(1) and (2).

In the first five Terms after the 1954 Rules went into effect, about 970 petitions for rehearing were disposed of, and all but 15 were denied.[36] Of the 15 granted, only two—*Reid v. Covert*[37] and *Flora v. United States*[38]—followed opinions on the merits. It may be noted that, in 20 years preceding 1961, only five rehearings were granted following the decisions on the merits.[39]

In sum, a slim haul; and yet that is par for the course. In the earlier edition of this work it was noted that, at the 1946 through 1948 Terms, the Supreme Court granted 17 petitions for rehearing out of some 700 filed. All except three involved cases considered either on petitions for certiorari or on jurisdictional statements. Of the other three, one turned on an intervening decision; a second was granted after affirmance by an equally divided court and was then reaffirmed after reargument, still by an equally divided court.[40] In the third case, *Graveer Mfg. Co. v. Linde Co.*,[41] rehearing was granted after opinion, but on rehearing the same result was reached.[42]

In this connection, of the five rehearings granted after opinion in the twenty years preceding the last edition of this book, the result in the end was different in only two cases.[43]

Section 141. Rehearings in the Supreme Court of the United States; Mechanics and doubtful areas.—The Supreme Court, like some Courts of Appeals, does not permit responses to a petition for rehearing except at its own request.[44] When such a request is made,

---

[36] The overall figure includes motions to file a petition for rehearing, i.e., petitions out of time, as well as petitions for rehearing filed as of right. The basis for computation was the number of cases. I thumbed the reports and so the final figure is not guaranteed; "E.&O.E.," as the brokers say.

[37] Rehearing granted, 352 U.S. 901, following opinions at 351 U.S. 470 and 351 U.S. 487.

[38] Rehearing granted, 360 U.S. 922, following opinion at 357 U.S. 63.

[39] *Jones v. Opelika*, rehearing granted, 318 U.S. 796, following opinion at 316 U.S. 584; *Elgin, J.&E.R. Co. v. Burley*, rehearing granted, 326 U.S. 801, following opinion at 325 U.S. 711; *Graver Mfg. Co. v. Linde Co.*, rehearing granted, 337 U.S. 910, following opinion at 336 U.S. 271; *Reid v. Covert, supra* note 37; *Flora v. United States, supra* note 38.

[40] *Marzani v. United States*, 335 U.S. 895, 336 U.S. 910, 336 U.S. 922.

[41] 336 U.S. 271.

[42] 337 U.S. 910; 339 U.S. 605.

[43] (a) *Jones v. Opelika*, 316 U.S. 584; rehearing granted, 318 U.S. 796; different result, 319 U.S. 103.

(b) *Reid v. Covert*, 351 U.S. 487, and *Kinsella v. Krueger*, 351 U.S. 470; rehearing granted, 352 U.S. 901; different result and earlier opinions withdrawn, 354 U.S. 1.

[44] Rule 58(3).

the petitioner has every reason to be hopeful,[45] but in at least one recent instance rehearing was denied notwithstanding.[46] Conversely, while Rule 58(3) states that "No petition for rehearing will be granted in the absence of such a request and an opportunity to submit a reply in response thereto," this limitation has not been adhered to when rehearing is sought following affirmance by an equally divided Court.[47] It should be noted that, while the filing of a timely petition for rehearing during the Term stays the mandate until disposition thereof, a separate motion to stay the mandate is necessary if the petition for rehearing is filed while the Court is in vacation.[48]

Section 142. Effect of denial of rehearing.—The old saw, that it is better to have loved and lost than never to have loved at all, should not be applied to petitions for rehearing. A "rehearing denied" will frequently weaken a good point when that point later becomes critical. First, no matter how strong a point may be, it will be far weaker if presented in the last of a long series of requests for reconsideration, because by then the usual judicial attitude recalls General Forrest's turn-down of the lieutenant's renewed application for leave: "Dammit, I told you 'No' twicet!" And, lest any reader deem that comment overly cynical, let him look at the *Rosenberg* case.[49]

There, after six consecutive applications for review had been denied, it was finally contended, on a seventh, that, since the petitioners had been found guilty of a conspiracy alleged in the indictment to have continued from 1944 to 1950, they were not properly sentenced to death by the judge under the Espionage Act of 1917, but could only have been so sentenced upon recommendation of the jury pursuant to the Atomic Energy Act of 1946. Now, whether or not that contention was correct, it would be hard to urge that as an original proposition it was unsubstantial.[50] But it was not

---

[45] *Reid v. Covert*, 352 U.S. 813; *United States v. Ohio Power Co.*, 352 U.S. 987; *Flora v. United States*, 358 U.S. 871.

[46] *Detroit v. Murray Corp.*, 356 U.S. 934 (response requested), 357 U.S. 913 (rehearing denied).

[47] E.g., *Ryan Stevedoring Co. v. Pan-Atlantic S. S. Corp.*, 349 U.S. 926; *Indian Towing Co. v. United States*, 349 U.S. 926.

[48] Rule 59(2).

[49] *Rosenberg v. United States*, 346 U.S. 273. This opinion, filed after the final ruling in the case, sets out in chronological order all of the applications made on behalf of the petitioners.

[50] See 346 U.S. at 301–310 (opinion of Frankfurter, J.).

presented as an original proposition, it was first presented as a
renewed, warmed-over, and hence apparently unoriginal seventh
proposition, and under unusual circumstances that would have
entailed substantial delay in the final disposition of the case.[51] In
one of the opinions it was said that "The stay which had been
issued promised many more months of litigation in a case which
had otherwise run its full course."[52] In another it was said:

> Once the Court conceded, as it did, that the substantiality of the question
> raised before Mr. Justice Douglas was the sole issue, it became wholly immate-
> rial how many other questions were raised and considered on their merits in
> the District Court and in the Court of Appeals, or how many times review was
> sought on these questions and refused by this Court. It was equally immaterial
> how long a time intervened between the original trial of this case and the pres-
> ent proceeding, and immaterial that this was a last-minute effort almost on the
> eve of the executions. To allow such irrelevancies to enter the mind not
> unnaturally tends to bend the judicial judgment in a false direction.[53]

But—the Court by 6–3 held the question unsubstantial, and the
Rosenbergs were executed.

Second, lower courts attach far more significance to the
Supreme Court's "rehearing denied" than the intrinsic significance
of that action probably justifies. Lower courts normally look upon a
denial of rehearing as a solemn adjudication on the merits.

Take *Ickes v. Fox.*[54] Water-right owners on a federal irrigation
project in Washington State brought suit in the District of Columbia to enjoin the Secretary of the Interior from curtailing their supply of water. The defense was that, since the United States owned
the water, the proceeding was a suit against the United States,
which had not consented to be sued. The District Court granted a
motion to dismiss, a divided Court of Appeals reversed, and on certiorari the Supreme Court held adversely to the Secretary. A petition for rehearing was then filed, only to be denied with a slight
change in the opinion;[55] and the case went to trial.

Trial resulted in a judgment adverse to the water-right owners,
who appealed; the Court of Appeals reversed on the basis of what

---

[51] The stay which the full Court set aside was entered after adjournment for the summer, and was made on the application of a stranger to the cause. As to the latter point,
see 346 U.S. at 291–92 (opinion of Jackson, J.).

[52] 346 U.S. at 287, *per* Vinson, C.J.

[53] 346 U.S. at 302, *per* Frankfurter, J.

[54] 300 U.S. 82.

[55] 300 U.S. 640.

the Solicitor General had urged in his petition for rehearing six years earlier:

> A petition for rehearing filed in the Supreme Court by the Solicitor General makes it apparent that the principal issue in this case was before the Supreme Court on the former appeal. In that petition for rehearing the Solicitor General pointed out to the Court that the decision would lead to serious consequences in the administration of the Reclamation Fund because it gave applicants, on the sole basis of prior deliveries of water, a vested right in a larger amount of water than was stipulated in their contracts. The petition for rehearing pointed out that this amounted to giving them a prescriptive right based on permissive use. The petition also relied on a Washington statute which gave the government the right to appropriate water. We can see no difference between the appellee's position here and his unsuccessful argument before the Supreme Court of the United States.[56]

This second time the Secretary's petition for certiorari was denied.[57]

Let us review these cases: Suppose that, in *Rosenberg*, the question of the legality of the death sentence had been raised after the first denial of certiorari, without the complication of the other five applications that intervened. I suggest that it is unrealistic to suppose that this new point would not have received a more cordial reception had it been made on the second time up rather than on the seventh. Moreover, if, in *Ickes v. Fox*, no petition for rehearing had been filed, it would certainly have been more difficult for the Court of Appeals to have reversed the judgment entered after the trial.

I realize that the foregoing comments have the benefit of hindsight, which of course is always 20/20 in each eye. Nonetheless, I strongly urge that, except in the most unusual circumstances, it is the part of wisdom not to ask for a rehearing. It hardly ever helps, but it may do considerable harm. When you're licked, take your shellacking like a little man, and comfort yourself with the thought that you can't lose them all.

---

[56] *Fox v. Ickes*, 137 F.2d 30, 33 (D.C. Cir.).
[57] 320 U.S. 792.

CHAPTER 11

New Counsel on Appeal

Section 143. Professional specialization in England and in the United States.—The English division of the legal profession into barristers and solicitors, each with their respective areas of specialization, has long withstood the test of time, and, so far as we can tell "when we contemplate such a system from the outside,"[1] the test of utility as well.

It would of course be vain to hope that in this country we might somehow be persuaded to revert to the English system.[2] However, because of the increasing burdens cast on American lawyers by the mounting complexity of the law, and by their clients' inexorable demands for efficiency and expertise, there exists in this country a considerable degree of specialization within the legal profession, chiefly in urban centers. It is not too difficult, in a given community, to point out the lawyers who hardly ever go to court and those who spend most of their time there. Moreover, particularly in the larger cities, the institution of appellate counsel is constantly gaining in importance.

No single lawyer today can hope to be well versed in every field of legal endeavor that may face him in the course of his practice. Just as in medicine one of the timeworn but timeless jokes concerns the universal expert, the specialist in the skin and its contents, so in law: no one today can ever fairly claim to be even reasonably conversant with the entire corpus. Similarly, no lawyer can hope to be expert in all techniques, so as to be able to try a case before a jury or before a judge, or to brief and argue an appeal, with equal facility and skill, and with full and knowledgeable grasp of all the relevant—and different—techniques connected with each activity.

Section 144. Appellate counsel specializes in being a generalist.—The increasing emergence of counsel for appeals reflects a recognition

---

[1] *Diaz v. Gonzales*, 261 U.S. 102, 106.

[2] A strong argument to that effect is set forth in Chap. XIII of the late Lloyd Paul Sryker's *The Art of Advocacy* (1954), 251–270, entitled "Barristers and Solicitors—A Plea for a Divided Bar."

and a growing awareness of the inescapable fact that effective appellate presentation demands the services of a lawyer who is expert, not simply in particular fields of substantive law, but in a particular technique. Otherwise stated, the true appellate counsel specializes in being a generalist. Given a record, properly prepared, he is ready to brief and argue any appeal.

Appellate counsel faces, in an appellate court, a different audience and a different task than those faced in the trial court. It is undoubtedly safe to conclude that appellate counsel who specialize in subtly invoking the predilections of judges of courts of last resort will as a general rule fail to sway with equal success the popular prejudices of jurymen—and jurywomen. By the same token, a top-notch lawyer before a jury may do rather less than well when arguing an appeal.[3] In this connection, I have vividly in mind the comment of the Chief Justice of a State court of last resort, made about an argument presented by counsel in a negligence case: "He made the same jury speech three times—once to the jury at the trial, once to the trial judge on motion for new trial, and the third time to us on appeal."

Section 145. Can anyone argue an appeal?—Yet, to a surprising degree, the view that anyone can argue an appeal is still too prevalent. It certainly obtains among the many able jury lawyers who are rather less than able before an appellate bench, and yet insist on arguing there as well. Curiously enough, the same view also obtains even among the lawyers who are quick to retain specialized trial counsel but would not dream of consulting, much less retaining, specialized appellate counsel. And that view constitutes the inarticulate major premise of every lawyer, high in the hierarchy of his law firm, corporation law department, or government law office, who considers that his position alone supremely qualifies only him to present cases to appellate tribunals.

Indeed, it is fair to say that it is just this view—that anyone can argue an appeal—which is largely responsible for the generally mediocre level of appellate arguments. Three decades ago, Charles Evans Hughes wrote:

> The progress of civilization is but little reflected in the processes of argumentation and a vast amount of time is unavoidably wasted in the Supreme

---

[3] "The advocate, who sweeps the jury off their feet with his torrential eloquence, is rarely able to adapt his style to the colder and more judicial atmosphere of the appeal Courts." Walker-Smith, *Lord Reading and His Cases* (134), 41–42.

Court in listening to futile discussion; this has the effect of reducing the time for cases which should be fully presented.[4]

If any reader thinks that there has been an improvement in the quality of argumentation in the years that have passed since the above was written, let him just sit in the Supreme Court chamber and listen to as few as three consecutive arguments. (If it is inconvenient for him to come to Washington, he can make the same discovery in any courtroom occupied by a United States Court of Appeals.)

Section 146. Appellate argument requires specialization in technique.—The fact of the matter is that appellate argument calls for specialization in technique quite as much as does the trial of a case. As a distinguished member of an eminent State court of last resort recently said, "Nor is the argument of an appeal any less an art, any less a job for the skilled professional, than the conduct of the trial itself."[5] Like the trial lawyer, the appellate lawyer is a specialist in technique rather than in mere subject-matter. He is a generalist who presents his case to a bench of generalists, a bench that is frequently not as versed in the details of the specialty that the particular appeal involves. The specialist who prepared and tried the case is frequently so steeped in the specialty and in all of its assumptions that he finds it difficult to present the details of his specialty. The generalist is better able to sort out the significant issues, to bring analogies to bear from related fields, and to evaluate the contentions of the specialist just as the non-specialists on the court are likely to do.

Otherwise stated, the appellate generalist will thus be able to minimize arguments that lack appeal to a non-specialist audience, and, by parity of reasoning, to emphasize contentions that will have greater impact on that audience.

Moreover, quite apart from the differences in technique that stem basically from the character of the respective tribunals, quite apart from the comparative emphases on specialization versus generalization, the most vital and significant point is that experience teaches it is better, regardless of the talents of the individual concerned, to entrust the appeal to a lawyer other than the one who tried the case.

---

[4] Hughes, *The Supreme Court of the United States* (1928) 61.

[5] *People v. Breslin*, 4 N.Y. 2d 73, 80, 81, 149 N.E. 2d 85, 89, 90, *per* Fuld, J.

Section 147. Appellate specialization in the United States Department of Justice.—In that connection, let us see how the largest and busiest litigant in the land—the United States itself—conducts its appellate business.

At headquarters—which is to say, in the Department of Justice in Washington—all Supreme Court matters are under the direct charge of the Solicitor General. He has a small immediate staff that reviews and revises the draft briefs prepared by the several functional divisions of the Department—Criminal, Civil, Tax, Lands, etc. The Solicitor General decides who will argue the cases that are to be heard on the merits. And he makes the decision for or against appeal in every Government case that is lost below, at every level and in every court.

Only on rarest occasions does a Government lawyer who tried the case or argued it in the Court of Appeals have any significant part in its Supreme Court posture. Probably less than five cases in ten years are thus handled. *Per contra*, the lawyers who have the responsibility for Supreme Court briefs and, preeminently, Supreme Court arguments, have had contact with the case below even more rarely.

This division of labor is not due to any *prima donna* attitude, nor does it reflect the view that a lawyer on the fifth floor of the building is necessarily and inescapably superior in talent to one whose office is on a lower floor. Rather, it represents the recognition of long experience that a lawyer versed in appeals and therefore able to weigh appellate considerations is better qualified to evaluate cases, particularly where they will be disposed of by a single ultimate tribunal. It is for this reason that the Solicitor General passes on all appeals from District Courts to Courts of Appeals. The United States Attorney may feel, frequently with the reason, that "We wuz robbed." But the case may be a poor one to serve as a test; although it can, in all likelihood, be won on appeal, it may have overtones that will make it unappealing or undesirable as a vehicle on certiorari later on; those are considerations that the Solicitor General, with his finger constantly on the pulse of Supreme Court trends, can better appreciate and hence better evaluate. In short, the United States Government, in its appellate work, employs virtually independent appellate counsel.

Interestingly enough, lawyers who enter the Department with doubts about this practice become converted after they have seen it in operation. The following is from a letter by former Assistant Attorney General Rice, then in charge of the Tax Division, who commented on this chapter when it first appeared in a legal periodical:

> As you know, we have long had separate Trial and Appellate Sections in this Division. I was not accustomed to this division of functions when I came here, for, although I came from a large New York City firm, the practice there was generally to have the lawyer who tried the case argue the appeal. I am convinced, however, from close association with the work here, that there is merit in the separation of responsibilities, mainly for the reason that the effective trial lawyer is all too often not an effective appellate pleader and *vice versa.* I think there are times when the appellate lawyer, working from a cold record, loses some of the color of the case or tends to isolate issues without sufficient emphasis on the whole factual picture. By and large, however, I believe that the separation of functions is clearly advisable in any activity having volume litigation.[6]

Section 148. Appellate specialization in United States Attorneys' offices.—The same trend is evident in the large United States Attorneys' offices. In the smaller offices that are located in districts where the workload is fairly light, the Assistant United States Attorney who tried the Government's case will be expected to handle the case on appeal. However, in the busier districts—and those include the large centers of population—successive United States Attorneys have found that they obtain better results by setting up an appellate bureau or section, whose members brief and argue on appeal the cases that their colleagues from the civil and criminal sections have tried.

This division of function, however desirable or useful, is not rigid. By and large, however, it has been found to be helpful. Assistant United States Attorneys who specialize in appeals find they enjoy greater ease in participating in colloquies with the appellate judges than those of their associates who appear only occasionally in the Court of Appeals. Similarly, the appellate specialists find it less difficult to meet effectively issues that concern and disturb that court. And, preeminently in criminal cases, whenever an appellant complains of the conduct of the prosecution, it conduces to a more objective argument if that conduct is defended by an Assistant United States Attorney who did not participate in the trial.

The Hon. Oliver Gasch, then United States Attorney for the District of Columbia, kindly furnished a memorandum articulating his reasons for establishing an Appellate Section in his office; it warrants quotation in full:

> It has been my experience as United States Attorney for the District of Columbia that it is most necessary and desirable to establish and maintain an

---

[6] Letter from the Hon. Charles K. Rice, July 30, 1959.

Appellate Section in this office. Annually, for the past several years, we have been responsible for processing about 300 appeals. The large majority of these appellate cases are in the United States Court of Appeals for the District of Columbia Circuit. Approximately 60% of them are criminal cases which in this unique federal district run the gamut from ordinary common law offenses to prosecutions based on general federal criminal statutes. On the civil side there is also great diversity in the subject matter of these cases. Most of them involve efforts to enjoin the action of the heads of the Executive Branch of our Government. Quite a few Federal Tort Claims cases reach the appellate stage.

Assistant United States Attorneys, who by reason of their training, experience, and scholarly inclinations are assigned to the Appellate Division of the office, have demonstrated that they can most effectively represent the Government at this level. Our trial men carry a heavy load of trial cases. Most of them are in court in connection with trial matters each day. To expect them to brief and argue appellate matters in addition to assuming their trial obligations would, in my judgment, be expecting the impossible. This year, however, we have determined to have each trial man argue at least one appeal. Our reason for doing this is that it seems desirable to have trial men experience some of the difficulties encountered at the appellate level. I think it will cause them to be more concerned about the problem of making a good record.

Generally, however, the objective approach of the appellate advocate is more effective and more efficient. Appellate specialists are more familiar with the appellate rules, procedures, and the many applicable precedents in the appellate courts. Their presentation is more direct and less time consuming. Their ability to answer effectively the questions propounded during oral argument often spells the difference between sustaining one's position and being reversed.

Section 149. Appellate specialization in a large public law office.—The same differentiation between trial and appellate lawyers was similarly found desirable in one of the busiest public law offices in the world, that of the Corporation Counsel of the City of New York. Some years ago, Judge Paxton Blair, who for about a decade was Chief of the Division of Appeals in that office (and who is now Solicitor General of the State of New York), wrote as follows:

I have always held that the trial man is *not the best man* to handle the appeal, but may even be the worst. * * * In the office of the District Attorney, New York County, a case taken to an appellate court is handed over to what is known as the appeals division or appeals bureau, and briefed and argued by an appeals specialist.

There are, to my mind, overwhelming advantages in this method of handling appeals. The appeals specialist views the case precisely as does the appellate court, through the little square window of the record, so to speak, and not as something viewed from the great outdoors. The trial man's mind cannot free itself of matters which entered in during preparation for trial but which did not get into the record, either because a witness he interviewed failed to respond to a subpoena or was not allowed to testify because of failure to establish qualifications. Or if the witness did testify, some important facts may not have been established because objections to questions were sustained.

Then, too, the style of oratory a trial man develops, through his constant appeal to a jury less learned than himself, is out of place in an appellate court. A calm, conversational style is there appropriate; and his hearers' learning exceeds his own, or at least he should conduct himself as though it did.[7]

Because of the work load, Judge Blair found it necessary to assign many appeals to the functional divisions of the Corporation Counsel's Office, where the litigation had originated. "Statistics which I kept showed that the men of the appeals division had almost twice as high a batting average as their brethren from other divisions."[8]

Section 150. Appellate specialization in private law offices.—The larger law firms—frequently referred to as law factories (though only by the outsiders)—are generally staffed with enough lawyers of broad appellate experience to permit them to meet, with their own resources, a problem that is essentially one of function and specialization. Yet even there, as will be indicated below in Section 154, the question whether a different lawyer within the office should handle the appellate phase of a case raises problems identical with those faced by an office of moderate size that is considering, in an important cause, the desirability or otherwise of consulting or retaining new counsel on appeal.

Section 151. Advantages of new counsel on appeal.—Apart from the ingrained differences between trial and appellate techniques, and even in a case that does not involve a detailed, self-contained, or esoteric specialty, appellate counsel is frequently able to bring new ideas and a fresh new approach into a case that has already run a long course. No matter how able or talented a particular lawyer may be, after the same individual has prepared a case, presented it to a trial court, and then briefed and argued it on appeal, he will be pretty stale in his thinking if a second briefing and a second argument at any other level are required on top of that. Injection of new appellate counsel at that stage is not in any sense a reflection on original counsel; it is a recognition, among other considerations, of the fact that repetition makes for dullness and that a fresh mind may well be able to introduce a new and hence a more effective approach to what has become rather more than a twice-told tale.

---

[7] Blair, *Appellate Briefs and Advocacy*, 18 Ford. L. Rev. 30, 46–47.

[8] *Id.*, note 38, 14 Ford. L. Rev. at 47.

Indeed, even experienced appellate lawyers who have lived rather too long with a particular case are often eager to bring in a colleague for a fresh viewpoint, or to consult with friends on a law faculty for the same reason.

The foregoing considerations are particularly pertinent in connection with Federal litigation. Thus, a case before a regulatory agency starts before the trial examiner, goes to the commission or board, then is reviewed by a Court of Appeals (or a three-judge District Court), then is sought to be reviewed by the Supreme Court on petition for certiorari or jurisdictional statement, and, if review is granted, is finally presented on the merits. And that is the usual, not the unusual, travel of such a controversy, and of many others, as, for instance, civil tax cases. Very, very few lawyers can avoid the dullness, the warmed-over undertones, the effect of stale-sounding canned reasoning that inevitably accompany such a reiteration of arguments.

Section 152. New appellate counsel in the Supreme Court of the United States.—Finally, if the appeal in question—whether the first, or the second, or even the fourth—is taken to a court with whose reactions and current tendencies original counsel is unacquainted, it is generally advisable to retain appellate counsel who is. It is this principle that underlies the centralization of the Government's Supreme Court litigation in the Solicitor General's office. And, even more than briefs and arguments on the merits, the one-shot written argument made in a petition for certiorari or a jurisdictional statement on appeal requires an intimate knowledge of the Supreme Court's standards for review.

On this subject, additional experience leads me only to repeat what I wrote in 1950:

> I might make the following additional observation about Petitions for Certiorari and similar briefs seeking discretionary review, namely, that they constitute, certainly for the uninitiated, the most difficult form of written argumentation: They must persuade a court, not so much that the ruling below was wrong, but that it warrants review. This view is confirmed, substantially without dissent, by most of my former colleagues in the Department of Justice who deal with Supreme Court briefs, and by my own experience under controlled conditions, viz., returning to the law after nearly five years' service in the Army: I felt able to write a brief on the merits the day I reverted to civilian status, and in fact plunged right into the process of writing one before that day was out; but it took me six months more to get into the swing of composing an acceptable Petition for Certiorari.[9]

---

[9] *Effective Appellate Advocacy* (1950), pp. 241–242.

The same considerations are of course equally applicable to the writing of Jurisdictional Statements in cases on appeal.[10]

Section 153. Use of appellate counsel at the trial level.—There is one other situation in which it may be helpful to retain appellate counsel, namely, in the important case involving large sums or large principles—and there the retainer should precede the appeal, while the record can still be shaped with the appeal in mind.

This other situation is not that of the "Big Case" exclusively; by no means. For bigness is relative, and the remarks that follow are not addressed to the familiar if happily infrequent instance of the monster antitrust litigation with its galaxy of talent,[11] but to the far more usual and indeed not uncommon case, whose facts can by and large be established without too much difficulty, but whose essential problem is that of shaping a record so as to sustain a carefully formulated proposition of law on appeal—in this instance, on the inevitable appeal, which both sides are prepared to take if the judgment is adverse to either.

Too often—far too often—appellate counsel is called in at the hospital stage, when the case is in the last stages of terminal illness. Similarly, too often appellate counsel finds that an essentially sound case has been seriously weakened by careless handling that did not have the record on appeal in mind.

I am not suggesting for a moment the second-guessing of trial counsel, the hindsight as to that famous just-one-more-last-question on cross-examination. As to these and similar unavoidable risks of a trial, appellate counsel must take the record as Cromwell preferred his portrait—warts and all. But if, when the litigation starts, it is obvious that there is a great deal at stake; that the case is certain to be appealed, regardless of outcome; and that the ultimate result will turn on questions of law, then the time for appellate counsel to assist is at the outset, when he can consult with trial counsel and work with them with a view to making up the record for the ultimate appeal.

Such work will include research on the law, not the once-over-lightly that all too commonly precedes a trial, but extensive study of

---

[10] See Stern and Gressman, *Supreme Court Practice* (2d ed. 1954) ch. VI(F), pp. 233–246.

[11] "The court judicially recognizes an array of talent seldom equalled in history." *United States v. E. I. du Pont de Nemours & Co.*, 13 F.R.D. 487, 489 (E.D. Ill.); for the decision on the merits, see *United States v. du Pont & Co.*, 353 U.S. 586; for the final decree, see *United States v. E. I. du Pont de Nemours & Co.*, 177 F. Supp. 1 (N.D. Ill.), probable jurisdiction noted, 362 U.S. 986.

the uncharted areas and the factors that may be expected to affect the appellate court in those areas. Before the trial, these labors will also include the preparation of trial briefs, and memoranda on the admissibility of disputed but highly material evidence. During the trial, appellate counsel will advise on the making or withholding of objections and on offers of evidence that will adequately safeguard the client's legal position before the appellate court. Thus appellate counsel assists in shaping the record that he will later defend, and in addition avoids what is so fruitless for the client, the brilliant trial victory doomed to reversal on appeal because of errors in the record.

Section 154. Considerations underlying retainer of new appellate counsel.—Of course, the run-of-the-mill lawsuit will not support such an elaborate and—necessarily—expensive apparatus. In many, many cases, all too plainly, what is involved will barely yield a reasonable fee to a single lawyer. But in a substantial zone of cases on appeal, the question whether to retain new appellate counsel necessarily arises.

First, should someone else be retained at all? That question includes the subsidiary inquiry, in the large law firm of diverse talents, whether a different partner should be entrusted with the appeal, regardless of his personal relationship either to the client or to the subject-matter of the controversy. The entire problem is one that must be carefully pondered, not only in the light of the considerations already outlined above, but also in its bearing on the very heart of the attorney–client relationship. For, if the client can afford first-rate professional assistance at the appellate level, and his trial counsel who lacks appellate experience insists on arguing the case—either on the basis that "This is the first time I have ever had a case in the Supreme Court, and I don't intend to lose that opportunity," or else on the view that "I have fought this all the way and so I propose to see it through"—there is a genuine conflict between the interests of the client and the interests of the lawyer.

Second, if it is decided to retain someone else, who? The "big name" lawyer who will not read the record? Or the lawyer who is somehow supposed "to have the ear of the court"? Both are equally without utility. One Justice of the Supreme Court wrote in an opinion, "Intrinsic professional competence alone matters. The name or fame of counsel plays no part whatever in the attention paid to argument, and is wholly irrelevant to the outcome of a case."[12]

---

[12] *Dennis v. United States*, 340 U.S. 887, per Frankfurter, J.

Another declared in a published lecture that "it is a grave mistake to choose counsel for some supposed influence or the enchantment of political reputation, and, above all, avoid the lawyer who thinks he is so impressively eminent that he need give no time to preparation except while he is on a plane going to Washington. Believe me when I say that what impresses the Court is a lawyer's argument, not his eminence."[13]

Third, if it is determined to proceed with the lawyers already in the case, is there any advantage to seniority unrelated to professional competence? In other words, does the very real importance of a case mean that it cannot be entrusted to anyone junior to the senior partner, or the general counsel, or the assistant attorney general?

Here again, a proper answer turns on function and specialization. The person best qualified to conduct an orchestra is not necessarily the most competent soloist; and the talents—or the accidents—that make X the appropriate and indeed logical choice to head a law firm or a government law bureau may be entirely irrelevant to technical appellate competence. Conversely, the ablest advocate may be quite unable to direct or administer even a small group of lawyers or to formulate policies that reach beyond litigation tactics or strategy.

Whatever may be the case as to appellate briefs, where cooperative effort is always helpful, appellate argument is necessarily a solo performance. If counsel is unprepared, if counsel lacks a firm grasp of the controlling issues, if counsel becomes flustered to the point of sputtering silence by questions from the bench, then the little slips his associates hand him—the only help anyone can offer at that juncture—will not rehabilitate either him or his argument. In today's complex society, there is wide scope for the talents of the organization man, but appellate argument is not his pigeon; the man on his feet arguing an appeal must be a well-contained individualist.

If the bar gave as much consideration to the selection of appellate counsel as is now generally given to the selection of trial counsel, there would be fewer arguments in appellate courts by lawyers whose talents lie in other directions, and hence far less "not good" arguments than are now heard. The cynical comment that "Many a rich client has a poor lawyer" was uttered by a distinguished appellate

---

[13] Jackson, *Advocacy Before the Supreme Court: Suggestions for Effective Case Presentations*, 37 A.B.A.J. 801, 802.

judge, since deceased. Considering what is at stake when cases are on appeal, it is indeed surprising why there has not been universal acceptance of the obvious criterion for selecting counsel on appeal, namely, that "Intrinsic professional competence alone matters."

Section 155. Should new appellate counsel be selected on the strength of his percentage of victories?—A baseball manager will— and should—select pitchers on the strength of their won and lost records, other players on the basis of batting averages. But an appellate lawyer's percentage of wins is apt to be irrelevant in any consideration of his qualities.

I once knew a Solicitor General of the United States—not, be it noted, one of the ablest incumbents of the position—who was inordinately proud of his percentage of cases won. But his pride was doubly misplaced. First, the volume of litigation in that Office is such, and the winning cases generally so obvious, that anyone with the right to pick his own vehicles for argument is well nigh certain, quite regardless of his qualities or lack of them, to win at least nine out of ten. Second, this gentleman in fact lost a number of cases that might well have gone the other way, and that advocates more generously endowed with forensic talent in all likelihood would have won.

Moreover, when we consider private litigation, it is at once apparent that the lawyer with a case that will probably be won is not going to retain an appellate specialist; those lads will be retained only in the difficult matters, the uphill fights and the forlorn hopes, areas in which batting averages necessarily tend to be low.

Here is a wry comment on that point from Professor Samuel Williston's delightful autobiography:

> I may add in reference to the frequency with which my aid was unavailing to lawyers who sought my assistance, that it was not generally sought unless the case was one of some desperation. In cases that are easily won, lawyers generally prefer to keep the labor and the compensation entirely to themselves.[14]

To the same effect is a passage from Augustus Garland's musings, written after he had argued *over 130 cases* in the Supreme Court:[15]

> In casting up the account of loss and gain in the foregoing list, the balance is rather against me: I have lost more than I gained. * * *

---

[14] Williston, *Life and Law* (1940), 287.

[15] Appropriately enough, he was stricken on January 26, 1899, while arguing *Towson v. Moore*, 173 U.S. 17, in the Supreme Court, and died in the Clerk's office the same day. See 172 U.S. 651; 43 L. ed. 598, note; J. Sup. Ct., Oct. T. 1898, pp. 101–02. He was also the protagonist of *Ex parte Garland*, 4 Wall. 333.

Upon one occasion, on opinion day, the tide ran so heavily against me, losing about five cases and gaining not one, I was quite ill at ease and moody. Coming out of the court, I got in with Judge Harlan[16] and passing the civilities of the day, he asked me how I felt and I told him quite badly, and the reason for it, and that I did not believe I could even get an attorney enrolled in that court any more, and recalled to him my fate on that day. He chided me somewhat, and remarked it was not unusual with the very best lawyers, and told me of his observation here and elsewhere that bad or difficult cases fell to the lot of good lawyers, and they were sought for to deal with just such cases.[17]

It will be appropriate, by way of summary, to conclude with a short sentence from the pen of one who was first an outstanding advocate, and then a great judge, the late Mr. Justice Jackson:

"A lawyer's stock in trade is not merely that he always wins his cases, but that he puts up a good fight."[18]

---

[16] The elder.

[17] Garland, *Experience in the U.S. Supreme Court* (1898), 91–92.

[18] Gerhart, *America's Advocate: Robert H. Jackson* (1958), 44.

Index